BUNCH OF AMATEURS

BUNCH OF AMATEURS

A Search for the

AMERICAN CHARACTER

Jack Hitt

Crown Publishers
New York

Published in the United States by Crown Publishers, an imprint of the Crown Publishing Group, a division of Random House, Inc., New York.
www.crownpublishing.com

CROWN and the Crown colophon are registered trademarks of Random House, Inc.

Library of Congress Cataloging-in-Publication Data is available upon request.

ISBN 978-0-307-39375-3
eISBN 978-0-307-95518-0

Printed in the United States of America

Illustrations by John Burgoyne
Jacket design by Christopher Brand
Jacket photographs: (Astronaut) Francesco Reginato/Getty Images; (barn) Samuel Hicks/Gallery Stock

10 9 8 7 6 5 4 3 2 1

First Edition

For Yancey and Tarpley

Contents

1

GUNGYWAMPING

In a forested bottomland of southeastern Connecticut, amid stony outcroppings and strewn granite boulders, lies an unusual cluster of nine beehive-like stone shelters. As far back as anybody can remember, including the Pequot Indians, the area has had a funny name: Gungywamp. When I first heard about the place, I called around and found David Barron, then the president of the Gungywamp Society. He invited me to join him on a walk in the woods with some fresh recruits, mostly married couples in their fifties. He told me that Gungywampers believed the odd stone huts are Celtic dwellings, an abandoned camp left by Irish monks who visited America fifteen hundred years ago.

After parking our cars on the side of a remote road, a dozen of us slipped into the woods. Barron, a tall man with sprouts of white hair exploding out from under a Greek fisherman's cap, marched with vigor, bubbling with enthusiasm. As a guide, he cut a familiar figure. He possessed a partiality for crippling puns. When someone had to peel off early from the group, he shouted to them, "Shalom on the range!" He smoked so much his white mustache was tainted yellow. He had a salty way of sprinkling his comments with innuendo that amused the wives, yet affected a Victorian coyness about cursing. When I found some trash—beer cans and cigarette butts—obviously left at one shelter by some teenagers, he let fly the foulest term possible: "Sheitzen!"

Then Barron led us to a large rock. He wanted to know if we noticed anything. There were some lichens on it, not much else; we stared intently. Barron explained that the rock had faded carvings on it and that one of them was a Chi-Rho, a symbol that superimposes the letter X over the stem of a capital P and served as an early emblem of Christianity. We all squinted.

"This particular style of Chi-Rho was common among Irish monks during the fifth to seventh centuries A.D.," Barron told us excitedly, linking the symbol to a time when a certain Brendan the Navigator of Ireland, according to legend, sailed west in search of the Promised Land of Saints. "Do you see it?" We all leaned over, carefully scanning every blotchy divot. An uneasy silence, broken only by the cracking of twigs beneath our boots, seized the forest.

Slightly annoyed at our befuddled postures, Barron turned an exasperated, upturned palm toward some mild indentations. He sneeringly referenced skeptics at Harvard and Yale who had looked at this evidence and were unimpressed. "Haaaavard," he said with thick snark. Right away you got the sense that there were two kinds of esoteric knowledge at odds here. The elite evidence-based world of "Yaaaaa-uuuull" and this other kind of knowledge—Barronic knowledge—that meant you had to see things differently. Barron took a piece of chalk from his pocket and traced over some worn dimples and there it was. A white Chi-Rho leapt off the speckled gray of the boulder like a 3-D trick. Many in the crowd ooo'd and aaah'd. It was an emotional moment to stand in this quiet hardwood bottomland and suddenly feel it instantly transform into a place of antiquity. A new idea had us in its grip, this notion that Irish mariners once stood right here fifteen hundred years ago. Then again, a few of us eyeballed another nearby chiseling, smoothed down by weather in much the same way, and we wondered what runic name it went by: JC III.

When you come across a guy like David Barron, you think, Haven't I met him before? The eccentric demeanor, the cocksure certainty for his ideas, that panting cascade of arcane information about things like Chi-Rhos. He's the guy with enough self-accumulated knowledge about local archaeology and medieval orthography and lithic architecture to cobble together a theory about this place. He's a type, right? Individuals like Barron can be men or women, old or young, but chances are their gusto for their singular obsession is captivating (or irritating, depending on your mood that day). And one other thing—I'm speaking from personal experience now—part of this package typically involves an unusual hat.

We all know these people. They are recurring American characters. These people are amateurs.

I say American characters not because the rest of the world doesn't have amateurs. Of course, every place has them and they are everywhere. At its most fundamental, an amateur is simply someone operating outside professional assumptions. The word derives ultimately from the Latin but comes into English via the French word *amateur*, meaning "lover" and, specifically, passionate love. Or obsessive love. This powerful emotion usually indicates someone's embrace of a notion (invention, theory, way of life) as a compulsive passion for the thing—not the money, fame, or career that could come of it. But there are differences.

In Europe and on other continents, the word hints at class warfare. Credentialism in the Old World suggests the elevation of those occupying a certain station. Amateurs may be taken seriously but, almost by the power of the word, are kept in their place: isolated outside some preexisting professional class, some long-standing nobility.

In America, amateurs don't stay in their place or keep to themselves. So once the word crossed the Atlantic Ocean—whether by St. Brendan or a more traditional way—it came to mean all kinds of, often, conflicting things. "Amateur" can signify someone who is nearly a professional or completely a fool. The word also encompasses a sense of being pretentious (mere amateur) or incompetent (the meaning one first hears in this book's title). In fact, look it up in *Roget's Thesaurus* and it's a wasp nest of contradictions—falling under five rubrics of meaning: dabbler, dilettante, bungler, virtuoso, and greenhorn. In America, we're a little touchy about this word, and for good reason.

Historically, our amateur ancestors grew out of the Ben Franklin tradition of tinkering at home. In the mid-nineteenth century, the homebrew style had to contend with a societal drive to professionalize, a movement that accelerated with the arrival of the Industrial Revolution. That was an era when, for example, the American Medical Association (formed in 1847) sought to distinguish legitimate doctors from snake-oil salesmen, itinerant abortionists, and other makeshift charlatans peddling miracle tonics. Many disciplines organized professional guilds like the AMA or created university departments to grant credentials to the serious practitioners of a craft over the self-schooled.

But the outsiders never really went away. American professionals have had to grow up right alongside their striving, awkward, amateur cousins in the same way that the first attempts at gentry in the Old South had to contend with their toothless cousins named Fishbait or Elrod, sleeping in the bushes outside the mansion. The embarrassment of our amateur origins, in every estate of American endeavor, is always lurking just around the corner.

In European popular culture, amateurism is practically feared. It's

Europe that gave us the "mad scientist"—an amateur straying into the realm of forbidden knowledge—whose models are Drs. Frankenstein and Jekyll. In America, we soften that image from mad to absentminded. We admire that kind of risk-taker. Our amateur scientists might resemble the character in *Back to the Future* played by Christopher Lloyd (whose hair has a passing resemblance to Barron's). The mad scientists of Europe spawned monsters. Our absentminded professors created flubber, an absurd confection whose most unusual property is that it enables our dopey hero to attract a girl.

So we think amateurs are hopeless dreamers, made practically adorable by their obsessive love for some one true thing, and each and every one of them charged with the potential of being a genius and making a crucial discovery. There's something quintessentially American in that version of the character, isn't there? The lovable Poindexter who just might possibly stumble upon the next big thing.

While the word may be complicated and full of contradictions, the American amateurs that constantly pop up throughout our history are, basically, one of two kinds of characters. They are either outsiders mustering at some fortress of expertise hoping to scale the walls, or pioneers improvising in a frontier where no professionals exist. If every country forms its national character at the trauma of birth, then we are forever rebelling against the king or lighting out for the territories.

On a late afternoon, Barron and I hung out for a while at the Gungywamp structures. They are charming shelters—about the size of a good tool shed built with flat stones stacked closer together as they get to the top, which is formed by a large, flat capstone. The entire construction, except the opening, is often covered in dirt, which in turn is overgrown with grasses. Being inside feels extremely ancient. Barron wanted to show me the main building. He believed it to be an oratory, a one-room chapel, examples of which are still standing in Ireland. These edifices began going up in Ireland after A.D. 400, when the Christian church opened for business there. In this particular hut, there was a "vent hole" whose orientation, it was accidentally discovered in 1987, admitted light only twice a year—on the equinox.

Barron gave me a sharp look, flaring his eyes and nostrils. His hat seemed to pop up a bit and meant to signal that the proof was fairly conclusive, right? That I was a convert, right? I flashed a neutral smile. Earlier that day, I had spoken to Connecticut's state archaeologist, Nick Bellantoni. He let me know right away he was quite tired of this crowd and couldn't they see already that the stone buildings were just colonial root cellars or pigsties?

Across from the vent hole was another small opening at the ground level that Barron wanted to show me. In Ireland, Barron continued, such doorways were common in these chambers. They led to hidden rooms where Celtic farmers might wait for the passing of an invading horde of Vikings. The dark hole was not more than a foot and a half square.

"A secret passageway," Barron said. So I crawled in.

When I originally hung out with Barron, I loved all this. Stories about crackpot amateurs like the Gungywampers are a journalistic chestnut. First and foremost, they require a slightly oddball protagonist who can supply lots of character detail (some editor is always urging the writer to "make it zany"—that word is practically jargon in the modern magazine business). And in order to really bring it—the zany—you not only need a Gungywamp zealot who curses in weird German like Barron, but you also need his foil, an official expert bristling with skepticism. So I was good to go, article-wise. I had the two key characters in the crackpot subgenre.

I was thinking about all this when I crawled out the other end of the secret tunnel. I was in another conical room also shaped into a rounded pyramid. It was just tall enough for me to set my six-foot self into a crouching stand.

I sat down on the dirt floor in the secret chamber and illuminated the drywall masonry with my flashlight. Even though this story was coming easily, some of the details weren't dovetailing. Sitting in this little room, and touching these old stones, I began to ask myself: Why would any colonial build nine very labor-intensive root cellars so close together? A collection of outbuildings like this doesn't occur anywhere else in the United States, and how many storehouses for potatoes and squash do you need in the eighteenth century? Who would ever build a solar-oriented root cellar? Why would any farmer create a crawl space in a pigsty that led to a hidden chamber? So instead of rushing to my computer to write the usual crackpot story, a new question popped into my mind: What if David Barron were right?

The first thing one usually hears about the era of the self-taught theorist and the garage inventor is it's supposed to be dead. The Golden Age of American Amateurism is over. You can read all about it in countless books with tombstone titles, such as Thomas P. Hughes's classic *American Genesis: A Century of Invention and Technological Enthusiasm 1870–1970*, or any of a shelf full of books with titles beginning *The End of . . .* More broadly, the entire American experiment seems to be shutting down, if you read Naomi Wolf's book *The End of America: Letter of Warning to a Young Patriot*.

I'm not sure I'd write America's obit just yet, for the same reason that I wouldn't write the closing chapter of amateurism either. Every generation likes to think that its time has grown too complex and sophisticated for any real homebrew breakthroughs. But then, each generation also discovers that what they thought were very expensive, highly unobtainable technologies suddenly turn into the next generation's play toys.

A few years ago, the technology for looking through surface materials—like those full-body scanners at airports—was incredibly complicated and expensive. Already, amateurs online have hacked the technology and created cheap DIY versions involving little more than certain cameras, a combination of filters, and specific wavelengths of light. This homemade method for peering beneath people's clothes is about to do for those old "X-ray specs" ads in comic books what the cell phone did for *Star Trek*'s "communicator badge." Make it real, and cheap. Like it or not, nude imagery is about to undergo the same change-up that personal information on Facebook did only a few years ago. And on we go.

Like so many trends in this country, amateurism is no different. It's not a moment that ends, but a cycle that's always coming around.

Business scholars have attempted to deconstruct how such amateurs succeed and one noted theory, published in the *Harvard Business Review*, argues that outsiders are not burdened with the "curse of knowledge." It turns out that ignorance *is* bliss and, in many cases, a more productive perch to start from. Not knowing anything about something is often precisely what's needed to see something new. And then the cycle starts over.

That's why, in the 1970s, IBM's top executive could say that the world would only need a few computers, because that's how they saw it. Steve Jobs and Steve Wozniak were not cursed with such presumptions and so famously went into Jobs's Cupertino garage and roughed out an early desktop computer from parts sold in the local electronics store or improvised with skills picked up at the now-famous Homebrew Computer Club.

Amateurism mysteriously summons America back, like some

Great Gatsby imperative, to that very mythological garage to begin once again the work of thinking about things far away from expert prejudices. It's not a coincidence that Hewlett-Packard recently restored the original garage at 367 Addison Avenue in Palo Alto, California, where Dave Packard and Bill Hewlett first formed their company in 1939 (and then provided Disney with some of the sound equipment used in making *Fantasia*). That quintessential location is the temple of American amateur ingenuity, and after stepping out to report the stories in this book, I found that plenty of folks still hie to this sacred space (literally) every weekend, hoping to make the big breakthrough.

In the pop culture itself, the evidence is constantly emerging that Americans are figuratively returning to this fertile place too.

There are the thriving new magazines like *Make* and a host of others catering to the resurgence of the DIY—do-it-yourself—impulse in America. Contests summoning amateurs to their workbenches and offering millions in rewards are now sponsored by the Pentagon (to invent robot cars), NASA (new lunar technology), the X Prize Foundation (space tourism), Congress (hydrogen energy), Al Gore (carbon emissions abatement), and even Google ($20 million reward for a robot that can get to the moon and explore).

There is also a steady stream of interest in weekend hobby clubs, where Americans have long retreated to tinker—depending on the decade—with their radios, remote-control vehicles, computers, and robots. The Internet has set loose a massive new style: open-source amateur collaborations that completely restructure entire disciplines. My own field of journalism is being thoroughly undermined, crashed, and rebuilt by the blogosphere, Slate, the Daily Beast, Facebook, YouTube, and Twitter. There is now open talk among the most fuddy-duddy editors that the dead-tree format—i.e., the newspaper—may be the illuminated manuscript of the twenty-first century. The old financial models are crumbling. Between 2000 and 2008, Craigslist alone eliminated about 49 percent of newspaper revenue that once came in from classified ads—as bloggers swarm every news story with fact-checking and commentary. They've created a heightened sense of being observed and have fundamentally altered the way journalism now gets reported and written.

There is almost no field that isn't experiencing similar tectonic quakes. Just casting about, it's not hard to find outsider collaborations. Amateur weather freaks, "storm spotters" who now communicate online, have long been relied upon by local governments and are acknowledged by the National Weather Service as "the Nation's first line of defense against severe weather." The world of biodiesel (not to mention the latest emblem of American freedom—the solar-powered car) has launched a thousand backyard inventors, as well as roving salesmen peddling devices that home-brew gasoline from table scraps. Google maps have inspired a new generation of self-appointed spies to scout enemy landscapes. Do-it-yourself builders of submarines, or "personal submersibles," now explore the ocean floor (PSUBS.org). Thiago Olson is a kid in Oakland Township, Michigan, who is now classified as the eighteenth amateur to create nuclear fusion in his backyard. It's the number 18 that's arresting.

Once you start looking for it, the only real shocker is how ubiquitous a figure the aspiring amateur is in America and yet how seemingly invisible these people are in our journalistic media.

The title of the nation's most watched program—an amateur hour, mind you—captures it: *American Idol*. The amateur breaking out and getting recognized—that is our secular God. We are the land of fresh starts *and* second acts; the promised land of immigrants starting anew.

The elevation of the amateur is not just this season's top-rated TV show. Prime time is now jammed with knockoffs and spinoffs of *American Idol* (*America's Got Talent*, *America's Next Top Model*, *Project Runway*, *Dancing with the Stars*, *The Apprentice*, *The Voice*). Before *American Idol*, which discovered Kelly Clarkson, there was *Star Search*, the show responsible for Britney Spears. But the pedigree of such programming goes way back, possibly all the way back. In the 1970s, the amateur show had already been such a staple that its parody was a huge hit. *The Gong Show* was straight-up ridicule of the genre (and yet managed to discover PeeWee Herman, Boxcar Willie, and Andrea McArdle—the first of the ginger 'fros who played Little Orphan Annie).

Before that was *Amateur Night at the Apollo*, which gave us Ella Fitzgerald and Pearl Bailey. At that time, there was another glut of these shows. One could also watch *Ted Mack's Amateur Hour*, a prime-time show that launched the career of Gladys Knight and Pat Boone. The other big one was called the *Arthur Godfrey's Talent Scouts*, where we first saw performers ranging from Patsy Cline to Lenny Bruce.

Mack got his television show because he had been the band leader for a radio show called *Major Bowes' Amateur Theatre of the Air*, which dates to the early 1930s and gave us the careers of Beverly Sills and Frank Sinatra. And before radio, various small theaters thrived on weekly amateur shows, like Miner's Bowery Theater in Manhattan, which discovered Eddie Cantor, or Halsey's Theater in Brooklyn, where Jackie Gleason first appeared. And before that, vaudeville would tour the country and perform in the local opera houses. The shows typically featured a local amateur contest—both to draw nearby audiences into the seats to watch their neighbors perform and, given the chance, to discover someone they could convince to tour with them, as they did Bob Hope and Milton Berle.

These amateur nights weren't just entertainments but confirmations of what Americans believe is true in every sphere. There is no realm that is understood to be off-limits to the lowest or newest citizen here. Americans affirm this idea in every aspect of their vernacular life ("Anybody can grow up to be President"). It's the essential faith of the amateur and the creed of America. It's why George Washington opted to be called Mr. President instead of going with the pompous alternative "Your Excellency." Every four years voters typically affirm their suspicion of "professional politicians" by elevating an inexperienced pol to the White House (with, arguably, a very wide range of results). The amateur narrative is encoded in our national DNA.

The cyclical return to the garage is happening now, as Americans sense that some great turn in history has come. It's time to tear down the fortresses and build them again, which is always traumatic. When one of the *New Republic*'s professional writers, Lee Siegel, was discovered to have posed online as his own fan, fluffing himself with cringe-inducing praise, he was suspended. The people who brought him down were bloggers who figured out that he was engaging in sockpuppetry (yes, there already was a word for online onanistic praise). Later, Siegel wrote a book about how horrible these amateur journalists were that were attacking him. "I love the idea of the amateur—that's what popular culture is all about," he told *New York* magazine. "But what the Internet's doing is professionalizing everyone's amateuristic impulses."

I don't quite understand what that sentence means, but I think it's safe to say that the pros occupying the barricades of expertise never like it when it happens. *The Cult of the Amateur: How Today's Internet Is Killing Our Culture* was a bestseller devoted to the lament—also a perennial when amateurs appear—that the great palaces of tradition are being wrecked by constant attacks from unschooled outsiders. It's one more entry on the bookshelf of apocalyptic American literature. But this is not the end of anything. This is the gyre of our own history coming around once again. What I want to argue here is that the cult of the amateur, once you step back, is the soul of America.

After hiking out of the Gungywamp, I went back to the state archaeologist, Nick Bellantoni, and pressed him on some of the details. He suddenly shifted his tone, if not his position. "It's well within the range of probability that Irish monks came here," he told me. "It's just that we still have no physical evidence for it." It seemed strange that he would hedge so quickly, but once I looked into the history of this kind of history, Bellantoni's caution did not seem so strange.

The source of Gungywampers' optimism about their theory goes back to 1960, when scholars ate a big helping of archaeological crow with the discovery of a Viking encampment in the New World, specifically at L'Anse aux Meadows, in Newfoundland. The man who made the find was a self-taught amateur and one-idea obsessive. Helge Ingstad was a lawyer by training and small-town politician (governor for three years of a Norwegian territory in the Arctic, the Svalbard Islands). Eminent scholars such as Harvard's Samuel Eliot Morison sniffed at him, regarding his theories as crackpot stuff. As if it weren't enough that the guy had been known to wander Mexico looking for a "lost tribe," his claim to the Viking landing in America relied entirely on his reading of the Norse sagas.

He had studied specifically the texts of *Graenlendinga Saga* and *Eirik's Saga*. If scholars thought that these were fanciful poems full of invented imagery, Ingstad disagreed. He believed that buried in the heroic verse was a core story of journalistic truth and factual exploration. He insisted that the place called "Vinland" and the ferocious savages known as the "skraelings" were not metaphors but were North America and the Indians.

Using the vague geography in the stories, he began triangulating the possible landfall sites along the northwestern Atlantic shore and spent years devising ways to visit harbors and inlets to examine the land for clues. In 1960 he was visiting a small village in Newfoundland on an unrelated medical mission. He happened to ask a local named George Decker if the village had any prehistoric sites.

Decker said it did, and after nearly eight years of digging, Newfoundland finally yielded physical evidence: foundational remains of three long houses, a bronze ring-head pin, some nails smelted from a

bog iron, and a spindle whorl for spinning wool—all of Norse prov-
enance. As a result, the Viking presence in the New World in the year
1000 is now accepted as absolute fact. Canada has made the place a
park. And even the Ivy League establishment has recast the story ever
so slightly to make it fit the model of a properly credentialed expert
whisk-brooming away dust from the Truth. In later editions of his
books, Harvard's Samuel Eliot Morison worked in a tiny tweak of
stately revisionism. He referred to the Norse voyage, stiffly, as confirmed by "archaeologist Dr. Helge Ingstad."

If amateurs always seems to be fading away, it's because that's what
most of them do. Most are failures, and that is a dead-end path to
immortality. Those amateurs simply disappear. And if they succeed,
then they spend a great deal of time trying to erase their amateur
past. They collect piles of honorary degrees or massive stock options,
either of which makes it very easy to look like a pro. And it makes
it easier to write that memoir that explains how it was all inevitable
anyway and airbrush out all that stumbling amateur striving. The first
of these was, of course, *The Autobiography of Benjamin Franklin*, an
amazing piece of revisionist history. It's what helped set up the image
of the wise old jolly Puritan inventor at the expense of the naïve
screwup, the liar, the rutting boy-satyr, the atheist, the self-promoter.
The amateur's redemptive memoir is practically its own genre in this
country; evidence of them can be found on every year's bestseller list.
You can find the same structure in the summoning of the log cabin
in William Henry Harrison's presidential biography—all true, but
part of the narrative of unpolished origins that begins so many of
these stories. Patti Smith's *Just Kids* opens on her birth in a room-

ing house and with an evocation of a humble family learning how to pray. What awaits is a lovely tale of pluck and inevitability. It doesn't matter who's telling it: Jack Welch of GE or Helen Keller. We love these stories. It's a world where we sweep away a lot of the details and make the path to glory seem inevitable. It can be a treacherous task, which is why this bookshelf is afflicted with so many scandals (*A Million Little Pieces, Three Cups of Tea* . . .).

The cover-up is a key element in the amateur story and the main reason why the whole narrative feels like a hidden history of our country. We're ashamed of our amateur status, so Americans love awards that deliver us from our low origins and elevate us in some way. Think of the famous prizes given out each year by the MacArthur Foundation. The intent is not merely to honor the already famous but also to find unknown people just following their bliss—amateurs, in other words—and reward their obscure good work with a large sum of money. But the money's not even half of it. What better title (and cover) could any American hope for than the award's nickname: the Genius Grant.

When I started thinking about this idea, I considered focusing on just such characters. One could start with Ben Franklin, who famously broke with his apprenticeship in Boston as a teenager and ran away to Philadelphia to reinvent himself as a Great Man. And then I could have carried that idea into any of the hundreds of American success stories that seem to follow the Franklin model. Dropping out is a great American tradition, the very essence of amateurism, another recapitulation of the pioneer/immigrant narrative, the ultimate in starting fresh: no school! It begins with Franklin, and one can find these dropouts popping up in every era of American history—Thomas Paine, Davy Crockett, Mark Twain, George Eastman, Horace Greeley, Thomas Edison, D. W. Griffith, John Jacob Astor, Samuel Gompers, Jay Gould, Andrew Carnegie, Adolph Ochs, Charlie Chaplin, David Sarnoff, William Saroyan, Will Rogers, Al Smith, Henry Kaiser, Orville and Wilbur Wright, August Wilson,

Bill Gates, Steve Jobs, those Stanford undergrads who invented Google, and Facebook's Mark Zuckerberg. But if that book hasn't been written a dozen times over, it sure feels like it has, and then I had an even better idea.

Why not try to break down the specific attributes and types of amateurism into different categories and then put them back together as a unified theory?

Turned out, squirreled away in a corner of sociology was a man named Robert Stebbins, an American teaching at the University of Calgary in Canada, who has published scores of books on "leisure." Stebbins found that some people took their weekending seriously, so he concocted a subdiscipline he called "serious leisure"—an ungainly phrase but one that circumscribed the same world, more or less, that interested me.

To develop his grand unified theory of amateurism, Stebbins constructed a fairly complex framework he calls the "Serious Leisure Perspective." Just to show you how large an idea it is, he always capitalizes it in his books. For example, Stebbins writes that "the Perspective has simplified and organized an undifferentiated mass of free-time core activities and experiences."

That's right, Stebbins is literally attempting to categorize the world of amateur pursuits, aka "free-time core activities and experiences," by breaking it all down—and down and down and down. His ability to map every cul-de-sac, blue highway, and back alley of amateur pursuit and compartmentalize the results recalls the Spanish bureaucracy that oversaw New World exploration, or maybe the final warehouse sequence of the first Indiana Jones movie. He calls this task the "Project," and he capitalizes that word, too. If the Perspective is the process, the Project is the result. His analysis reveals that amateur pursuits possess certain "qualities" and that some of these can be further broken down into "dimensions," and these divisions go on and on too.

In one amateur sub-category he offers examples: "entertainment magic, Canadian football, stand-up comedy, barbershop singing, volunteering, and selected map hobbies." No writer since Walt Whitman can list items in a series quite like Robert Stebbins.

Another newly discovered sub-sub-category called "project-based leisure" can include: building a stone wall, making a relative a sweater, surprise birthday parties, a genealogical project, developing a basement, setting out Christmas decorations, volunteering for an arts festival, climbing Kilimanjaro, and "knot making from kits."

Knot making from kits? What century is this? Where am I? What bellum am I ante?

As I read one of Stebbins's books after another, what I had thought was a gold mine turned out to be a rabbit hole. I read almost all his books, mostly in a state of wonder at Stebbins's Project: One study brings the Perspective to tournament bass fishing, and then turn the pages, and the same Perspective is bearing down on dildo parties in England. (Swear to God.) One book compares "tolerable deviance," which includes "cross-dressing, homosexuality, watching sex . . ."), with the other sub-sub-sub-category, "intolerable deviance," which covers "incest, vandalism, sexual assault. . . ." These lists are luxuriously odd—considerations of elderly shuffleboard players alongside mushroom collectors alongside figure skating. I don't know how Stebbins will ever finish this Project unless he calls in Jorge Luis Borges and his infinite library for backup. Many splendored things happen "outside work." Maybe another word for the Project is "Life."

If you spend too much time looking at amateurism this way (and I have), you wonder if you'll ever end up seeing it at all. Like peering through a telescope, constrict the aperture too much and you get the Ten Success Stories. Open it too wide and you end up lost, Fitzcarraldo-style, macheteing a trail across the Continent of Stebbins.

Somewhere in the middle ground was where I had to be. I wanted to catch amateurs before they got famous, observe them in action, and not be lured into the usual quicksilver arguments about creativity. I wanted to catch a glimpse of what improvisation looked like and how one went about pioneering into the muck of a new frontier (or idea); or to understand how constant assaults by amateurs shaped the profession attacked; or to see a new idea emerge among those unconvinced by familiar habits of mind.

One organizing idea immediately jumped out at me as I began to collect evidence of amateur enthusiasm. It's not as if amateurs can be found in *every* discipline and pursuit. Like any invasive species, amateurs gather where there has been some kind of stress to the system, some kind of disturbance. When they clump together by forming a group of websites or a weekend club, it reveals something about where the inventive surges in a culture are located. I began one line of research by hanging out with weekend robotics clubs until I realized that those were already past their maturity. It was a while back that the Pentagon would regularly send talent scouts to sit in the back of robot club meetings in order to recruit the freshest thinking for DARPA (Defense Advanced Research Projects Agency). One thing led to another, and I quickly learned that another kind of gathering was beginning across town, in abandoned warehouses, and the aim was not a mechanical robot but a living one—synthetic biology. It was easy to find truly good examples of pursuits that revealed precisely how the amateur impulse asserts itself against a well-known, well-defined professional elite. One I considered was the rise of amateur porn on the Internet and its sudden takedown of all those old film and video outfits in California's San Fernando valley. I ultimately decided against porn as a story because, honestly, porn as a story is always boring. Visiting the set of a porn movie or the porn awards banquet is another of those journalistic chestnuts (the word "zany" shows up in editor conversations on this one, too). I have read so many of these over the years—including Martin Amis and David Foster Wallace—and the results are always disappointing, even in the hands of masters. Turns out porn stars are about as articulate about their craft as, say, hockey players. And yet, the elements of the story I was looking for are right there: the professional elite who have reduced their work to known points of order—massive breast implants, shaved pubic hair, clichéd plot lines (the hitchhiker, the pool boy), the four or five basic moves, the same essential sets (gilded parvenu mansion, suburban den, a van), and the well-worn conclusion, the money shot, as predictable as the suspect on a detective show tearfully breaking down in the interrogation room in the last four minutes of the program. Into this plasti-coated, stylized world of same ol'/same ol' arrived a handful of amateurs, actual real people, who videotaped themselves with real bodies in their own homes, fooling around. And there it is: Amateurism is often about reclaiming some kind of primordial authenticity. (Think of punk music in the late seventies trying to recover some primal thing lost under the similarly plasti-coated sound of Lionel Richie, ABBA, Captain and Tennille, Rupert Holmes, and the canned world that produced them.) It's easy to see in the exponential growth of amateur porn websites and online video sales that this new porn is a classic story of weekend dabblers trying to reclaim some important, lost, funky thing. It's a classic story; I just won't be telling it.

Out in the forest with the Gungywampers, I came to understand that the conventional wisdom about the Age of Discovery is deeply flawed (even if they never won me over with their Chi-Rho evidence). I would hear one withering critique of Christopher Columbus after another. Not of the anti-imperialist sort; there were no mentions of blankets infected with smallpox. The Gungywampers trash Columbus because they think his big, bold, much ballyhooed "risk" of sailing across the Atlantic was in fact not that big a deal and has been hyped by academics who don't want to even consider the possibility that crossing the ocean was not that difficult. Goaded by the Gungywampers, I started calling around the history departments and wound up talking to a historian who had taught at Brandeis and NYU, Cyrus Gordon, who specialized in archaeology and ancient languages.

"Plenty of people were capable of crossing the Atlantic. They just didn't make a big deal about it," Gordon said. He argued that what really marked the Age of Discovery was not so much that Columbus sailed the ocean blue but that it also coincided with the Dawn of the Book. Unlike the previous era's illuminated manuscript, with its labor-intensive efforts making it suitable only for extremely valuable texts like scripture and maybe a little science or history, this new book medium was faster to produce and more easily distributed. In its own time, the book's impact on culture was not unlike our Internet's. A lot of things could be published, and new stories could get told. Columbus, for instance, published his letters after his voyages, as did most of the name explorers. This new medium was drawn more to stories of individuals and their great achievements. If and when Brendan returned, he had to wait for an epic poet to compose a saga. That's some serious lag time in publicity (although one that bitchy authors nowadays believe they can understand). And sagas weren't written down but existed in the oral tradition, a second-rate venue back then, the tabloid media of the Dark Ages.

When Columbus returned, Professor Gordon told me, he "practically held a press conference, that's all." And there were publishers there to take it all down.

Gungywampers hold that there were plenty of accounts of people sailing to America. It's just that we don't read sagas the right way anymore. Brendan the Navigator has his poem too. Eventually it was written down and called the *Navigatio Sancti Brendani Abbatis* (*The Voyage of the Abbot, Saint Brendan*). It's a ripping yarn of a band of Irish monks who left home around A.D. 500 in leather boats called currachs. They sought to escape European corruption by sailing west in search of a remote place they called the "Promised Land of Saints."

As the poem goes, the monks endured the frights of a moving island, a giant who hailed fire down on them, and a dangerous sea of crystal pillars—very colorful images, clearly the fictional embroideries of a poet. But what if they were metaphorical descriptions of a whale, an Icelandic volcano, and icebergs? the Gungywampers argue. Suddenly the story can be read somewhat journalistically, too.

Although Brendan was a historic character and the Irish monks of that era were known for their maritime talent (currachs can still be found among Atlantic fishermen, and *National Geographic* sailed one from Ireland to America in 1976 for a TV special), few historians agree with the Gungywampers that there was a voyage. But it's no longer absurd to try and prove with solid material findings that it did happen. And the era that preceded Columbus looks a lot less dark and far more interesting than it once did. Adventurers did sail and improbable journeys did take place, and it just might be that one of them sought out the Promised Land of Saints and found it just off I-95 not far from the Foxwoods Casino.

This is a book called *Bunch of Amateurs* because that last word most accurately captures this essential quality that runs through these stories. I also call it a search for the American character, because there's just something fundamentally American about heading off to one's garage to reinvent the world.

Amateurs are often wrong, crazy, fraudulent, or twisted. There is typically a pomposity among amateurs that, well, one just has to get used to. They are often nerds, if younger; cranks, if slightly mature; eccentric, if aged; and—it should be said—at just about any age they can be total jackasses. But these are just the characteristics of people obsessed with a new idea, following their bliss, in love (*amo, amas, amat*—amateur) with one true thing.

Who cannot love amateurs like the gungywamping David Barron? Not merely because these people are loopy and fun in a knight errant sort of way, but because even the amateurs who have it all wrong but are obsessed are typically on to something. It's just often not the something they think they are on to.

I've hung out with a lot of amateurs who were misguided or, for now, lost in a world defined mostly by their own private conspiracy theories. But their views of the larger profession or frontier against which they were pushing usually led to some cool thoughts. What I always liked about hitching my own curiosity to someone else's amateur passion was that it granted me access to a world, like a travel writer, in a way that few others get to see. Think of this book as a hitchhiker's guide to amateurism. In each chapter I get in somebody's car and go somewhere, and often no place near where the driver thought we were heading.

I sought out the venues where amateurism seemed to be thriving—those multimillion-dollar contests and those weekend hobby clubs hoping to break out into something important. Some disciplines are just teeming with amateur passion right now and long have been—astronomy and paleontology, for instance. It's probably not a coincidence that both fields take us into the biggest questions. If you're going to fiddle around on the weekends, why not solve the secret of the universe or the mystery of life? I hitched a ride on the ongoing controversy of Kennewick Man in part because the amateur anthropology in that case drove so revealingly off the rails. And I couldn't resist the story of the ivory-billed woodpecker because no amateur pursuit takes us so far afield, lost in bureaucratic thinking, the drama of experts failing, the hidden history of Dixie's postwar destruction, and the very American fantasies motivating the restoration of the land.

In this book, there is a search for the original American amateur and the baptismal moment of defining this country as a nation of garage invention and second acts; the story of a fortress of expertise under attack by banshees eager to bring down the walls; an expedition into the world of weekend warriors meeting in their clubhouses plotting scientific revolutions; an intermission of error and total amateur fiasco; and, finally, a visit to one of those perpetual frontiers where amateurs continuously have (and always will) come to discover—in this case, literally—new worlds.

It's a series of stories that glimpse the ongoing American experience, the one told repeatedly throughout our pop culture's sacred art, such as *The Wizard of Oz*. Just who is the Wizard? A cranky old expert whose breakthrough achievement occurred long ago (during the Omaha State Fair, if the balloon is to be believed). He is no longer certain that his expertise will sustain his reputation, so he hides out in his fortress and engineers a mighty façade of smoke and fire he can belch at others who challenge what he has to say.

And who challenges him? Rank amateurs improvising their way through the deep dark forest. Their roundabout journey is a way for them to discover their own emerging capacities as unfinished creatures of intellect, compassion, and courage. Sure, that story might have been a metaphor for the qualities needed to get Americans through the Depression (what I always heard growing up). But *The Wizard of Oz* is also an American narrative about self-invented outsiders overwhelming the domain of professionals.

What does happen in the finale? The Wizard is revealed to be merely a washed-up blowhard who's been dining out on the tattered remains of a dated and jejune credentialism. And what is it that the Wizard offers the three great amateurs—the scarecrow, the tin man, and the lion? Emblems of expertise: a diploma, a testimonial, and a medal.

"Back where I come from we have universities, seats of great learning, where men go to become great thinkers," the Wizard tells the Scarecrow, assuring him in most un-European terms that he's as smart, if not smarter, than any credentialed thinker. "And when they come out, they think deep thoughts—and with no more brains than you have. . . . But! They have one thing you haven't got! A diploma!"

The adventure's the thing, of course, but it's always nice when a self-made pioneer winds up with, say, a genius grant—something that happens all the time in our culture. We're Americans. We love that stuff. This is our temple and our American idol. We're Gungy-wampers all the way down.

2

ONCE MORE, TO THE GATES

I. The First American Is Born

It's spring in Paris, 1778, and I have always pictured this particular moment happening in front of the golden baroque gates of Versailles. One of the weekend rituals of King Louis XVI was the formal reception of arriving ambassadors in order to chat them up a bit and get a sense of just what kind of new men were in town. That day, His Majesty was scheduled to meet the latest American envoy—John Adams, the Yosemite Sam of the founding fathers.

By Yosemite Sam, I don't mean that Adams was a short, barrel-chested, overly suspicious, fuming hothead with a fondness for flyaway hairstyles and a taste for poofy neckwear. That's a *given*. Rather, I mean that Adams, like Sam, spent a great deal of his life aggravated that the world would not conform to the story line he thought should be playing out around him. Adams was a man of protocol and schedules, reasoned decisions and a disregard for foolishness, all work and no play—the kid who always did his homework on time.

When he was twenty-one years old, he set down a schoolwork plan in his diary that would last a lifetime: "I am resolved to rise with the Sun and to study the Scriptures, on Thursday, Friday, Saturday, and Sunday mornings, and to study some Latin authors the other 3 mornings. Noon and Nights I intend to read English authors. This is my fixed Determination, and I will set down every neglect and every compliance with this Resolution. May I blush whenever I suffer one hour to pass unimproved."

Adams rarely blushed. Life was a homework assignment to John Adams, and the right answer to every question was always self-improvement leading to virtue: "I will strive with all my soul to be something more than Persons who have had less Advantages than myself."

Impressed by his improved self, Adams got distraught if he thought his moral achievement wasn't properly recognized. When it wasn't, which was often, Adams would plunge into the colonial version of a pity party and unload to his diary or his wife, Abigail, just how unfair it all was.

"The English have got at me," he wrote to Abigail regarding British press coverage of his reputation in Paris. "They make fine work of me—fanatic, bigot, perfect cipher . . . awkward figure, uncouth dress, no address, no character, cunning hardheaded attorney." When he witnessed others getting ahead by cunning or luxuriating unpunished in debauchery, he flipped: "Modesty is a virtue that can never thrive in public. Modest merit! Is there such a thing remaining in public life?"

Adams had this vague sense that others had figured out how to get ahead *without* all the homework, and he felt clueless and even injured when he found himself in the shadow of such shrewdness. It was all so horrible, especially because no one was noticing Adams's magnificent virtue and his strict adherence to the rules. In fact, people seemed to *prefer* the company of insufferable wretches who swanned about town and grasped at popularity. And he despised it all as a cheap trick, as he explained to his wife, Abigail: "A man must be his own trumpeter—he must write or dictate paragraphs of praise in the newspapers; he must dress, have a retinue and equipage; he must ostentatiously publish to the world his own writings with his name . . . he must get his picture drawn, the statue made, and must hire all the artists in his turn to set about works to spread his name, make the mob stare and gape, and perpetuate his name."

Here's the problem, though: This trumpeter Adams grumbled about was Ben Franklin. And Franklin was the reason Adams was in Paris, ostensibly to work as his partner in the war effort to get French support for America's struggling armies in 1778. Already the rumors of Franklin's boozing and womanizing were legendary. How could he party all across Paris and attend to the business of salvaging the failing American Revolution? The Continental Congress had sent Adams there to watch over this old and famous man whom many of the founding fathers had come to see as America's very own Falstaff, a mead-guzzling, woman-flirting raconteur, handy with the pithy one-liners but not very efficient at getting the hard work done. As a result, Adams simply mistrusted Franklin. Yet that was the man Adams was slated to meet at Versailles on that May morning to make proper introductions at the Court.

At the time, an appearance before the king was a highly ritualized affair. One had to dress the part of a formal gentleman, which meant a stylized version of a knight pledged to the chivalric code—i.e., clean breeches, fine boots, laced cuffs, a sword, and a powdered wig. There were actually shops nearby to Versailles that catered to this getup, just as teenagers attending the prom today can rent a tuxedo. Near the gates, one could even find a sword-monger to rent you a fine-looking cutlass with gold hilt, an essential piece of the entire costume. So, picture it. There is John Adams in formal French court clothing, standing around, expectant. He has his sword and powdered wig. His cuffs are perfectly set to reveal the stitched finery of rich lace. Slay me, Percy, if he isn't a dashing pimpernel. Don't say John Adams doesn't know the rules! His perfumes are an exquisite blend. His breeches are fresh and pressed, his over-jacket cut just so, all according to court protocol as pronounced by the effete chamberlains who literally looked you up and down and vetted the costume of each man approaching the king's personage and/or his representatives.

So Adams is feeling quite good about himself. He is here to meet the King of France, win over more support, and do his fetal nation proud. And now, here comes his partner's carriage. I like to imagine the horses halting, the wheels braking, and Adams's moon face tilting slightly to catch a partial glimpse of the, even then, world famous hangdog eyes and sly smirk of Ben Franklin. The carriage door's iron latches turn with a tiny crunching sound and the door opens wide.

But I'm not going to bring Franklin, the notorious trumpeter, out of the carriage just yet, because, at this point, you won't get the joke. (This is always the problem with history, so much huffing and puffing.) You can't really appreciate the unbearable lightness of the moment until you have a sense of the petty soap opera playing out between these two crucial Americans and the broader quarrels that dominated French society at that time. Along with the mud, Franklin stepped from his carriage into all of that, too.

More important, what happens here is one of those great moments in American history, specifically in the way our nation comes to be thought of as a bunch of amateurs. We often apply that word to garage inventors or athletes who can't make the cut. Or we think of it as a broad word that implies poor quality or mediocre talent. I want to argue that the word took on several meanings when it crossed the pond and that together they form a kind of story, an American story. And this story often involves, at the beginning, an act of fraudulence, of assuming a new name or donning a disguise, of pretending that you are something that you are not. This story gets repeated over and over again and far more often than people might think. It constitutes a hidden history of America. And while there are many places in our past where one could say it began, I am going to locate it right here, with Franklin's exit from the carriage, because it was an instant in history as daring as it was hilarious. With nothing but a bit of ad-libbing on Franklin's part, a fresh figure is about to be born: the New World amateur and the soul of the American character.

II. Bowling Alone, Colonial Style

During the Revolutionary War itself, few really understood just what Ben Franklin was up to. From our point of view, we see him as just another founding father. But the other revolutionaries didn't see him that way at all.

At this time in Paris, Franklin was seventy-two years old. John Adams was forty-three years old, Thomas Jefferson was thirty-five, and James Madison was twenty-seven years old. They had not yet earned their bones. Franklin already had one gouty foot in the history books. He was not just famous. He was world famous. The subject of his fame—the taming of lightning—had about it a kind of pre-Darwinian grandeur. He had demystified one of the last natural phenomena widely perceived to be God's direct and immediate interferences in man's events. Some felt he had overstepped the bounds of humility. Others thought that, having literally stolen God's thunder, some of it had rubbed off on Franklin himself. In many quarters, he was considered not simply a scientist, but perhaps the greatest scientist since Isaac Newton. It's a role every century or so assigns to one individual.

Consider how the twentieth century elevated Albert Einstein as scientific genius who rose from patent clerk to fuzzy-haired icon with twinkling eyes and mischievous sense of humor. By the time I got into college, that ideal of intellect was yielding to the computer and so our new icon would become a great mind literally bound inside a machine. We see it every time Stephen Hawking's crumpled body is wheeled out into a lecture hall to talk to us. Withered and slumped to one side, his face a human rhombus, Hawking flashes an elfin smile as his B-movie metallic voice explains his central idea, so monstrously big it is actually called the Grand Unified Theory of the universe.

Ben Franklin was this character in his time. All the world saw him as both the most mysterious and the perfect creation of the New World. He had not only bottled lightning, he had cranked out hundreds of inventions. With his stringy hair and Buddhist paunch and sly grin (the puckish sense of humor seems to be the common denominator of genius), he looked the part as it was conceived then.

Given the generational difference and his insurmountable greatness, no one quite knew what to make of Franklin's conversion to the Revolution. Especially John Adams. So how perverse was it that destiny would throw these two opposites together at so many crucial moments—they both were chosen to edit Jefferson's first draft of the Declaration, they parleyed with the French about wartime alliances, and later they went to Paris to negotiate the end of the war.

The two men had a history, long before they ever got to Paris on this trip, and they would have a history long afterward. Think of them as the twin poles of the American psyche. They show up at nearly every crucial event of our founding, two cartoon figures standing on Lady Liberty's shoulders, whispering in her ear.

John Adams was a man who believed in civic virtue, that the core measure of a man was his essential goodness (or absence of it). Adams believed you said what you meant. He fervently believed that you got smart decisions by promoting good people to make them. Franklin believed in civic action and that words could (and maybe should) be deceptive. As Franklin put it to Adams on this trip: success in Paris would "depend more on what we do than what we say." Good people were never a suitable replacement for good deeds.

Or to put it another way, Franklin thought Adams was an officious prick. Adams thought Franklin was a decadent blowhard. Their relationship is key to the creation of the mythic American tinkerer of the Old World's imagination.

Adams came to his disgust with Franklin slowly. When he and Franklin were sent to New York during the earliest days of the fighting, in the hopes of negotiating some resolution with Admiral Howe after the Battle of Long Island, the two of them had to bunk together at the various inns as they traveled. One night, in New Jersey, Franklin threw open the window to ventilate the room even though many people thought that illness came from "out there." Adams explained to Franklin that he was "afraid of the evening air." But Franklin had long ago noticed that "nobody ever got a cold by going into a cold church, or any other cold air." Adams knew of Franklin's theory because he'd read it, but he'd written that "the theory was so little consistent with my experience that I thought it a paradox."

"Come!" Franklin shouted to Adams. "Open the window and come to bed, and I will convince you." Then he added a line in which, despite the intervening centuries, one can hear the insufferable preamble of the pompous know-it-all. "I believe you are not acquainted with my theory of colds."

Of course, Franklin's theory is right, but in Adams's writings you can sense his—for now, friendly—weariness: "The Doctor then began a harangue, upon air and cold and respiration and perspiration, with which I was so much amused that I soon fell asleep, and left him and his philosophy together."

By the time Adams arrived in Paris, Franklin had long been

working the salons and parlors trying to win over the locals. His strategy was to go slow and grasp the lay of the land before deciding how best to make the approach. To do this, he spent a lot of time socializing and indulging in French life of that time. Literally, he just partied.

To a man like Adams, Franklin was sunk in debauchery and doing unspeakable things with the ladies. Franklin was known to have played chess with a notorious lady named Madame Anne-Louise d'Hardancourt Brillon de Jouy while she bathed in her tub. He had attended dinners where women just plopped into Franklin's lap, showered him in kisses, and purred, *"mon cher papa."* Women who might otherwise seem honorable would casually flop an arm around Franklin's shoulder. It was outrageous, Adams complained, such "incessant dinners and dissipation." Why couldn't they just go to the king and ask for help and money?

Franklin had already figured out that was premature. France had lost a war to England, and other nations were rising up. Russia under Catherine the Great had just recognized Poland and for all intents and purposes had declared itself a new and major player in continental affairs. The foreign minister of France at this time was Comte de Vergennes, a cunning militarist who desperately wanted to re-arm France and challenge England via the American conflict. (The scholar Jonathan Dull told me he considered Vergennes the Oliver North of the eighteenth century.) Vergennes had let Franklin know that building support in the town, sitting quietly, and waiting for the propitious moment were crucial.

France was ruled by one of the most famous kings on the earth, Marie Antoinette's husband, Louis XVI. But he was only twenty-four years old at the time, and straight talk would probably spook him. Sure, the French hated the Brits, and on that level, no problem, but here come some American bumpkins who want his support in overthrowing another . . . king? Might that not come back to haunt him?

Franklin chose not to confide in Adams about his own strategy because Franklin had long ago learned that secrecy in diplomacy is key. Before Adams, there had been a succession of co-diplomats who despised Franklin for the same, understandable reasons. When Franklin forgot to tell Arthur Lee that he'd changed messengers, Lee exploded that Franklin's neglect was "one of the deepest injuries that can be offered to a gentleman, a direct and unjust judgment of his veracity." Another, Ralph Izard, found Franklin equally despicable and told Adams when he got to town that "Dr. Franklin was one of the most unprincipled men upon earth: that he was a man of no veracity, no honor, no integrity, as great a villain as ever breathed."

Franklin simply ignored his partners, and he expressed his true thoughts in a letter to Izard that he never sent: "It is true I have omitted answering some of your letters. I do not like to answer angry letters. I hate disputes. I am old, cannot have long to live, have much to do and no time for altercation."

He also realized that the Parisians' interest in him as a Great Man drove his partners insane: "I am too much respected, complimented and caressed by the people in general," he wrote, and so when it came to his diplomatic partners in Paris, he simply chose to dismiss "those unhappy gentlemen; unhappy indeed in their tempers, and in the dark uncomfortable passions of jealousy, anger, suspicion, envy, and malice."

Into this matrix of disinterested disregard came John Adams. What he saw when he observed Franklin's behavior was a man sunk in immoral frivolity and Parisian decadence. This urbane love of Franklin was seen by Adams from the other end of the telescope, and he charged that Franklin had "a monopoly of reputation here, and an indecency in displaying it." Or he was jealous of it: "When they spoke of him, they seem to think he was to restore the Golden Age."

To Adams, there *was* no strategy, but how would he know? Franklin mostly neglected him, too. Thus the letters of John Adams and his wife, Abigail, paint a portrait of a most despicable Ben Franklin. Adams is enraged when he realizes he's traveled all this way to do nothing of any importance. He's reduced to the role of clerk to Franklin, figuring out the accounts and balancing the books. Franklin barely talks to him. And it was the hypocrisy that galled him. Here he was neglected by Poor Richard himself, who had lectured Americans like some Puritan saint that "a little neglect may breed great mischief."

Sunk in despair and self-pity, Adams in another letter said that he was simply "hated." He was a man "treading among burning plowshares, with horrid figures of jealousy, envy, hatred and revenge, vanity, ambition, avarice, treachery, tyranny, insolence, arranged on each side of his path and lashing him with scorpions all the way, and attempting at every step to trip up his heels."

Over the years, Franklin repeatedly observed Adams's aimless rage (and possibly his baroque metaphors), and he later wrote: "I am persuaded, however, that he means well for his country, is always an honest man, often a wise one, but sometimes, and in some things, absolutely out of his senses."

The difference between the two boiled down to a moral split in approaches to the wider world—between "I say what I mean" (Adams) and "Actions speak louder than words" (Franklin). Adams's entire worldview was a variation of the Protestant work ethic, the strict bearing of the Quaker, the virtue of the Puritan. Franklin possessed more of the pioneer's make-do ethic, the down-to-earth philosophy of the dabbler fooling around in search of a working solution, the pragmatism of the Deist. This division between a Puritan's view of the world, with its emphasis on revealed truth and expert ways of doing things, versus the Deist's view of the world, with its emphasis on seeing what works and an improvisational way of doing things, is a fundamental tension between these two men. It is a tug between how you're supposed to do things and how you might try to do things, between a kind of professionalism and amateurism.

In Paris, Adams was up at 5 A.M. every morning and was distraught that the man who had penned the words "Early to bed, early to rise . . ." could rarely be found before lunch. The hypocrisy offended Adams's Puritan sensibility. Every day seemed another fresh outrage, such as when Adams finally got command of enough of the French language to realize that Franklin was, in fact, a terrible speaker. He was just winging it, faking, and getting by with gestures and wit. "Never was a country more imposed on by finesse," Adams wrote.

Soon enough, Adams and his sour attitude got left behind with Izard and the others. Franklin would not have much use for him, either. Adams was once again isolated, alone with his pen and his poisoned thoughts. "The longer I live and the more I see of public men, the more I wish to be a private one," he concluded. When David McCullough, in his biography of Adams, wished to capture the seclusion and melancholy of this journey, he wrote this sentence about Adams: "'Dined at home,' became a frequent note in his diary."

As a man, Adams made the perfect foil to Franklin, in part because if Franklin was the undisputed master of his own talents, then Adams was the unforgiving amanuensis to his most hideous defects.

When he did get invited to those parties with Franklin, Adams would come home disturbed that he lacked the "power of the face." By "my physical constitution," he wrote, "I am but an ordinary man." Adams was a short, fat man with a doughy face, and he understood that this somehow hurt him. Think about what an insight this is in the pre-television era: "When I look in the Glass, my Eye, my Forehead, my Brow, my Cheeks, my Lips all betray this Relaxation."

There is a raw, honest quality to Adams in his own determined examination of his essential loserness. Again, here he is looking into the mirror: "I have insensibly fallen into a habit of affecting wit and humor, of shrugging my shoulders, and . . . distorting the muscles of my face. My motions are stiff and uneasy, ungraceful, and my attention is unsteady and irregular." When he was a young man, even his friends ridiculed him. "I talk to Paine about Greek; that makes him laugh. I talk to Sam Quincy about Resolution, and being a great

Man, and study and improving Time, which makes him laugh," Adams wrote (strangely sounding like Robin Gibb when he sang that Bee Gees hit "I Started a Joke"). "I talk to Hannah and Esther about the folly of Love, about despizing it, about being above it, pretend to be insensible of tender Passions, which makes them laugh." Unlike most kids with the KICK ME sign pinned to his backside, Adams knew it was there. Instead of taking it off, Adams spent a lifetime writing about it.

When he considered, as a young man, that he might try to be cool and well regarded, he of course wrote about it: "Shall I look out for a Cause to Speak to, and exert all the Soul and all the Body I own, to cut a flash, strike amazement, to catch the Vulgar? In short shall I walk a lingering, heavy Pace or shall I take one bold determined Leap into the Midst of some Cash and Business? That is the question. A bold Push, a resolute attempt, a determined Enterprize, or a slow, silent imperceptible creeping. Shall I creep or fly?"

Here's why Adams is amazing: He decided to creep.

Imagine his despair when a letter from the colonies flits over that February in 1779 appointing Franklin "minister plenipotentiary"— that is, the single and sole representative to the King of France. Arthur Lee was reassigned to Madrid. And what did the letter say about Adams?

They *forgot* about him. The founding fathers back in the colonies neglected to reassign Adams. They didn't even mention his name, as if they no longer remembered he was even in Paris. (We know Yosemite Sam's reaction: Both six-shooters now firing in all directions, a funny dance, and lots of frontier gibberish at the top of his lungs.) Well, rhetorically, Adams almost got there: "The Scaffold is cutt away, and I am left kicking and sprawling in the Mire," he wrote. "It is hardly a state of Disgrace that I am in but rather of Total Neglect and Contempt."

He immediately left Paris to catch a boat back to the United States. He had come to France to save his country, and instead all that happened was more mockery of John Adams. He fancied himself a brave paladin in the chivalrous service of freedom itself. Instead the world saw him differently, but why? He would contemplate that one on the way home, a trip for which Adams selected a great work of literature to study for his usual self-improving drudgery on the long trip across the sea. What book did Lady Liberty's knight errant choose?

Don Quixote.

III. Franklin Steps from the Carriage

But I can't let Adams leave Paris just yet. Before he quixotically stormed off, there was this moment, his appointment at the gates of Versailles, when Franklin exited his coach. And Adams didn't seem to quite understand what Franklin did understand: how different this particular visit was from all the others. On every other voyage, Franklin had been a British citizen. Now Franklin and Adams were *Americans.* But it was Franklin who understood that he was being looked at for the first time—gazed upon and studied . . . as an American. We had separated from England and were now being referred to as Americans. The sense that we were somehow different occupied people's thoughts. How would they see us? What would they make of us? Franklin knew that he, as the most famous American, was suddenly cast in a role that went far beyond just being a diplomat. The center of all European culture was here, and they were anxious to see what Americans looked like and how they behaved. They were looking, specifically, at the person and character of Ben Franklin.

So when he stepped from the carriage, it's crucial to understand what the French were hoping to see when they looked. A fight was going on in Paris then about the very nature of Man, and in that quarrel the New World played a crucial part. A common view then held that the geographical climate of a place affected one's very physical development. Others believed that what really mattered was the nature of the government under which one lived. It was a nature versus nurture fight; we still have them today.

In the time that Franklin and Adams arrived in Paris, much of France believed that the relatively "new" climate of the New World stunted your growth and your mind. No, literally. It just seemed obvious to the French that Americans were smaller and somewhat stupider. American animals were understood to be punier, and our food crops were practically bonsai.

According to Europe's top scientists, the cooler American climate produced animals "mongelized, undersized, cowardly and a thousand times less dangerous than those of Asia and Africa." The American Indians found on the land were understood to be "a mere animal of the first rank" who "lacked vigor and endurance, were sexually frigid and perverted, unprolific, hairless, insensitive to pain, short-lived, and afflicted by a list of ills and perversions ranging from irregular menstruation to the eating of iguanas." Once Europeans moved to America, the men actually started to shrink, the women ceased to be fertile, and the domesticated livestock shriveled and became lethargic.

If things weren't more flaccid and dull-witted, then they were just very, very strange. A widely known *fact* at the time was that American bears attacked cows and bit a hole in their side. Then the bear would blow into the wound until the cow exploded. American snakes, it was said, just lay back with their jaws unhinged and waited for our retarded squirrels to fall into their mouths.

The New World was a place of climate-controlled degeneracy, which explained why, according to Durand Echeverria, the "universities of America had not produced a single man of reputation, not a single individual capable of writing even a bad book, not a single teacher, philosopher, doctor, physicist, or scholar whose name had ever reached Europe."

Such notions were regularly advanced by the top thinkers of the day. This was not just conventional wisdom but known fact. One of the most ferocious theorists in this school was a Dutch scholar named Cornelius de Pauw, and when Diderot was deciding just who among the world's experts should write the nineteen-page article in his famous encyclopedia on America, he chose this guy. De Pauw considered the discovery of America the "most disastrous event in the history of mankind." Another of these theorists was Abbé Raynal, who later would dine with Franklin. When this issue of the puny American came up, Franklin asked his fellow countrymen at the table to stand. Franklin was tall, as were the others. Everyone laughed, because, as Thomas Jefferson, who loved to tell this story, once wrote, Raynal was "a mere shrimp."

A second school of thought of the day held precisely the opposite view: America was, in fact, an arcadia of pastoral simplicity. Here man got back to the land, improved himself naturally, expanded his worth according to grounded agrarian economics, and matured into a natural philosopher. The basics of this notion dated all the way back to Rousseau and his concept of the noble savage, which is exactly what these thinkers believed the American Indian to be, and even the colonialists, whose virtue was hewn from the hard labor of civilizing the land.

A popular novel of the time explained America this way: "Every day of your lives is serene, for the purity of your souls is communicated to the skies above you. You are free, you labor, and bring forth all about you, besides your abundant crops, a harvest of all the virtues. You are as nature would wish us to be." Here's a metaphor of freedom, from that time: "a life as innocent and as imperturbably happy as that of the inhabitants of Virginia."

Abbé Raynal was eventually converted, and when he crossed over to the pro-America camp, he opined that "the inhabitants of the Colonies lead that rustic life for which the human race was originally intended and which most favors health and fecundity."

This argument invaded every major discipline. Economics, for instance. One view held that only agriculture created new wealth and saw in America's largely agricultural economy proof of these ideas. These were the Physiocrats, who were opposed by the Mercantilists, who didn't see anything wrong with importing stocks of gold and silver from the New World. Again, America was either a source of inspiration with its pastoral simplicity or a pit of degeneracy into which France threw all its good raw materials and got back, as one Physiocrat put it, nothing but "gold and syphilis."

What the French knew of the homeland of John Adams and Ben Franklin was, therefore, fairly twisted. If Americans saw the typical Frenchman as a fop in silk and lace, then the average Frenchman saw the typical American as a withered homunculus. If, as a Frenchman, you took the more benign view of the New World, then the picture you had in mind ran to one of two images: the virtuous farmer in the coonskin cap or the Good Quaker in an outsized hat and enormous buckle shoes. The latter image was introduced some forty years before Adams's arrival, by Voltaire. In a 1743 letter, Voltaire presented the image of the Good Quaker, an earnest and simple man, who served as his argument against the institutional church. This Good Quaker had escaped the confines of the traditional clergy in Europe and developed into an anticlerical pacifist, a man devoted to the benevolence of the human spirit and a sense of liberty hewn in the rough woods of the American eastern seaboard.

You know this guy. He's the pilgrim who is resurrected as a series of construction-paper cutouts in schoolrooms across America every Thanksgiving Day. Right, *him*—decent to a fault, kind to the Indians, delighted to have discovered maize, and known almost exclusively by his outfit: the funny hat, buckle shoes, and white stockings. And this costume was how the French knew him as well.

Often Franklin would go to the formal salons in Paris dressed in this outfit, or he might go in the clothes of the other stereotype of that period—the American pioneer farmer, wearing a coonskin cap and a rustic coat as if he had recently stepped out of the freshly cut forests of Pennsylvania. One of the widely read works in Paris at the time was a book by colonist James Dickinson entitled *Letters from a Farmer in Pennsylvania to the Inhabitants of the British Colonies.* You know this guy too. He's Daniel Boone.

Franklin spent a lot of time cruising Paris in one of these two costumes. The French loved it. And so, while John Adams waits at the gates of Versaillies at last, the door of the carriage opens and out steps Ben Franklin. History doesn't record which costume he wore, but I have always imagined him in the frontier outfit. There is a famous Parisian drawing of Franklin from this very period in a coonskin cap. Despite the passing of two centuries, he still looks ridiculous in it. And, according to one chronicler of this meeting, "Adams left the palace surroundings with the feeling that the situation could be compared to Indian leaders addressing the Congress. . . ." Why? Because there standing at the gates of Versailles was John Adams in his official wig, his rent-a-sword, his fresh breeches. Imagine his reaction at the sheer audacity of a known libertine like Franklin, a woman-letching, Paris-loving gourmand costumed in the humble garments of a colonial bumpkin.

Certainly, Adams was embarrassed by Franklin's breach of etiquette and fretted that he had made them both look like fools. Or, as a second thought, Adams probably feared that Franklin's prank *would* work and there Adams was, the dope who dressed properly. Suddenly, wearing the wig and lace would make him look the naïf, the fool, the loser with the KICK ME sign once again pinned to his breeches. (Time to write in the diary!)

What would be the comparable moment for us? Imagine being invited to the White House for a state dinner and someone shows up in bib overalls and a baseball cap that reads SEX INSTRUCTOR—FIRST LESSON FREE. Now imagine just *who* that person would have to be for everyone in the Blue Room to turn, see it, and say, "Oh, that's brilliant, let him in."

It was a crucial moment in the development of the idea of America—all of France was looking and talking. It was the moment our image as a land of improvisationalists solidified in the minds of people abroad. They not only loved Franklin's costume, they loved that he was *in* costume. They got the joke better than Adams did. This was who the French thought we were, and Franklin indulged it, camping it up.

When Franklin stepped from that carriage, and all the moments when he'd visited the various parties in Paris and the salons, he had been consciously participating in arguably *the* first modern media circus. But he invented it, right then and there, as the thing that would get him what he wanted. When he had stepped off the boat in Marseilles months earlier, he was old and bald, with that stringy long hair down his neck—just as most of us remember him. He had donned a coonskin cap and a plain brown coat just to keep warm. He quickly realized that people were reacting to his outfit and looking at him in a useful way. He decided to run with it. Forget the great scientist. He'd work the Daniel Boone angle. His coonskin cap became so popular that it was merchandized in Paris. People bought souvenirs depicting this image of Franklin the trailblazing woodsman of America. On other occasions, when the French saw Franklin with his bifocals, they thought his glasses were cracked and that he didn't get new ones because of his frontier frugality. He never bothered to correct them. He knew what people wanted to see. So he made sure that they did.

But Franklin's time in Paris was about more than his costume. He was literally received with cheers. People lined the streets. Portraits, mementos, and images were stamped out and sold. His face became familiar everywhere. Artists sketched him, and his portrait appeared on small figurines, snuffboxes, vases. An overnight fashion of the time, suddenly, was to have a portrait of Franklin over the mantel, in much the same way that one finds portraits of Martin Luther King in various homes today.

The man who gave Franklin free quarters in Paris, the Comte de Chaumont, was also franchising Franklin ruthlessly—convincing the king's portraitist to paint him and mass manufacturing medallions showing Franklin in high-minded profile with a Latin slogan that translates, "He snatched the lightning from heaven and the scepter from tyrants."

Adams thought all this excess was scandalous. But the Parisians couldn't get enough of Franklin-mania. Close friends to the king were unable to shut up about him. One of those aristocrats was Marie Antoinette's close friend the Comtesse Diane de Polignac. King Louis XVI was so annoyed by the hype that he presented her with the ultimate piece of Franklin kitsch—a magnificent Sèvres porcelain chamber pot with a portrait of Franklin's now notorious face positioned, you know, just so.

Enraged as always, Adams never quite understood what was happening around him. He saw it all as vulgarity (and who can argue?), but he also understood that Franklin was creating a different way of seeing the world. Of course, Franklin's flimflammery got us the money, the arms, and the men. But later Adams fumed that such stunts would rob history of the truth of his own role and that in time people would say "that Dr. Franklin's electrical rod smote the earth and out sprung General Washington." Which, if you read your average grade school textbook, is not that far off.

Meanwhile, Franklin continued to ignore Adams and actually whined about how time-consuming all this eighteenth-century hype was. He complained of having to spend so many hours sitting for so many portraits. And he noted that his profile was as recognizable as "the man in the moon." All the world was watching and *Franklin* was what they saw. He was not just a pioneer (trying to improvise his way into the hearts and wallets of the French), but our meta-pioneer. He created this image of us as clean-living bumpkins but also as the pioneering amateurs we often are, fiddling our way into becoming something new by pretending to be something we're not.

IV. The Next (and the Next After That) Frontier

Adams was always there to claim that the "real and everlasting excellences" were "piety and virtue." He knew that these fine qualities were always put at risk by the mob whose unwashed ambitions lusted for vulgar fame. Naturally, Franklin saw it precisely the other way around. Success and fame were not ends in themselves but the flattering sideshow that came of heroic action. Like two figures of Greek mythology, Adams and Franklin battle in the American heart.

They fought bitterly throughout the founding era of the country and tried to establish two very different kinds of America. They managed to produce both, through their contempt for each other's view and life. By struggling to create a single coherent America, they instead discovered a force and a counterforce whose ebb and flow guide the tides of our history. The one believes he is erecting a noble fortress to tradition and virtue; the other appears to be tearing it down.

Between the two of them were twin impulses, one more improvisational and experimental, the other more tradition-bound and knowing. There is no fixed American meta-narrative, but there is this ebb and flow between Adamsian veneration of piety and Franklinian love of improvisation, between Calvinist certainty and Deist doubt, between head and heart, virtuocracy and meritocracy, good character and cunning action, between security and freedom, between professionalism and amateurism.

The reason these cycles have little to do with daily politics is that these qualities very easily (however slowly) shift from one party to the other. A little more than a half century ago, it was Franklin Roosevelt who could wink at his aristocratic past, his John Adams virtue, while the Republican candidates who ran against him were often self-made outsiders who claimed the mantle of Main Street. By 1960, self-made Richard Nixon tried unsuccessfully to knock over the glamorous scion of a family already seen as Boston Brahmin (the truth being more complicated). Dynasties have no lock on any party. A century that opened on Tafts and Roosevelts closed with Kennedys and Bushes.

By our time, it was meritocrat Bill Clinton, son of a dog track regular with a fondness for men and a racing stripe in her hair. Clinton didn't know who his father was, but he clawed his way to the White House. He was followed, like clockwork, by the very essence of noblesse oblige: George W. Bush, a man with no accomplishments other than his birth. He claimed to consult his gut and instinct because to allege that any of his decisions were made through his own reasoned contemplation was a pose not even his aides thought he could carry off. So Bush preferred to cast his decisions in the language of virtue, which in our time takes up words like "faith" and "morality." Bush was fond of publicly pronouncing his loyalty to others' virtues. He introduced members of his cabinet with language that would have thrilled John Adams. George Bush typically explained that a certain man was chosen for a task because he was "good" or "strong." Judge John Roberts was elevated to the Supreme Court, Bush said, because he believed Roberts had "a good heart." And General Mike Hayden was elevated to head of the CIA because he was a "strong leader."

What decisions they made sort of didn't matter. They were "good men," so what they did, it followed, was good. This view of virtue—very John Adams—explains why Bush held on to abject failures like Michael Brown at FEMA and Donald Rumsfeld at the Pentagon long after their own friends had kicked them to the curb.

For now, the virtucrats dwell mainly on the right of our political spectrum. It's why a public scold like William Bennett could write a tome called *The Book of Virtues*, in which he describes the essential qualities of all "good men and women." John Adams could have written that book, because that book gets written every generation. *McGuffey's Eclectic Reader*, a collection of patriotic piffle and accounts of civic virtue, was its name a century and a half ago.

When Arthur Schlesinger Jr. wrote a book called *The Cycles of American History*, he tried to define this movement as some variation between American political liberalism and conservatism and happening every generation or so. His father, Arthur Schlesinger Sr., had a similar theory but crunched different numbers, computing a turn of the wheel every sixteen and a half years. Others had different time frames. Karl Mannheim put it at fifteen years. Henry Adams conjectured a turn every twelve years. De Tocqueville played it safe: "Among democratic nations," he wrote, "each generation is a new people." All of them were making a Freudian argument—that the time more or less coincides with the period of time it takes for one generation to age enough that it gets its head handed to it by the next one coming up. None of these cycles work out, because history doesn't play by the clock. But switch out the idea from one of *time* to one of *creativity* and it works a little better.

It's knee-jerk to believe that American history is a linear progression. For a long time in the past, it was arguably true—our narrative rolled along with the folks from the east as they pushed west. In 1893, the historian Frederick Turner wondered in an essay, "The Significance of the Frontier in American History," if the closing of the American frontier would change the nation. Americans have answered his question by proving themselves over and over again capable of finding all kinds of new frontiers to invade, settle, and abandon—disastrously sometimes (the Philippines, Vietnam, Iraq), often beautifully (the North Pole, the moon, the ocean), even virtually (radio, Hollywood, cyberspace). From time to time, we go so far as to demand from our President that he find us a new frontier to swarm.

In American culture, the cycle of amateurs clawing at the walls of professionalism has no fixed origin or duration. One can find it playing out continuously. The two need each other, feed on each other, and in the mythic course of American time—given new costumes, new eras, new characters—find themselves squaring off over and over again. In 1987, Allen Ginsberg (radical poet, destroyer of tradition, and nude protester) confessed in an interview that he admired his lifelong nemesis: conventional writer, defender of tradition, and clothed intellectual Norman Podhoretz. Ginsberg said that he didn't know what he would do without him. Ginsberg and Podhoretz had gone to school together, dreamed of becoming poets together, and set off with their ambitions together. Podhoretz, though, recoiled at the amateur improvisations of the beat poets and retreated to the fortress of tradition. From there, he hurled invective at Ginsberg for the rest of their lives. But Ginsberg confessed that he needed the unmovable whetstone of Podhoretz's intransigent tradition to sharpen himself against. "If he weren't there like a wall I can butt my head against," he said, sounding very much like a certain bespectacled founding father, "I wouldn't have anybody to hate."

3

THE TRUTH ABOUT BIRDS

I. The Biggest Story in the World

One morning I got a call from a friend inside the Nature Conservancy who asked me, first off, if I could keep an incredibly huge secret. We all know the answer to that question.

Breathlessly, he told me that his organization was sitting on one of the most amazing stories in history and would I be interested? I'm not sure I even got to answer that one. He immediately told me that a team was on the ground in a primeval cypress swamp in Arkansas and that they had found the ivory-billed woodpecker. Honestly, I didn't know much about the critter other than that the very name, like the yellow-bellied sapsucker's, was cartoon shorthand for bird nut.

I typically avoid daily journalism, especially announcement stories (New Asian Weasel Discovered!), because I've spent most of my life in weekly or monthly magazines and breaking news was always tantalizingly out of reach. But this one was different; there was time. So I asked him to let me check it out and immediately sped off to learn that, yes, this was North America's largest woodpecker, but it also came with a backstory so bizarre, epic, covert, and overwrought that if we included birds among mythic Americans, the ivory-bill would keep company with Charles Foster Kane and Jay Gatsby.

Rumors among ornithologists and hunters that the bird still existed floated out of Southern swamps from time to time, and so the bird had become a kind of rural legend. No one had confidently seen it in more than sixty years. No doubt, it was the most sought-after bird in the world.

Native Americans long ago prized those white bills as emblems of power. John James Audubon marveled at their remote swampy habitats, the "favorite resort of the ivory billed wood pecker" with "the dismal croaking of innumerable frogs, the hissing of serpents, or the bellowing of alligators!" Early colonial hunters were stunned by the bird whose mostly black plumage at rest unfurled into a glitzy burst of white trailing feathers beneath a nearly three-foot wingspan. There was something aesthetic at work here, something unutterable, something semiotic. Its shape and style beguiled people, like the stride of a panther, the eyes of a koala, the sway back of a rhinoceros, the rolling shoulders of a gorilla.

The adult ivory-bill is a large bird and is exquisitely colored. Its yellow eyes, red crest, ivory bill, black feathers, and (when perched) the white lightning bolt marking on its neck—the mark of Zorro, the forehead of Harry Potter—give the whole bird a garish charisma. Connecticut's state ornithologist Margaret Rubega wrote: "This is the Dennis Rodman of woodpeckers."

In rare 1930s moving footage of the ivory-bill, it hops around the side of a tree with a cocky certainty, glancing about, seemingly aware of its ostentation. Back in the days when they were plentiful, the sight of them startling away from a tree in an explosion of white

light was said to provoke blasphemous cries from the virtuous. The
"Lord God Bird" is what the profane helplessly nicknamed it on
their way to Hell.

I liked the idea of pursuing this story because I have a lucky streak
with woodpeckers. I spent a week once with Beau Turner, Ted Turner's son, in northern Florida as he explained to me how he was garden-
ing an entire thousand-acre wood of longleaf pine with an eye toward
its most fragile and reclusive tenant, the red-cockaded woodpecker.
Standing amid the cathedral pines that afternoon, I instantly spotted
one making a ruckus in the canopy. Another time, I was reporting a
story in Tierra del Fuego. I wandered off in the woods trying to get
as close as I could to the tiptoe of the Americas, as one is inclined to
do down there. On an otherwise lonely path, an enraged Magellanic
woodpecker, another Goliath of the clan, swooped in and landed for
a face-to-face. This particular specimen wasn't too pleased with me
being near her nest, I guess, and she stood directly in my path, flapping her wings and making a racket. This was a really big woodpecker.
But it was still a woodpecker. Maybe a foot tall, stretching it. But I'm
city enough to know my Hitchcock movies, so I gave ground.

My friend at the Nature Conservancy called back that day to as-
sure me that this woodpecker tale was a high-octane story. This was
not merely the most sought-after animal in our mutual phylum—
I was being let in on an expedition that would inevitably get headlined environmental story of the century. This was a lead with real
players: the Nature Conservancy, the Department of the Interior, the
state of Arkansas, and the prestigious Cornell Lab of Ornithology.
Several rich tycoons had been smuggled in to see it. Private jets, my
friend told me, were clandestinely dipping in and out of the Arkansas
bayou on a regular basis. The bird had its own Secret Service–style
moniker: "Elvis." The president of Citibank as well as the President
of the United States had been briefed. Arrangements were under way
to have Laura Bush make the announcement at the ranch. Oh, man.
I would do this. I was pumped.

The next day, April 29, 2005, the story leaked and blazed across the front pages of 459 newspapers. EXTINCT? AFTER 60 YEARS, WOODPECKER BEGS TO DIFFER declared the *Washington Post*. The head of the Nature Conservancy intoned, "This bird has materialized miraculously out of the past but is also a symbol of the future." The eminent director of the Cornell Laboratory of Ornithology, in an ironical choice of metaphor, said, "This is dead solid confirmed."

II. Resurrection Accomplished

I awoke that morning to a National Public Radio reporter tromping through the bayous of Arkansas. "These swamps are like flooded cathedrals with thousand-year cypress trees rising like columns out of the water," said Christopher Joyce. I am always riveted by those radio pieces that take you to some exotic location—the crunching of the sticks, the trickling of the water—and create the place on the soundstage of your head lying on a pillow. In this case, though, I enjoyed it while simultaneously feeling like Wile E. Coyote after a misfired boulder lands on his chest.

Knowing that Christopher Joyce had probably received the same phone call I got drove me to manically consume these accounts as they broke in magazines, radio, television, and websites. I knew the punch line already and I knew that it had all been orchestrated. I knew the main characters and that they had been prepped. I knew the background. I had done the homework. Once I quickly worked through the usual Kübler-Ross stages of reporter despair—denial, anger, jealousy, I hate everybody—I watched something I had never seen before.

I observed a massive new truth stand up in American culture. Right away, the ivory-bill came to represent issues much bigger than a single bird. The Lord God Bird signaled to America that maybe all that news of environmental destruction was overstated. The Bush administration seized upon this story—and the Department of the Interior's Secretary Gale Norton took command of it—for precisely this reason.

It wasn't quite as if Galileo had called a press conference to announce that the earth revolved around the sun or as if Darwin summoned the scriveners of Grub Street to explain for the first time how changes in species can occur through natural selection. But it was a small-picture version of something like that, where a brand-new understanding totally at odds with accepted opinion becomes fact in one fell swoop.

The story of the ivory-billed woodpecker is a case study of how professionals in our time can deploy new tools and media to proclaim a new truth. But it is also about how outsiders, many of them amateurs, can swarm this new fact with questions and contradictions to uncover an even more intriguing reality. An absolutely opposing reality. The story of the ivory-billed woodpecker is a tale of professionals erecting a citadel of expert opinion around a new truth, with a sequel about a messy band of amateurs assaulting that fortress and tearing it brick by brick to the ground.

All fortresses get declared by a flag, and the ivory-bill was no different. That press conference on a bright spring day in Washington, DC, was magnificent in an Andrew Lloyd Webber way, an impressive display of contemporary institutional theater. The Department of Agriculture was there. The Cornell Lab of Ornithology was in full force. Secretary Norton headed up a full-on Capitol press event. Standing on a stage backgrounded by the snapping flags of proud departments and bureaus, Norton stepped up to the podium as giddy as an Oscar-winning supporting actress. It was as if the emperor's legions had returned from a campaign in Africa and had brought to the seven hills the exotic spoils of the jungle—the brawny gorilla, the stealthy panther, the subdued rhinoceros. The masses were assembled and invited to gawk not so much at the bird, which wasn't there, as at the grand power of the state and the institutions that had found this bird.

"This is a rare second chance to preserve through cooperative conservation what was once thought lost forever," declared Norton.

Here, too, was a new and thoroughly contemporary character in the drama. America got to meet the modern environmentalist: John Fitzpatrick, that morning, was a man in full. In his early fifties, Fitzpatrick was ruggedly handsome enough that if it had been a few decades earlier, he'd have been recruited for a Marlboro ad. He sported a whitening brush of a mustache and just enough pink in his face to suggest a career in the woody outdoors, schooling himself in the nuances of Nature. He was a really friendly guy. His friends called him "Fitz." And now it seemed impossible for a nation not to join them.

"The bird captured on video is clearly an ivory-billed woodpecker," Fitz told us. He said they had also recorded the bird's distinctive sounds and that seven professional ornithologists had personally spotted the bird in flight. The basic story was an adventure yarn. A kayaker named Gene Sparling had spotted the bird and blogged about it. Then, a bird journalist named Tim Gallagher read the post. With another enthusiast named Bobby Harrison, they slipped into the swamp and, in an emotional encounter, saw the bird. Gallagher returned to tell Fitz, who was convinced of the details and who launched a massive, yearlong cover operation to confirm the bird story of the century.

For the next twenty-four hours that story was inescapable. There were three hundred thousand searches for it on Google; birding sites crashed. Cornell rushed into publication (on the Science Express website operated by the scholarly journal *Science*) the necessary peer-reviewed article to give the story the empirical imprimatur of High Truth. The scientific paper boasted seventeen acclaimed authors. In it,

Cornell detailed the seven confirmed sightings of the bird by trained Cornell ornithologists. They had the video "clearly showing an ivory-bill" performing its signature move—bursting off a tree in a flare of white light and flying away. There were hidden devices recording its distinctive cry, and numerous photographs of scalings—the signature marks an ivory-bill makes when it strips bark from dead trees to get at beetle larvae.

Despite the story having leaked, Cornell managed to flood the media zone. There were 174 television programs and 43 radio shows featuring segments on the bird. Cornell launched www.ivory-bill.com, and the marketing department fired off electronic press releases to one thousand members of the media. Cornell's press office beefed up its Washington presence. One of the authors on the scholarly article had also prepared a popular book. Tim Gallagher, the editor of Cornell's bird periodical, had written *The Grail Bird*, now rushed into print. The only medium neglected in those first weeks was, paradoxically, opera.

But it didn't stop there. Add to all this effort the stunning fact that the ivory-bill was blessed by a miraculous sense of timing and coincidence. The area of Arkansas where the sightings had occurred was known, like something out of a child's tale, as the "Big Woods." It was spring, too, and the announcement of the bird's resurrection came within days of Easter. And its nicknames are the Grail Bird and the Lord God Bird?

Irresistible. Interior Secretary Norton declared that work toward habitat restoration and protection of the ivory-bill would receive $10.2 million in federal money, an astoundingly massive sum for a single species. Norton announced that the area in Arkansas where the bird was spotted would now be known as the Corridor of Hope.

When the technical paper appeared, *Science*'s editor in chief, Donald Kennedy, wrote an editorial that quivered with excitement, an unusual public display of affection for a sober, technical journal. His mash note ended solemnly, though, casting over the entire spectacle a patriarchal prayer. Kennedy wrote: "An appropriate salutation would be the ancient Hebrew blessing: 'Baruch Mechayei haMetim: Blessed is the one who gives life to the dead.'"

III. A Single Spear Hits the Fortress Wall

Like any professional group, highly credentialed ornithologists comprise a cozy ecosystem of people all pursuing the same subject. That is the essence of any such group. They meet annually as, say, the American Ornithologists' Union and give the most eminent member the keynote address. In this small world, they may not know one another personally, but they know *of* one another. So they all simply know that, say, a professor named Jerome Jackson has always been the go-to guy for the ivory-bill or that Fitz himself made his name studying the Florida scrub-jay. And in this micro-climate of specialized professionals, the Darwinian competition among species is fairly intense and arguments about scientific evidence can often get distorted, if not collapse entirely, into battles of ego and pride. Which is why Mark Robbins, an ornithologist at the University of Kansas, at first kept his stirring concerns to himself.

He had just returned from an overseas trip to discover America in the full grip of ivory-bill fever. The first person he spoke to was Tim Barksdale, who is a world-renown photographer of birds—"tenacious in getting the shot," Robbins said.

"I said, 'Tim, did you get this on film?' And he goes, 'No.' And I asked him, 'How much time did you spend there?' He said, 'I spent over two hundred days, over twenty-three hundred hours.' And I'm thinking to myself, something is wrong here. That was my first red flag." The next day, Robbins met with some graduate students who were very excited about the rediscovery and wanted Robbins to share in the pleasure of seeing the bird on film. To the delight of birders everywhere, Cornell Lab had posted the brief movie on their ivory-bill rediscovery website for anyone to watch.

Almost every birder has seen a pileated woodpecker, which shares many of the ivory-bill's traits—white panels of feathers on a different part of the wings—but its beak is nearly black and it's somewhat smaller and it's very, very common. "I wanted to see the film," Robbins said, "so one guy downloads it onto his computer. I look at it and now I'm feeling sick. I'm almost at the point where I'm going to vomit on the floor because I realized that it's a pileated woodpecker."

The video itself is now legendary, possibly the most studied four seconds of moving images since Abraham Zapruder filmed his home movie in Dealey Plaza. The cameraman was a computer programming professor and ivory-bill enthusiast named David Luneau. He kept a camera mounted on a central post in his canoe. And when he visited the swamp, he kept it running all the time, just in case. As it happened, his brother-in-law Robert was in the front of the canoe on this day, and the automatic focus gives us a very clear image of him. Off to one side of him, in the blurry distance, a bird startles and flies away. A non-birder would not be able to tell you if it was a woodpecker or an eagle. It's a tiny blur of white and black, and after being blown up, it's an even blurrier blur.

But to a professional, the bird's white panels permit an interpretation. To Robbins, good science requires that you make the most likely interpretation: "The proportion of white to black on this bird can't be the dorsal of the ivory-bill," Robbins told his grad students that day. "We pulled our specimen," he said, "and sure enough it didn't fit and everybody is going, 'Holy shit.'"

Robbins kept this skepticism to himself but only for a day, at which point his old officemate Rick Prum called. Prum had since moved on to Yale (and he's a neighbor of mine now), but he and Robbins maintained their old water-cooler chats by phone. And without so much as a howdy-do about Robbins's overseas trip, "Rick was right off the bat with 'What do you think about this ivory-billed proof?'"

Turns out Prum had seen what Robbins saw—a pileated. Still, it seemed crazy to question it since there was so much other proof—the numerous sightings by professionals, the telltale bark scalings, and other evidence. Yet by the end of the conversation, Robbins and Prum felt compelled to make the scientific case, especially about the ambiguity of the video. They would prepare a paper and submit it to a peer-reviewed journal, in this case, *Public Library of Science Biology.*

This was how we are all taught science is supposed to work. Data and conclusions get set down, then presented to other people in the field to review (or duplicate), and then those peer reviewers give the paper a thumbs-up or -down to publication. This idea of peer review is what makes science different from other forms of truth construction. Originally, the scientific method might have been an effort to keep the language of miracles and faith and Scriptural Authority out of observations and conclusions. But now we understand that it's also meant to scrub secular flaws as well—logical holes, rhetorical leaps, insistence based on seniority or ego.

As he and Robbins wrote the paper and finished it, I got a call from Prum. He was asking me for advice about how to get the word out about his paper. I immediately told him of my own failed involvement in the story so far and, frankly, was excited to hear that there was a controversy. Again, my magazine deadlines would not be fast enough, and it hardly mattered. Just before they were set to publish, Prum and Robbins received a call from an acquaintance inside the Cornell lab who had heard about their upcoming article. She warned them that Cornell had put audio machines throughout the woods and were still analyzing the numerous calls and knocks picked up on the tapes, but that the sound prints looked like the rock-solid evidence everyone wanted. And yet, in the paper, Cornell refused to say anything about the sounds other than that they were "suggestive but not proof." Prum and Robbins were permitted to hear the audio and compare it to the soundtrack of the only film of ivory-bills made in 1935, shot by a legendary ornithologist named Arthur Allen, then also the director of the Cornell lab.

The recordings convinced Prum and Robbins that while they might be right about the video specifically, perhaps they were being too impetuous about the general claim. So they did what scientists are supposed to do. Faced by better evidence, they held their article. Given the fame of the bird by now, Prum and Robbins's retraction itself became national news.

I remember Prum called me the day this happened. I was on my cell and stood in my driveway. Prum talks fast to begin with, but he was a flywheel that afternoon. The words zipped by. He said he was pulling his paper because that is what good scientific method mandated. But he was also saying that he still didn't believe the video. It was an important distinction but one I felt helpless telling him would never survive the blunt instrument that is our national media. Indeed, within hours, the whole story became a parable about a failed attempt to bring down Cornell. But it was much weirder than that. For the time being, the bird existed in the most bizarre way. Prum and Robbins believed the video showed nothing, while Cornell said it showed an ivory-bill. And Cornell pooh-poohed its own sound recordings as "suggestive," while the other ornithologists considered them compelling.

IV. Fitz in Glory

When John Fitzpatrick ascended to the podium at the annual meeting to the American Ornithologists' Union, it was as if Perry had re-

turned from the North Pole or Armstrong from the moon. All honor
and glory would be showered upon Fitz.

In his career, he was known as the scrub-jay guy, but he'd also become
famous as a *packager* of birds. At various organizations in his career,
he had shown that he could unite conservation mascots—photogenic
birds, for instance—with money from mega-donors and the sweat
equity of well-intentioned environmental groups to create massive
partnerships. The work on the ground was carried out by the do-
gooders, while the backers were welcome to proclaim their public virtue and the two "synergized" to get the hard work done. His most
famous achievement—a bird program called Partners in Flight—says
it all in the title.

The stage for the annual meeting was massive, with a huge drop-
down screen, and was set perfectly for the arrival of the great man.
Sure, there had been a peep of controversy with Prum and Robbins,
but that was over now. Fitz was prepping himself for the history
books. You know that scientists are thinking about history books
when they dare to use religious metaphors—as Stephen Hawking did
in the last line of his *A Brief History of Time*, about how science will
"know the mind of God."

Fitz's own words were solemnly quoted as if he'd already ascended
to the great canopy and sitteth on the right hand of John James
Audubon: "These woods are my church," he prayed.

From the beginning of his presentation, he spoke rapturously of
nature. The first few minutes were about big old trees and haunting romantic landscapes and the loss, long ago, of virgin forests. He
spoke achingly of earlier folks like Allen who got to walk in woods we
can only imagine or see in mournful photographs.

It's in this context that the discovery of the bird became the birth
of another cute-animal mascot. Koala bears, baby-faced marsupials,
charming fuzzy critters? This is how Fitz presented the ivory-bill, as the
new animal that would launch a decade of fund-raisers. The larger mission was, in fact, so huge—reviving entire deltas and massive swaths

of land, the Big Woods—that it made accepting the rediscovery of the bird seem minor. Fitz was in Hawking mode, sure, but it was not history he was reaching for really. It was a new partnership.

By the time he got to the evidence, he cheerfully encouraged the audience not to be troubled by the flicker of a speck of an image. In the video, the bird is no bigger than the brother-in-law's thumb, and as it flies off it only gets smaller. Fitz says it's crucial to get "the whole gestalt" of the bird coming off the tree. Yet it's not as if the nuanced differences between ivory-bill and pileated perch-departing gestalts were then common knowledge. If anything, that very odd word permitted the audience to fill in the gaps of what was not seen. If you're looking for a gestalt—instead of clear identifiable proof—then you'll see the gestalt and be convinced. Fitz's audience in Santa Barbara that day saw it and cooed.

The various complaints from Prum and the others who had questioned his evidence—what did he make of those? They were useful, he said, because the brief controversy lent an air of scientific struggle and, by extension, legitimacy. Barely an air, though. At the end, he posted a slide in his PowerPoint presentation that read "Scientific Spice" and then listed Prum, Robbins, and three other minor skeptics. His body language and vocal tone formed its own communication, suggesting that while he should obviously feel nothing less than contempt for these pathetic apostates, he had conquered the world and so it was easier to be generous in a chuckling, belittling sort of way.

"I particularly want to especially thank these guys for adding scientific spice to the discussion all summer long," said a bemused Fitz.

Science was less than an appetizer. It was a pinch of herb sprinkled over the main dish. Even the bird was not the entree. Throughout the talk, Fitz invited his peers to journey with him past the shaky evidence to the larger marketing campaign for big-scale land conservation. In his very last line, before he accepted the grateful applause of a thousand ornithologists, he intoned: "We can save these forests, and we can do it with a great badge of a bird at the top of the treetops if things work out right."

Words betray us. To Fitz, the ivory-bill was not a bird. It was a logo.

V. Shotgun Blast at the Wall

By the following winter, the aimless discontent of some professional ornithologists exploded in a small magazine called the *Auk*. It's not a scholarly journal, but it is respected. The author was Jerome Jackson, the man whom the cozy club of ornithologists had long known as the go-to guy for ivory-bills. Just why Fitz had not brought Jackson in from the beginning is still one of the great mysteries. Jackson was to have been an author with Prum and Robbins on that suppressed paper, and now he let fly with a cri de coeur all by himself.

He charged that Fitz's proof was "molded more by sound bites than by science." He said that the massive federal funding was a ruse. Jackson charged that the big money Secretary Norton had pulled together from the Interior budgets "was not a new appropriation, but a re-allocation of funds from other budgeted projects, including ongoing efforts on behalf of other endangered species, resulting in cutbacks to those projects."

Jackson slammed what is known as "story creep." Tim Gallagher's popular book on the rediscovery, published in May 2005, had described his sighting of the bird when he was in the swamp with Bobby Harrison. He estimated his distance from the bird at "less than eighty feet." That July, though, his wife wrote in *Audubon* magazine that it was "less than 70 feet." In an interview on *60 Minutes* in October, Gallagher said the bird was "about sixty-five feet away." At one news conference, Fitzpatrick observed that if Gallagher and Harrison had not shouted, the bird "might even have landed on the canoe." Jackson wrote: "Observations can become more and more 'real' with the passing of time, as we forget the minor details and focus inwardly on the 'important' memory."

He noted that Prum and Robbins never did retract their assertion that the video showed nothing other than a pileated. He said that when you examined the evidence carefully, Fitz's stuff wasn't science or even scientific spice, but rather "faith-based ornithology." Jackson closed by alluding to the paranormal TV show *The X-Files*: "Whether truth is in the presence of Ivory-billed Woodpeckers or in the perception of the presence of Ivory-billed Woodpeckers, we now have hope. But hope is not truth. It is only the fire that incites us to seek the truth. The truth is still out there."

Fitz fired back immediately, charging that it was Jackson dressing up dubious evidence as science: "Despite being neither peer-reviewed nor fact-checked by the Editor, that article was treated as a scientific contribution by the public media, a perception actively fostered by its author in public appearances and interviews." Fitz rebutted each point and—being standard media advice in the age of the marketing rollout—he accused Jackson of precisely the failings Jackson had alleged: "We agree with Jackson's statement that 'sound bites must not pass as science.' This is why we were flabbergasted by Jackson's own use of the phrase 'faith-based ornithology' in referring to our work. Who, exactly, is compromising science with sound bites here?"

VI. Audubon's Children

So it sat for a while—another gnarly scientific quarrel—until I heard from another bird person, David Allen Sibley. Like Audubon or

Roger Tory Peterson before him, Sibley is a careful field birder who studies birds in the wild and paints them.

I met Sibley years ago through a mutual friend, and one day he was telling me that *he* was going to come out with a paper in *Science*. He was joining the ranks of the video skeptics. Up until now, the complaints about the video had been broad—"I think it could be a pileated." Sibley and three other authors got right into the details, questioning the video frame by frame.

For example, when the blurry image was blown up and "de-interlaced," according to Cornell, a portion of the perched bird could be seen as a droplet of white that is peeking out from the tree's edge. The Cornell team saw this image as the tucked-in feathers of a perched ivory-bill. Sibley provided a drawing in which he argued that it was just as likely a pileated in the first explosion of flight be-hind the tree. The white-feathered droplet was a pileated twisting its wings frantically in those first big beats of taking off, scooping huge pockets of air to skedaddle.

It's one thing to say that the image is just "too blurry." It's quite another to show, frame by frame, how much more easily one can look at each frame and see a super-common bird. It was like one of the optical illusions where you think you've been looking at the soft-focus image of a beautiful young woman in the nude until someone points out that tilted this way it even more perfectly forms the face of an old hag wearing a babushka. Afterward, it just becomes impossible to look at the image and see the nude anymore.

In a single scientific article that is what happened to a lot of birders. The most famous ivory-billed woodpecker of the twenty-first century became, overnight, one more startled pileated, flying away.

The Cornell team published their rebuttal simultaneously. For some, there was another way to dismiss Sibley as a disgruntled com-petitor: Sibley is a Cornell dropout, a man whose dreamy obsession with birds kept him wandering in the woods, never able to get his degree. There are stories of him going out into the woods for days on end to look at birds and never getting around to the homework. And it's true: He is *not* a professional ornithologist, in the technical sense. Sibley is a working stiff, a mere painter, to a professional ornithologist, and outsiders like him live beyond the daily concerns of their esoteric and expert sphere of knowledge.

But that distinction is also what made this paper devastating. The earlier questioning of Cornell's proof could be easily bracketed as "part of the scientific debate." Professional rivalry. Scientific *spice*. But Sibley's paper exposed a rift between folks in the field and those in academia, between outsiders and the fortress-dwellers.

"One of the dirty secrets of ornithology," said Chris Elphick, the fourth author on the paper and a professor at the University of Connecticut, "is that the ornithologists in the university are not experts in identification anymore. They were a hundred years ago, but for the most part university researchers study one species or a small set of species. They spend most of their time in front of a computer rather than in the field."

Bird professionalism is like every other specialty. It emerged from a more hands-on world of gritty, hairy grunts in the field, but as it developed more tools for exploration and more theories, it tended to move indoors. To the academy. Sometimes to industry. But, most typically, to a *desk*.

And it left behind the generalists, the mechanics, and the amateurs doing basic research. In this case, those people were the lovers of birds happy to organize group tours or whatever it took to keep them out in the field, the dreamy open field where the occasional sighting is a profound pleasure.

"The whole expertise of bird identification is not in the realm of the university anymore and hasn't been for some time," Elphick said. "All that expertise is out among the amateurs and the bird-watchers."

VII. How to See a Bird

If you look at the history of professionalization of any kind, you'll see that it tends to follow this route. In America and Europe, a great deal of professionalization occurred in the nineteenth century, when most gentlemen of breeding considered themselves amateurs at all kinds of disciplines. Go all the way back to Jefferson, who collected fossils and wrote about botany and invented household tools and studied animals. He was an amateur anthropologist and even an amateur theologian who famously cut all the miracles out of the New Testament because he thought Jesus made a whole lot more sense without the supernatural material mucking up the good moral philosophy.

Throughout the nineteenth century, however, different professions began to emerge. The invention of the telegraph and the railroad—a bricks-and-mortar version of our Internet—sped communication and interaction, permitting groups to form more easily, hold meetings, trade notes, and determine what was good for the field or bad. One of the earliest examples was the formation of the American Medical Association in 1847. Previously medicine had been a private guild. It was held together by little other than the Hippocratic Oath, which didn't pledge members to "do no harm" so much as to "spill no secrets."

The professionalization of medicine, as with any discipline, established standards and practices. It set rules and created a cohort of insiders. In the case of doctors, it would go on to establish medical schools and then credentialed medical schools, then board tests and board examiners. For most disciplines, the grand credentialer became the academy.

And that was the case with birding as well. It came out of a long history of amateur pursuit. Birding developed from the gentlemanly world of collecting, which was part of the hunter tradition. John J. Audubon painted his birds after *shooting* them. But in the course of time, that method fell into disfavor and bird-watching trended to the less intrusive, less brutal way of making distinctions. The modern birder in the field had to become good at sighting on the fly or in a matter of seconds as the bird perched. This change in identification is what led to the shift from the grand paintings of Audubon to the guidebook work of Roger Tory Peterson and David Sibley.

Audubon was painting his work to show people the flora and fauna of the New World. His work was expeditionary and meant to enlighten the world generally about the vastness of America's varying environments. Audubon's paintings have a nearly British feeling when you look at them—magnificently staged birds in some fantastic tableau. They might be captured on paper in the middle of feasting, like the red-tailed hawk dining on a half-eaten bloodied rabbit. Audubon's long-billed curlew stands in a patch of muddy marsh probing the muck with its improbable bill. I own an old engraving of this image in part because if you look at the distant horizon, you'll see the skyline of my hometown, Charleston, South Carolina, with Fort Sumter in the harbor. But all of that is tiny imagery in the background. For Audubon, he is showing the fauna's POV. He's found and identified these creatures, and his paintings invite us to see the world from the bird's and the New World's perspective.

Sibley's work has a different purpose. The naming and grandeur of New World birds is a done deed. His paintings are not trying to show us the bird's perspective but Sibley's. He wants his readers and viewers to come away knowing how to distinguish an ivory-bill from a pileated and a red-cockaded from the hairy variety.

If you've ever been in the field with a really great birder, then you know that this skill requires years of practice. Birds are identified not merely by their color and plumage but by the mastery of thousands of pieces of learned information about size, age, feet, beak formation, eye, crest, wing shape, flight path, the way they land, the company they keep, where they perch in a tree, or how they stand on the ground. After you've learned the boomerang curve of a swallow's wing, then you learn the nuance differences among the nearly one hundred swallow species. Once, when I was in the Florida woods with Beau Turner, he quickly pointed out to me a tree swallow that was in the northernmost sweep of its range—a rare sighting in winter. Nothing quite convinces one of another's bona fides than an easy intimacy with the unusual and outermost details of a field of knowledge.

To spot such nuances and to know in your gut that you have that nailed is a deep physical pleasure. Any birder will tell you so. When people obsess about collecting their "life list" and seeing all these birds and checking them off, in a sense they are re-creating the long journeys of John J. Audubon, the first birder obsessed with his life list, only he painted his.

When I first met Sibley, it was through a mutual friend. There were a bunch of kids with us, and Sibley offered to take us around the woods of Shelter Island at the end of Long Island to look at birds. It was a marvelous afternoon, but at one point the kids had fled. Sibley was left with just me, standing in a meadow with a distant view of water. He has a charming obsessive quality when you're with him. Sibley is laconic, even shy. But in time, he opens up and reveals a wonderfully funny and ironic personality.

That day, I did most of the talking (not unusual). I found out, for instance, that there were only a half dozen species of birds in this hemisphere that he had never personally seen—birds which nested on the ocean and required super-expensive boat trips in harsh environments to see. But when, during the course of this (or any) casual conversation, Sibley's peripheral vision senses a slight speck scoring a thin black line in the sky, he immediately cuts off everyone and tunes out the rest of the world. When I was with him, he turned mechanically, instantly, and precisely in the direction of the bird. His high-powered binoculars were on his eyes and the bird was centered in his field of focus in half a second.

"Yellow-shafted flicker," he might say. Meanwhile I'm squinting at a distant circumflex and then struggling with my binoculars until finally I get a glimpse of a departing speck. Throughout all this, I might try to keep the conversation going, but Sibley's body language has a way of communicating that he's no longer there for you. He is inside the binoculars for those few seconds. It's as if he's gone, left his body, literally ecstatic.

On several occasions, I didn't even bother to look at the bird, so riveting was it to watch a man in the grip of an irresistible thing. It always seemed sacrilegious to continue talking. This was hallowed time, bird identification time, concentration time.

On this very afternoon, Sibley was looking in one direction and I in another. And I spotted a bird first and raised my binoculars. I got it quickly in focus and could see right away what it was.

"It's just a seagull," I said and lowered my binoculars. I saw that Sibley nevertheless had his gaze fixed intently on the bird. Sibley's body language and radiant silence was telling me that, even if I didn't think so, the bell jar of avian solemnity had descended over this entire meadow. Sibley was in the bird zone, his face tense with study. I slammed the binoculars back to my eyes and fixed my field of focus on the bird. Had I missed something? Was it a wayward albatross? But I grew up on the ocean. I know my gulls, and unquestionably that was nothing more than an everyday seagull.

"It is just a seagull, isn't it?" I said, again lowering my binoculars and looking at him. And then he said this simple, little thing. He didn't say it pretentiously or ominously. I could make it sound like the Buddha talking or Yoda training his Jedis. But it wasn't like that.

Sibley has a nearly petit way of talking. And this was Sibley at his most fragile and vulnerable, as if he wanted me to understand something but lacked the words for it. So he just said this thing that has stayed with me ever since.

"It's a bird," he said. Again, I got the glasses back on my eyes. But I realized there were no binoculars powerful enough to show me what he was seeing. I was furious, silently berating myself for my fatuous dismissal—so quick to see the tiresome seagull, the bird of landfills, the ocean pest, the flying rat, the scavenger gull of my teenage years when we all repeated the shoreline legend about what happened when you fed them Alka-Seltzer.

Later I saw him pleasantly lost in a reverie of crows. For Sibley, he's always looking at birds he's seen a thousand times as if he's seeing them for the first time. That's a skill born of love, amateurism in the best sense. It's an obsession, the kind that makes you drift off into the woods in college, so consumed with the unutterable pleasure of the work that you forget, ultimately, about earning a degree.

One thing that marks the amateur, the best of them, is this talent for not seeing things according to the dominant paradigm. One of the traits Thomas S. Kuhn describes in his *The Structure of Scientific Revolutions* is this ability not to see things according to the reigning paradigm of the day. The much abused phrase "paradigm shift" is a regular feature of scientific breakthrough in part because certain people can see through the frame within which everyone else dwells and see something different.

A 2006 *Harvard Business Review* article detailed the Curse of Knowledge, reporting that many breakthroughs are achieved by people who don't know the jargon and minutiae of a field, who work outside the realm of day-to-day expertise. Lacking that detailed scaffolding of understanding, they can often see things that insiders look right past. Think of those instruction manuals that came with the computers of the 1990s. They were written by the computer programmers who had lived deep inside the vast world of alt-shift-return-F7. To them, those instructions were easy because they lived inside the paradigm. To those of us outside, their manuals were frustratingly opaque, eventually hilariously so. We had to wait for some outsiders to write those *PC for Dummies* books so we could find out how to work a computer.

Once, in between sightings, I asked Sibley why he painted birds at all when you could so easily just take super-detailed digital pictures of what he saw in the lenses. He explained that a picture is a specific bird, and each bird is slightly different from the *essential* bird of that species.

Each oriole is different in the way that every person is different, yet there are certain qualities that capture the very essence of oriole-ness. And the way the brain works, he said, makes it crucial to paint. If we see the quintessential oriole, our brains can typically pick out all the variations and make that call. Sibley doesn't paint any one oriole but (and this is part of what he's looking for when he glues the binoculars to his eyes) a stylized oriole all of us can see.

Every time he lifts his binoculars, he is looking for tiny elements—secondary feathers, some tuft, a unique shape to the tail—that essentially capture the bird in view. What does a platonic seagull look like? And that's why he can get lost with every winged creature that flaps within view. It's a bird, to Sibley, but one that may yield one more detail, moving his understanding that much closer to the platonic bird of that species. There's always time for one more look at some impish blue jay or pudgy owl. That's why Sibley's explanation of the Luneau video ended the argument for a lot of birders. They know that almost no one on the earth can see a bird the way that Sibley can. They know what I know. He may not be a credentialed ornithologist, but he is among the best bird spotters alive. Yet Sibley's paper was careful. He didn't say the ivory-bill didn't exist. He carefully said that the Luneau video was not the proof.

Still, plenty of birders refused to believe Sibley's evidence. And

forget about wingbeats and de-interlacing, what about the seven ornithologists who saw the bird personally? And the sound tapes? There
was still plenty of hope. And just before this latest challenge emerged,
the hopeful convened in Brinkley, Arkansas, for what was headlined
as the first annual ivory-billed woodpecker festival. I was offered a
free tour of the swamp to try my hand at seeing the bird myself, so I
booked a plane ticket.

VIII. Got Pecker?

First day out, I spotted an ivory-billed woodpecker.

Or at least I can now add my name to the list of those who make
that claim. It was a mild February in the swamp when I visited the
bayou with Bill Tippit, a friendly bear of a birder. We were expecting
to spend the day in the swamp with an expert guide, but in the chime
of a cell phone, we found ourselves suddenly guideless, standing there
with our waders, a canoe, and a big desire. "I'm game," he said in his
slow, deep twang. So we put in and spent the day drifting around the
primeval beauty of Arkansas' most famous bottomland swamp.

Even though I grew up among South Carolina's cypress swamps, I
had never seen cypress trees this huge and haunting. Towering beside
them was the ancient tupelo, like some Devonian Period beta version
of "tree." These thousand-year-old senator trees are large enough at
the base to garage a car, and then they suddenly narrow like a wine
bottle before shooting up into a regular tree. Tippit and I spent the
day paddling into swampy cul-de-sacs and just hanging there, strictly
quiet, for half an hour at a stretch.

"You can't find the bird," Tippit said in his most casual Zen. "The bird has to find you." By late afternoon, the swamp had come to life with a dozen birdsongs. Blue herons flapped through the trees, while above, the canopy was a rush hour of swallows and sweeps. At times, the dimming forest could be as chatty as a crowded cocktail party, filled with the call of the pileated woodpecker.

Then: "Ivory-bill!" Tippit urgently whispered from the back of the canoe. I looked ahead but saw nothing. I turned to see precisely where he was pointing. I whipped back around to see the final movements of a large, dark bird disappearing like a black arrow into the dusky chill of the swamp.

I knew the drill. To confirm the sighting, I asked Tippit to report to me precisely what he had seen. As with any witness, it was important to set the interview down on paper as soon as possible. Tippit called out: "Two white panels on the back of the wings! It lit on that tree. It was large. Also saw it flying away from me with flashes of white." He called it in on his cell phone. And since that winter evening, I have been able to say, "I saw an ivory-billed woodpecker."

And yet I have not said it. Later that night, during the festival, when people would make conversation, they'd ask, "Did you go out today?" And I'd say yes and move on to marveling at the size of the cypress trees. I just didn't have it in me to make the boast, and it felt especially odd because "ivory-bills" were everywhere.

The little town of Brinkley (formerly Lick Skillet, Arkansas) had really gussied itself up for the Call of the Ivory-Billed Woodpecker Celebration. I fully expected to see a parade led by Robert Preston sporting an ivory-bill haircut (available at Penny's Hair Care for $25). A modest motel had been renamed the Ivory-Billed Inn. Gene's Restaurant and Barbecue offered an ivory-bill cheeseburger. There was even ivory-bill "blue": I bought a T-shirt that read GOT PECKER?

There were lots of T-shirts and tours, and www.ivorybilled expeditions.com offered the cheapest rate at $325 per person. The deluxe was $2300 and your guide was Gene Sparling, the kayaker who first spotted the bird.

Soon enough there were limited reproductions of Audubon's famous ivory-bill drawing from 1829, issued by "Discovery Editions." Governor Mike Huckabee issued ivory-bill stamps. On a television set one might see a public service announcement asking for funds, which piped:

"Emily Dickinson said, 'Hope is the thing with feathers.' The Nature Conservancy in Arkansas would like to add that hope also has an ivory-colored beak and eats wood grubs."

Ivory-bills were everywhere, and yet talk of *seeing* the bird was conscientiously absent. It's hard to describe, but it was like saying you'd walked on the moon or been anointed by the Dalai Lama. It was a boast of immense magnitude, exalting to claim.

For instance, I went to a talk given by Sharon Stiteler, a perky, witty, smiling blonde who is the host of birdchick.com. Everyone knew that she had been invited by Cornell to spend a few weeks in the swamp. This very fact gave her an air of privilege and her talk a sense of potent authority—and she was discussing bird feeders. During the Q and A period afterward, she pointed at me for a question. So I asked: "Have you seen an ivory-billed woodpecker?" It was as if I'd dropped a glass on the floor. The room went weirdly silent. The smile on Stiteler's face flickered away, quick as a chickadee. "I am not allowed to comment on that," she said. "I was out with Cornell in December and had to sign a lot of confidentiality agreements."

The act of birding, ultimately, is a very stylized form of storytelling. For instance, if someone said to you, "I saw this cardinal fly out of nowhere with yellow tips on its wings and land on the side of a tree," even the least experienced amateur would counter that cardinals don't have yellow wingtips and don't cling to trees but rather perch on branches. Each bird is a tiny protagonist in a tale of natural history, and this is what I picked up with Sibley: The story gets told in a vivid but almost private language of color, wing shape, body design, habitat, bill size, movement, flying style, and perching habits. The more you know about each individual bird, the better you are at telling this tale.

Claiming to have seen a rare bird requires an even more delicate form of storytelling and implies a connoisseur's depth of knowledge. Saying "I saw an ivory-bill's long black neck and white trailing feathers" requires roughly the same panache as tasting an ancient Bordeaux and discoursing on its notes of nougat and hints of barnyard hay.

If you don't pull it off, then superior birders diss you. It's all about cred. And this is where birding gets personal. Telling a rare-bird-sighting story is to ask people to honor your skills—to trust you, to believe you. So just who gets to tell the story of seeing an ivory-bill? I spent the entire festival trying to find that out. Cornell claims that seven members of their search team saw the bird, but they weren't gabbing in the halls about it either.

That intimidating institutional demand for silence was everywhere. There *was* a great ivory-bill story, but this, too, was very carefully stage-managed, coordinated, and controlled. I picked up the festival guide and saw the schedule. Cornell was holding it back—the telling of the most famous ivory-bill sighting. This was the dual sighting by the editor of *Living Bird* magazine, Tim Gallagher, and his good friend Bobby Harrison. These two men saw the bird together, and for this festival they were going to tell all about it. The story itself was the central event of the entire festival—an evening affair, after dinner, standing room only.

IX. In the Beginning

The fantastic story of the bird's rediscovery begins with its Genesis tale. Every great find has one and the ivory-bill is no different. It's the story of the first confirmed sighting and the written version can be found in Tim Gallagher's book *The Grail Bird,* a history of the search for the ivory-bill and the book that was rushed into print with the rediscovery. Gallagher intended to interview every living person who had claimed an ivory-bill sighting. It turns out that there's a whole subcategory of bird aficionados known as ghost-bird chasers, who look for birds presumed to be extinct. Gallagher himself was one, and over his years of searching, he met Bobby Harrison, a photography professor at Oakwood College in Alabama, who was also in this game.

The two men were made for the Chautauqua circuit and the kind of postprandial entertainment promised in Brinkley. Gallagher is a tall middle-aged man with white hair and a pleasantly restrained Yankee demeanor. In Arkansas he amiably confessed that he'd always thought the South was weird and that he considered Harrison his "interpreter and guide." Harrison, a fun good ol' boy with a head like a mortar shell, had his own schtick, like saying that he didn't know "damn Yankee" was two words until he was twenty years old. The audience laughed wildly at their tale, which was, like the best sightings, a great adventure story full of snakes, mayhem, mud, bugs, and a bird.

Harrison is the kind of guy who loves his outdoor gear. When I first met him, he showed me his canoe draped in shredded camouflage material. He could climb in beneath this small bunker of camo, smear gobs of multicolored camouflage greasepaint all over his face, and float through the swamp—looking like nothing more than a drifting pile of leaves (or some whacked-out survivalist hiding deep in a bayou). By contrast, Gallagher is a restrained gentleman whose posture and courtesies make it easy to believe that he's spent a great deal of his life at a desk on an Ivy League campus.

Their story was why everyone had gathered in Arkansas. And, it began in early 2004 when Gallagher was alerted to an online posting by another Southerner, the kayaker Gene Sparling, who reported that he'd seen an unusual woodpecker in the Bayou de View. Gallagher and Harrison each interviewed him and were convinced that Sparling had seen *the* bird. They rushed to Arkansas and entered swamp in canoes. The second day they were there—February 27, 2004—the two saw something burst into the sunshine. "Look at all the white on its wings," Gallagher shouted. "Ivory-bill!" they both screamed. And it was gone. They wrote down their notes and drew sketches. Gallagher had a new ending for his book. Bobby got on the phone to his wife, Norma, and sobbed.

The audience was laughing one minute and stunned into teary solemnity the next. These were the two emotions of the night. We might be carrying on at Harrison's schtick as a good ol' boy making fun of the straight-man Gallagher or listening to the Yankee talk about how wacky it was to be in the swamp with Bobby and all that rednecky camouflage. Then the story might grow solemn as they took us into just enough detail to relate how emotional it all was: how they shouted when they saw the bird, how they flipped out as it flew by, and how they cried like babies as they wrote down their descriptions.

If you read the *Science* article, it's clear that the other academic sightings aren't nearly as entertaining as this Billy Yank and Johnny Reb rendition. So the Cornell rollout carefully controlled this crucial part of the narrative. Only the official speakers—the courtly intellectual Gallagher and the hilarious swamp rat Harrison—did the talking.

As they explained, after they had their emotional sighting, Gallagher flew back to Ithaca, New York, and back to the Cornell Lab of Ornithology, headed by John Fitzpatrick.

As with any convincing rare-bird narrative, Fitz listened carefully and then, based on his judgment, he believed. So Fitzpatrick decided to throw the lab's prestige and best resources into the search. Right away, Fitz learned that the Nature Conservancy had heard about the same Gene Sparling sighting that had attracted Gallagher to Arkansas.

"A few days after February 27, Fitzpatrick called me," said Scott Simon, the state director of the Nature Conservancy, "and we danced around trying to find out what the other knew." When they discovered that they knew the same thing, Simon became a partner and agreed to supply aerial photographs.

"Fitz emphasized the need to keep it quiet," Simon went on to tell me. "They wanted to get in one full year of research uninterrupted and focused. For fourteen months we did that. We called it the Inventory Project, and we talked about it in code." IBWO became the preferred shorthand for "ivory-billed woodpecker." Cornell's swamp operation moved swiftly into place in Arkansas in the spring of 2004 and kept thirty-six people on the ground at any one time. "Twenty-two paid staff; fourteen volunteers," field supervisor Elliott Swarthout told me. Scattered throughout the forest, time-lapse cameras were mounted on trees. The ornithologists had also drawn up grids and transects and were systematically moving through the area with human eyes to conduct regular bird counts and spot roost holes.

There were twenty-four autonomous recording units, or ARUs, stationed at strategic flyways in the swamp. Hundreds of hours of audio recordings were clandestinely flown back to Cornell, where they were computer-searched for the patterns of the ivory-bill's two most famous sounds. There is the "kent" call, a funny *bweep* that sounds like a kid's toy horn. And there is the double knock—two heavy bill blows into a tree, so close together they almost register as one sound.

Eventually, when all the necessary groups were brought in, the Inventory Project had a sixteen-person management board. "And it was really fun," Simon said. "These people met on a conference call every Tuesday night at eight thirty P.M., Central Time."

The ivory-billed woodpecker—aka IBWO—became the subject of the greatest super-secret mission in the history of ornithology.

By the end of the first year of searching, Cornell had many sightings but decided to put forward only seven of the best ones in the *Science* paper.

But those very sightings would eventually become their own controversy. Originally, Fitz sent down several people who were well known for being able to identify birds. But those specialists did *not* see the bird. That was the red flag Mark Robbins mentioned. How could Tim Barksdale, who almost never failed to get the shot, spend twenty-three hundred hours in the woods and return without a single decent frame?

It was only after these skilled birders failed that *other* researchers—who happened to be in the employ of Fitz and also inside this bubble of emotional secrecy—went down to Arkansas. All of them had, essentially, the same sighting. The bird never stopped and perched. It was always flying by. Of all the field marks that one might see—the famous white bill, for instance, so noticeably different from the pileated's black bill—well, no one saw those field marks. Every one of them saw the burst of white trailing feathers—the one field mark most likely to be confused with a pileated.

And in each case, the sighting occurred in a surge of emotion. "As soon as Ron's canoe rounded the bend, I began shaking all over and feeling as if I would cry," wrote Melanie Driscoll of the day she made her sighting.

Could this be a case of group hysteria? That would ultimately become the claim from a lot of outsiders. When I first heard this charge, I thought that Cornell probably had seen the bird. I mean, "group hysteria"? Wasn't that one of those TV diagnoses, like "amnesia" or "catatonia," that show up as some kind of lame excuse in our pop culture rather than an actual reality. But, well, no. Actually, it turns out, such hysterias do happen. A *lot*. In the introductory book *Sibley's Birding Basics* (published long before these sightings), Sibley warned against "the overexcited birder" and "group hysteria." He cited "one very well documented case in California" in which "the first state record of the Sky Lark (a Eurasian species) was misidentified for days, and by hundreds of people, as the state's first Smith's Longspur." Turns out, hysteria is practically a common problem among birders, ghost birders especially.

"There is a long list of well-studied effects," Sibley told me. "There is peer pressure, the expectation of what they were there to do, as well as the authority effect of finding what the boss wants you to find." Most of the Cornell sightings occurred in the surge of emotion immediately following Gallagher's return to Cornell. Shortly after the sizzle of that emotion faded away, so did all the sightings.

It's this emotion that almost every birder has described and has described at greater length, often, than the sighting of the bird.

I know what this emotion is like.

A few weeks after Tippit and I saw our bird, I went back into the swamp with none other than Bobby Harrison, the ivory-bill rock star. If you're going to spend a day in a swamp, there is no one better to spend it with than Harrison. He had a nearly silent trolling motor, so we were able to penetrate the darkness of the swamp this time without a peep, except when we were beating off cottonmouth snakes with our paddles or portaging the whole rig over frustrating logjams. After three miles we came into an area called Blue Hole, and we had puttered up the way just past a visible ARU when suddenly: *bam-bam*. "Did you hear that?" Harrison said. I had. No question. We pulled the canoe onto a mud bank and stepped out. Visibility was becoming limited, not because of light but because the forest was in early bud. Leaves were growing bigger, it seemed, by the hour, making the distant vistas close right up around us. As Harrison and

I stood there, a large black-and-white bird came from behind us and soared into the green. "Did you see that?" he said. I did. We both looked at each other. My face was a blank because, the truth is, I am a birder with greenhorn skills. Was that a woodpecker or a duck? Had I seen white on the trailing feathers? Honestly, I didn't know. The moment was brief, and when it passed, Harrison's eyes tightened with disappointment. "I couldn't tell," he said.

Had I declared that I had seen a panel of white, what might have happened? Would Harrison have then asked me: Was it on the trailing feathers? Well, maybe so. Was the bird large? Yes it was. Did it have a long neck? Yes, I think it did. And what if my editor, the day before, had told me that it would be a good story if I went out with Harrison but a cover story if I saw the bird with him? What if I knew that a confirmed sighting by a *New York Times Magazine* writer would land me on a half dozen prime-time news shows as the man who confirmed Cornell's sightings after long absence? Maybe I'd get that interview with the secretary of the interior?

Instead, I shrugged because I didn't see anything I felt comfortable confirming. And then we paddled on. But the adrenaline moment was right there. Had I given in—I could feel the tug, too—had we talked it out, the sighting would have been as real as if I had seen something. In short order, it would have been another sighting, pillowed as they all were by powerful emotions so that, recollected in tranquility, the details could be recalled with absolute certainty. Such emotions cushion every sighting.

The first sentence of Gallagher's book reads, "I think I've always been the kind of person who gets caught up in obsessive quests, most of which seem to involve birds." This sentiment of deep longing grips all those from Cornell.

"It's been a fixation since early childhood," Fitzpatrick told me. In many ways, Gallagher's book can be read not as a birder's adventure of discovery but as a fanatic's confession of self-delusion.

Gallagher admits he's prone to "quixotic quests." And in his own book, he notes that ivory-bill skeptics have long said things like "If you want to see an ivory-bill bad enough, a crow flying past with sunlight flashing on its wings can look pretty good." The code name used for the bird during the Inventory Project was "Elvis." As a Southerner, I immediately wondered if Cornell understood the joke. Elvis is, how you say, extinct. Only menopausal fans and postmodern ironists believe that bumper sticker: ELVIS LIVES.

If you read Gallagher's book closely, you see that he provides that pedigree of sightings that led to his own. He had heard about the location in Arkansas from Sparling, the kayaker. But Gallagher also tells the story of how Sparling came to kayak in the Bayou de View. It involves a ghost-chaser named Mary Scott, who told Sparling that she had seen an ivory-bill in the Big Woods of Arkansas the year before.

Scott was a lawyer who in midlife abandoned her profession and decided to live in a yurt near her parents' house in Long Beach, California. On one birding expedition, Scott took along a friend who knew a "woodpecker whisperer." Mary called the clairvoyant on her cell phone from the swamp and learned that the bird wanted to be seen but was troubled by the group's "energy." Scott eventually wandered off by herself and, she says, saw the bird. In fact, Scott sees the bird quite a lot when she's alone, and she's also never able to get her camera out of the backpack in time.

"I must admit," Gallagher nevertheless writes in his book, "I had come to believe strongly in her sighting." And that's the pedigree of the ivory-billed woodpecker sighting. Set aside the Department of the Interior, the Nature Conservancy, and Cornell University, and you have Harrison and Gallagher. Go back before them and you have the kayaker. Go back before him, following the chain of sightings, all linked by fervent ghost-chasers in a state of high emotion, and it leads back ultimately to a yurt-dwelling, courthouse dropout charting her course in the swamp with the help of a woodpecker whisperer on a cell phone.

X. Blogging a Bird to Death

Watching the massive rollout of IBWO 2.0 during the Bush administration was to see how much the methodology of the Massive Product Rollout has dominated the first decade of the millennium. Back in the summer before the Iraq invasion, some press members asked if war was imminent. Andrew Card, then chief of staff, famously noted, "From a marketing point of view, you do not introduce new products in August." So we invaded the following March, a month whose very name seemed to synergize with the product (and/or service) being marketed.

The Rediscovery of the Ivory-billed Woodpecker was a product rollout that flooded the media pipelines and created a capital T Truth in the minds of the media and the public. So when it turned out that the new marketed truth was flawed, how could one push back against the Cornell publicity machine or the White House's sycophantic press corps?

As for the attempts by Prum and Robbins on the one hand and Sibley et al. on the other, all went to scholarly journals. They were banking on a system that may no longer function. They expected the scholarly journals to pronounce their findings and stamp upon them the imprimatur of authority.

But as critics of the Bush administration discovered in the new media ecosystem, one cannot rely upon the media at large to spread any particular idea other than one issued officially from the high perch of authority. So if you don't have a Cornell (or a White House) operation to flood the zone, it's not easy to get the counter-story heard. The marketing plan dominates, the array of speakers stay "on message," and the new truth continues to stand.

The quaint notion of old-school truth—just the facts, ma'am—cannot really compete with a Massive Product Rollout. It took a while for the public and the media to understand this new shift. By the time Bush had a national emergency to drive his marketing, rational truth had become so small a part of our national discourse that the Bush administration could easily dismiss it as the idle pursuit of the liberal media. The old Enlightenment sense that truth is mutually arrived at through dialogue and debate had been reduced to a hat tip and a slogan. The President would often proclaim that we had had a debate to get us past the fact that the marketing plan intended to skip that part.

The Daily Show's Jon Stewart and Stephen Colbert had a chat about journalism and the Watergate story of Woodward and Bernstein that ended with this exchange:

> STEWART: The truth is the media couldn't break Watergate today?
> COLBERT: That's right, Jon, it just no longer has the credibility.
> STEWART: The media?
> COLBERT: No, the truth.

The problem for the "truth" was made even more difficult for the skeptics confronting the massive IBWO 2.0 rollout. All Cornell had to do was take the discussion further and further into the academic weeds of mind-numbing specifics and stay on message. The slow pace of Enlightenment-style scholarship meant that it would take another six months to a year for the skeptics to write a formal reply.

Pretty soon, the "debate" about the ivory-bill got very weedy. At one point, Cornell examined the blurred bird and determined that it beat its wings 8.7 times per second, which was what the historic tapes from the 1930s recorded for ivory-bills. Pileateds on the other hand averaged 7 to 7.5 beats per second. Now, in order for the academic system to rebut this claim, someone would have to step forward with a professional understanding of wing-beat theory, knowledge of how best to count wingbeats, an acquaintance with the problems of wing-beats on video, as well as the unique controversies of wingbeats on blurred video.

Oy. It would take scholarship *years* to respond to these snooze-inducing details. In the flowering of all the new media in the new millennium, though, there appeared one that moved at precisely the opposite speed of a peer-reviewed journal, and it rode to the rescue. The blog. Specifically, Tom Nelson's blog.

Nelson was no expert. He's an electronics engineer and a passionate birder with a healthy skepticism. His casual blog—tomnelson .blogspot.com—quickly became the gathering spot for all the amateurs in the larger sense—non-credentialed and credentialed birders who were outsiders to the Cornell clique.

Reading this blog while also listening to Cornell's occasional statements is to see how amateurism at its best confounds uptight pros. Granted, Cornell had been fighting rope-a-dope ever since Mark Robbins and Rick Prum complained. But the bloggers simply delighted in the fight, while Cornell had empires to lose. Journalism critics who don't much care for blogs always complain how they are infected with an infantile, sometimes potty-mouthed glee—snark. When you watch a real amateur assault on an academic and government fortress, it's not hard to understand the pleasure. Cornell dug in and issued thin-lipped statements, while Nelson's blog ruinously hooted at the "six-pixel bird."

Amateurs are more likely to see what is actually there because there's no money, no power, no prestige (at least not immediately) attached to seeing anything else. Amateurs mainly just want to know. On the other hand, once you introduce the prospect of getting a piece of the Department of the Interior's $10 million ivory-bill habitat restoration fund (or a no-bid contract in Iraq), that becomes its own massive distortion field. The immediate prospect of money, power, or prestige obviously blurs one's ability to discern the truth. And it makes it much easier to look into the fuzzy image of some de-interlaced pixels and see not only 8.7 wingbeats per second but also, as Gallagher wrote insanely in his book, "what appeared to be a large bird with a black-crested head and a white bill peering out from behind a tupelo."

What Sibley and his coauthors did with their observations about the bird in flight on the Luneau video, the Nelson blog did to every claim, every jot and tittle, regardless of how small or specialized. The rolling conversation of several years permitted every tiny aspect of the Cornell claim to get aired, challenged, defended, but—ultimately— debunked.

No issue was so difficult that some reader couldn't provide a challenge and show that Cornell's evidence was far more slippery than it appeared. For instance, since Cornell apparently only saw one bird, how unlikely is it that that bird was an albino or a bird with abnormal pigmentation in the feathers, known as leucism? A common pileated with enough abnormal addition of white feathers would look, on the fly, very much like an ivory-bill. One amateur's posting slays Cornell in a simple pithy line:

> what are the odds of an albino—remote—but they are more likely than a single unattended ibwo.

What developed online was an amateur effort at peer review. In the arcane world of birding, this was not unlike the fight in the larger culture between Encyclopedia Britannica and Wikipedia—a fight between highly authoritative versus user-generated content, between credentialed experts and enthusiastic amateurs. *Science* magazine published Sibley's article and Fitz's reply, but *Science* refused to publish Sibley's subsequent answer to Fitz. Moreover, they kept most of their coverage out of the peer-reviewed section and ran a journalistic article or note about the ongoing coverage. It was all very delicate and *Science* is still afflicted by the fact that they ran this article. The original finding still stands and *Science* says it has no intention of retracting Fitz's original article. Officially, then, in the annals of peer review, the ivory-bill flourishes in Arkansas.

But on the blogs, there was none of this supercilious fragility. The bloggers wanted to debate the evidence and test every claim. And they did it with brio.

The argument put forward by Cornell's rollout formed a trio of claims—the video, the sightings, and the sound/scaling evidence. Each pillar of the argument crumbled—overwhelmed by amateurs dissecting it, testing it, reevaluating it outside the heat of Cornell's august authority. It must have been infuriating for Fitz.

Those sounds recorded in the woods: readers quickly provided the more likely counterproof, with source and page number. Jackson's *In Search of the Ivory-billed Woodpecker*, page 182, relates an account of hearing a blue jay give precisely the ivory-bill's call in New Jersey—far outside the range of ivory-bills.

One of Cornell's arguments for no one seeing the bird in the years after their small clique had a few emotional sightings was that the bird was elusive and shy—despite the bird's well-known reputation as a show-off. There are photographs from the old days of people putting the ivory-bill on their own heads and posing for the cameras. Woody Woodpecker's gregarious character is modeled in part on the ivory-bill.

Cornell argued that the more bashful birds had been selected out since the most gregarious and ostentatious ivory-bills would likely be the ones that got shot. Good point, until Nelson himself noted that the ivory-bill had been hunted intensively for two hundred years, which ends essentially around World War II:

I see no reason why the Ivorybill would stay half-tame through over 200 years of hunting pressure, then make a quantum leap to ultra-wariness during 60+ years of no hunting pressure.

Some of the blog posts do not address science at all, but just human nature. One writer pored over Harrison's various statements and publications and put it bluntly and without ornamentation:

Bobby [Harrison] has seen an Ivory-bill FIVE times now.

Another of the best sightings among the Cornell team was Casey Taylor's. She heard the double knocks and then saw the bird. That elevated her sighting in the minds of experienced birders since having more than one indicator is a pretty good index to authenticity. But Nelson read the account closely and noted:

In "The Grail Bird," page 246, Gallagher says that Taylor heard all the raps, and then: "Casey sat still for about a half-hour without seeing or hearing anything of interest." Only after this half-hour without rapping did she glimpse a woodpecker.

Open-source peer review brought up issues that individual scholars wouldn't be able to see in time. For instance, the bloggers kept a running account of how many details got nudged ever so slightly in the direction of confirming the bird.

Like Casey Taylor's sighting, there existed a form of evidentiary drift in Cornell's accounts, and Nelson's blog caught every speck of it. The Luneau video? When Bobby Harrison first watched it, he said, "It makes a bad Bigfoot movie look good." Then, slowly but surely, he found himself agreeing with Fitz that the blurry image was "clearly an Ivory-bill." Gallagher elevates the blur to solid proof, saying: "Virtually all of the ivory-bill's major field marks were there, albeit fuzzy."

When *60 Minutes* did a piece on the bird, Nelson questioned the description of Arkansas woods as some vast wilderness. The TV host purplishly described the bayou as "one of the most exotic and the most inhospitable environments in America, a vast primordial ooze, a place so wild, that the Big Woods have been called this country's Amazon." Forget the facts—constantly noted in the blog—that most sightings occurred within earshot of an interstate and the white noise of speeding traffic. (That was definitely true for my visits, too—the whine of distant high-speed traffic was inescapable.) But Nelson nailed it perfectly:

> Ok, the Big Woods isn't small, but let's not get carried away. According to this link, the Amazon's total drainage basin is about 2.7 million square miles in size. The Big Woods of Arkansas is about 860 (.00086 million) square miles in size. In terms of square miles, South America's Amazon is over 3000 times larger than "our Amazon."

Ultimately the blog settled on a metaphor for the Cornell sighting, and it was infuriating to the Ivy League ornithologists: Bigfoot. The bloggers organically generated a set of entertaining but serious Bigfoot rules to explain why the evidence in both the ivory-billed woodpecker and Bigfoot cases involved blurry video, fleeting sightings, and ambiguous proof of presence (scalings, footprints).

The blogger explanation for why the video is always fuzzy (whether it's Bigfoot, IBWO, Loch Ness, Chupacabra—doesn't matter) was brilliant: The minute the view of, say, a Loch Ness Monster gets clearer, then the person can see that it's a log. Similarly, the reason no one ever caught sight of the bird's eponymous field marking—IBWO's ivory bill—is because when observers did see the bill, it was black, like a pileated's. The reason Bigfoot is always looking away or at an angle is because if you saw him square on, the bear's trademark ears would give him away. The reason the bird never perches is because that would give the observer an extra second or two to calm down from the adrenaline rush of seeing an ivory-bill and realize that the markings are actually those of a pileated. And I should simply add, when I went out in the Big Woods with Tippit and later with Harrison—both times—the forest was full of pileateds. At dusk, especially, they rioted everywhere.

Nelson cited a quote from Benjamin Radford of the magazine *Skeptical Inquirer*, nicely summing up the problem of having so much marginal evidence serving as solid proof: "I liken it to a cup of coffee—if you have many cups of weak coffee, they can't be combined into strong coffee."

XI. The Explorers Club

The one great flaw of blogs and journalism is that they have no way of making grand pronouncements. Both of those media are about unfinished things, first, rough drafts of something or other—discussions, not declarations. That's the one thing about high authority. They do that declaration thing very well. Blogs and lowly reporters can get the word out, slowly, but they don't get pageantry, flags, granite-chiseled peer-reviewed findings, $10 million budget lines, or press conferences.

Today's exploded, highly niched media ecosystem has not yet worked out a meaningful way to accommodate the new forms of truth assessment, especially in light of the Internet's retooling of wikified amateurs into an uncoordinated form of (always ongoing) peer review. So what happens when the Great Citadel of Truth is assaulted successfully by the outsiders? In theory, it should be that the new facts get declared and everybody goes home to start fresh, working off the new reality. But it's not like that in the real world. In the real world,

you end up eating "Sweet-and-Sour Bovine Penis Braised, with Tes-
ticular Partners."

Let me explain.

Even while more and more birders were tuning in to the skeptics'
arguments, and as they were becoming more and more convinced
that the declaration of the IBWO was a perfect storm of misunder-
standing, the alternate reality of the flourishing ivory-bill was enjoy-
ing glamorous balls on Park Avenue. Not long after I returned from
the swamps of Arkansas, I got invited to the Explorers Club annual
gala. Among the highlights on the bill that night was the Harrison
and Gallagher show with kayaker Gene Sparling, too.

The Explorers Club is a grown-up version of the Boy Scouts,
minus the solemnity of tying knots. In the Waldorf Astoria's Grand
Ballroom, the evening required a tuxedo to join thousands for a
sit-down dinner. More than a few of the members literally paraded
about in pith helmets, and these members often favored entertainingly baroque mustaches, as well. The entertainment was exotic, of
the old-school aristocratic style. For instance, there was a visit, in the
ballroom, from a llama. A real-life march of the penguins occurred
on stage. At one point, a massive raptor hawk was released from the
balcony and swooped, on cue, above our dinner tables to the podium.
It eyeballed the crowd with stern accipitrine judgment and then flew
back. The ivory-bill trio mingled among the crowd, looking fairly
uncomfortable, especially Harrison, whose camouflage ghillie suits fit
him better than black tie. Tonight they would be honored with the
coveted President's Award for Conservation. Their sighting story was
the early party chatter, as we all hung around a banquet table loaded
with those braised bull penises with sweet and sour testicles, as well as
"Kangaroo Balls Bourguignon."

I have long kept my genitalia consumption restricted to the metaphorical realm, and my tradition survived the evening. I did try the
Spanish goat and the weird fish. Otherwise, the presentation that night
by the ivory-bill performers was their usual tale of derring-do, of ini-

tial disbelief, of high emotion, of sighting the bird and the Oprah moment of sobs that followed. The audience of thousands loved it. And even if anyone in the room had read the blogs or Sibley, the explorers appeared to think of the ivory-bill the way children think of Tinker Bell, and they clapped the fading specter back to life with insistent and thunderous applause. Here I witnessed what I had come to see in other realms. There are two phyla of media consumers—high-information voters versus low-information voters. The high-information voter knows the details, the facts, and the ambiguities—that the full story is "complicated." The low-information voter knows the surface contours of the story and just enough details to shake an affirming head when someone says that life, in fact, is "just that simple." And so it was at the Explorers Club. The chatter beneath the pith helmets was about the thrill of the ivory-bill's rediscovery. Reports of Sibley's critique were out there, yet here one heard not a peep of dissent near the "Mealworms with Durian Paste, on Toastettes."

XII. Ivory-Bills and Weapons of Mass Destruction

As the evidence crumbled, though, there almost seemed to be a battle afoot to see which metaphorical conceit could possibly capture the tragedy here. Was this a Bigfoot story, or was it more ominous? Some bloggers—furious that Cornell would not admit that it might have made a mistake—argued that persistence in a known mistake amounts to a kind of fraud and compared the ivory-bill to notorious hoaxes, the Piltdown Man ("fossil" of transitional early human dug up in England) and the Cardiff Giant ("bones" of a ten-foot petrified man found in New York State). Or was this more like

Bush's invasion of Iraq in search of nonexistent weapons of mass destruction?

"The Arkansas ivory-bill is the WMD of ornithology," Prum told me at one point. Or was Jackson's "faith-based ornithology" spot-on from the beginning with all that talk of "these woods are my church" and the nearly Calvinist insistence that not everybody is chosen to "see" the bird.

With all this metaphor-mongering, what was plainly evident was that something much deeper than bird-watching was tugging at this story. News storms like this one are no different than really great novels or blockbuster movies—the themes and the details manage to somehow gather up strands of wayward anxiety and pluck complex chords that resonate in ways far beyond the facts (or lack of them).

My first real hint of this came when I went out with Harrison to look for the bird. It was a chilly morning in Arkansas when Harrison and I drove just outside of Brinkley to visit with a Fish and Wildlife clerk named Karen, sporting ivory-bill earrings. She winked at Harrison as I got my permit, and she told us she'd been hearing something coming out of an area called the George Tract. The ground there was not exactly swamp—just wet, full of sinks and little bogs—but some had reported a few trees with scalings that might be indicative of the ivory-bill. We were grateful since her telling us this was like a competitive angler betraying a prime fishing hole. As our truck rattled down the road, I asked Harrison if he could remember when he first got bit by Ivory-bill Fever.

"Oh, sure," he said without pausing. "It was after reading Don Moser's article in *Life* magazine in 1972. I was seventeen years old."

I had been hearing about this article—an account of a search for the ivory-bill—since the festival. Gallagher had mentioned it in his talk, and I noticed how often it came up in lunchtime chats with visiting birders. "I remember reading that *Life* magazine article," Fitzpatrick later told me. So I ordered the old magazine. From paragraph to paragraph, Moser's story quivers with melancholy and wistful longing, and, as is typically found in Yankee writing about the South, the author's prose goes all damp as he contemplates a landscape of things lost and, at twilight, almost found.

"If the question of its existence remains unanswered it will continue to range the back country of the mind," Moser trembled, "and those who wish to trail it there can find it in their visions." The article speaks reverentially of the earlier two Cornell expeditions, the first one by the director, Arthur Allen, that resulted in the famous films and recordings in 1935 and the return in 1937 by Cornell graduate student James Tanner, who spent two years studying the birds.

"It's a funny thing about that magazine," Harrison said. "I cannot tell you how many people I stumble upon out here in the woods, and when we get to talking, I find out that they were inspired by the exact same article." The editor of *Science*, too, went on in his own pages about how a magazine article on the ivory-bill changed his life.

When I went back to read up on those original expeditions into the Singer Tract in Louisiana, I discovered that each time there was the indispensable local who knew the land, understood the ways of wildlife, and happily agreed to tell funny stories while leading the academics into the woods. In 1935, Allen made his way in the swamp working on a tip from a colorful local guy named Mason Spencer.

Two years later, Tanner was accompanied by another folksy local yokel, named J. J. Kuhn. The more I read up on these two expeditions, the more I found myself concerned less with the bird than with the characters.

Every time, these expeditions seemed to be remakes of the exact same buddy flick. The courtly intellectual from the Yankee Ivy League college gets taken into the woods by the joshing redneck who knows the ground instinctively. It was The Gallagher and Harrison Show *each* time—these two iconic characters partnering up to enter the woods, as if they were required to give the claim some kind of deeper credibility. Read about enough of these ivory-bill sightings, and they have the same eerie quality of those group pictures in the movie *The Shining*—the same people turning up in the picture, no matter what year it was taken.

In his editorial on the rediscovery, *Science*'s editor gushed over the authenticity of the local who "guided two members of the Cornell team into the right area." Kennedy added: "It is fortunate for science that it attracts people who may lack special training or higher degrees but have found the knowledge and confidence to know that they can do real science."

Despite all the press mentions that Fitz's sightings were the first in "sixty years," it turns out that there have been regular, notable sightings (later dismissed) every few years or so since Tanner left the woods with the last verifiable pictures of the bird: In 1950, Chipola River, Florida. In 1955, Homosassa, Florida. In 1958, Altamaha River, Georgia. In 1959, Aucilla River, Florida. In 1966, Big Thicket, Texas. In 1967, Green Swamp, Florida. In 1971, Atchafalaya Basin, Louisiana. In 1975, near Baton Rouge. In 1978, DeSoto National Forest, Mississippi. In 1982, Pascagoula River, Mississippi. In 1985, Loxahatchee River, Florida. In 1987, Yazoo River, Mississippi. In 1988, Ojito de Agua, Cuba. In 1999, Pearl River, Louisiana. Each sighting has mythic tones, and not just because the iconic bird could never be definitively seen. There was often that repetition of plot that marks the cultural myth—the Mutt and Jeff characters, the almost-confirmed sighting, the fuzzy image.

Some of these sightings led to vicious disagreements. The 1966 sighting by a very respected birder, John Dennis, was dismissed by none other than the godfather of ivory-bills, James Tanner: "Dennis wants to believe he saw something," Tanner said. "But he didn't." In 1971, George Lowery came forward with a story that he had befriended a knowledgeable local, a local Indian who trained his dogs in the swamp. Lowery refused to identify the Indian or the location of the sighting. But the Indian had given him two fuzzy Kodak instamatic pictures of an ivory-bill on two different trees.

After critics had a little time with the two pictures, they noticed that the ivory-bill had the exact same body posture in both pictures. The conclusion was that the bird was stuffed and put up in the tree. Lowery stood by his Indian friend, never revealing his identity, until his death. He died a disgraced birder.

The burden of the ivory-bill history runs from Tanner's beautiful book to Lowery's ignominious exile from ornithology. "Am I worried?" Fitzpatrick mused to me when I asked him where in that spectrum this sighting fell. "That if the ivory-bill is never seen again, that people will look back and say Fitzpatrick laid an egg? No, I did the right thing to jump on the story and put resources on the ground. We continue to focus on this as a conservation story whether or not the bird decorates the treetops." As always with Fitz, the bird is a decoration, a badge—on the large suit of forest restoration.

In South Carolina in 1968, a disputed sighting petered out when the professionals entered the woods with one of the most colorful men the state has ever produced: Alex Sanders. (Alex is an acquaintance of mine.) The hubbub around the possible sighting eventually led to the protection of the Congaree Swamp. That seems to be another mythic quality to the story: The result of a flawed sighting is the protection of vast forests, a desperate effort to reclaim some part of the past that is, well, past. After the 1971 disputed sighting in Texas, 84,550 acres would become the Big Thicket National Preserve. The Nature Conservancy says that it will simply carry on the work of expanding the Big Woods Conservation Area.

This repetitive quality to the stories, with so many of the same features—the experts, the fuzzy image, the pleas for belief and the collapse of the evidence, the Yankee intellectual and the Southern woodsman, the ultimate quest for land protection—meant that the search for the ivory-bill wasn't merely a Freudian story of childhood dreams. This was American mythology.

One afternoon while I was ivory-bill hunting, I stopped into the Gene's BBQ there on the main drag in Brinkley to catch an ivory-bill cheeseburger. Bobby Harrison was there, and a couple of locals started talking to us about the bottomland swamps. Talk like this in the South usually means you're going to be discussing special places to hunt—where to find the good turkeys, where the mallards feed. But at one point, one of the old guys referred to one spot as particularly hard to navigate since the growth had really come back after "all that cutting." When I asked when that happened—the cut—he said, "Oh, more than a century ago." This is one aspect of my native South that I have always admired: People carry around knowledge of long-ago events as if they just happened.

Most people couldn't tell you what happened on their own land a year before they bought it, but a century ago? Yet these guys talked repeatedly of the "logging" as if they were referring to 9/11. In terms of terrorism, the comparison is almost appropriate.

The swampy areas in the South are "hardwood bottomlands," and upland areas tend to have favored a longleaf pine forest. A century or so ago, these two interwoven, interconnected ecosystems had a wide range. During a lecture at the festival by a Nature Conservancy guy, he posted a slide showing the range of these ecosystems and the range of the ivory-billed woodpecker that used to flourish in them. It hit me like a slap in the face.

The longleaf pine system, for instance, ran down the East Coast from Virginia to Florida's panhandle and then ran west as far as Texas, covering ninety million acres, and was said to be the largest single-species ecosystem in the world. And when you set over that the range of the ivory-bill, which is a slightly smaller version of that image, and then step back, you realize you are looking at an ecosystem that already has a name.

Dixie. How coincidental was it that the world of this bird and this larger ecosystem roughly bracketed the world we would come to call the Old South?

Many early naturalists visiting the South looked upon the long-leaf ecosystem in awe. It was not the deep dark forest as most of us come to understand it. Almost *no* thickets grew in this forest. It was open, cathedral-like, populated largely by tall longleaf pine poles, which grew straight and true. A longleaf forest looks orderly and tidy and endless. Horseback riders could gallop through it effortlessly for hours. This ecosystem was also called the "fire forest" because it would naturally burn every year. The longleaf pines dropped their luxurious needles, some as long as eighteen inches, throughout the year. Coated in a highly flammable resin, they stacked up slowly, and by the really hot months of July and August, a lightning strike would catch them on fire. The fire was unavoidable, and so combustible are these needles, there are accounts of the forest burning even in a rainstorm. But it's a ground fire, more than a smoldering fire, not an all-consuming *forest* fire. It's just enough for the longleaf, which can survive a ground fire, to burn back its competitors—the oak tree, the gum, the hickory, etc. It's one impressive adaptation.

Even the animals that live in a fire forest have adapted to it, almost like some kind of Disney movie. In the southernmost portion of the fire forest, the gopher tortoise, a fairly large creature that grows a little bigger than a dinner plate, digs a burrow some thirty feet in length. During the fires, the burrow becomes a kind of air raid shelter for all kinds of insects, snakes, birds, mice, everybody. Biologists who've studied this arrangement have determined that some three hundred different species make temporary use of the gopher tortoise hole when the fires hit. Meanwhile, all their competitors flee. Evolution, doing its thing.

So a fire forest, when it is not burning, is distinguished by its open, sunny quality. The earliest settlers for instance found these woods so repetitive in appearance that it was easy to get lost in them. You would not enter them without taking a local guide. In Savannah, Georgia, the town fired a cannon at the day's end, so that men in the woods could follow the sound home. There were special laws governing widows whose husbands wandered off into the forest and never came back.

It was a place where, according to ivory-bill expert Lester Short, the ivory-bill could dine all day and where the bird preferred to live. "The habitat in the United States is usually cited as being deep, tall swamp forest," Short wrote in his classic *Woodpeckers of the World*. "However, it is my view that the species originally inhabited the virgin pine forests of southeastern North America. These pines were cut over rather early, because of their accessibility, probably restricting the Ivorybill to less optimal swamp hardwood forests."

The story of that cut-over is one of the hidden histories of the South, surviving mostly in the anecdotal remarks of men sitting around barbeque joints. It's the largely unknown story of what happened in the cruel decades after the Civil War when the survivors in the South, black and white, had no economy and struggled to find a way to make ends meet.

Beginning in roughly 1880, speculators saw the easiest business opportunity in the history of the world: ninety million acres of the most beautiful pine on earth and, living right on top of it, a desperate, starving labor force.

There was even a book published in 1880 called *How to Get Rich in the South*, written by W. H. Harrison Jr., who was either the grandson of the President by that name, or a man who never corrected the assumption. I bought an original copy off the Internet, and it is a breathtaking read.

The chapters have names like "Cattle" and "Duck," breaking the South down into every exploitable commodity no matter how small. There are chapters on "Beans, Snap" and "Cabbages, Early." And on down it runs until the last chapter on timber. It encourages speculators to hurry because "the lumbermen of the North are buying up large tracts of valuable timber lands and putting in saw-mills." Land in the South, the author tells his eager readers, that "is now for sale at $1 to $3 an acre will bring $50 to $100 within twenty years, for its timber. Southern timber land is an absolute certainty as a profitable investment."

And the speculators descended, and the timber companies also came, buying up land in 100,000-acre dollops. One can argue about the dates, but, effectively, between 1880 and 1920 the eleven states of the Old South were clear-cut into a confederacy of muddy stumps. Railroads were temporarily erected into even the most inaccessible areas. When Bobby Harrison and I fought our way three miles back into the Blue Hole area of the swamp, we came across the rotting remains of a raised railroad line, a century old.

These loggers were sloppy, wasteful, and reckless. In the slang of the day, they "cut out and got out." Rivers churned with what looked like and was the melting sludge of hills dissolving into plains. Ghost towns appeared after an area was "sawed out." The mountains of sawdust left behind often would catch fire from lightning and smoke for years. Visitors to the South in this time would comment on how no amount of travel could get a tourist away from smoke coming from somewhere.

The devastation was so extensive that state revenues dropped as taxable forest property had to be reclassified as nontaxable wasteland, thus extending the economic crisis of 1865 into an eighty-year catastrophe.

Other economies eventually arrived in the mid-twentieth century, such as planting over the old longleaf soils with loblolly and slash pine to feed the paper mills. Historians have written about the paradox of this timber era. It was a culture that was so remote and brutal, it left no songs or slang, no famous workers or evil foreman and barely any written accounts. Almost effortlessly, the shame of this massive clear-cut receded into history, largely without leaving one.

So the wild primeval swamps and the cathedral stretches of pine forest in the South were sheared into flat farmland by the time Allen and his party headed south. In fact their destination, an 81,000-acre stand of virgin forest, was known as the Singer Tract because the sewing machine company owned it to cut wood to make the cabinets for their sewing machines. It was the last, large section of Dixie's original forest.

It's hard to imagine that it's a coincidence that the story of the ivory-bill so often involves a re-creation of the outsider coming down and hooking up with a local guide for an expedition into the endless forest. The penitent Northern scientist coming South to find a smart-alecky good old boy from Dogpatch—these two light out for the swamp and find the elusive bird with mythic regularity.

The ivory-bill's habitat is the South's Eden, the haunting swamps, the majestic pine forest. The names of the areas where it's been sighted—the Big Woods of Arkansas, the Big Thicket of Texas—suggest the very landscape it needs to survive: a large and wild habitat, crowded with patriarchal trees and brimming with wildlife. To see an ivory-bill is to confirm that we haven't destroyed what feels like the very origin of life. The swamp's ivory-bill is Noah's dove, surviving improbably long after a catastrophe we'd rather not remember, to tell us we are pardoned. Lord God Bird, forgive us our trespasses.

After Tanner returned from his famous 1937 study, a massive effort was launched to save the ivory-bill and its last known address, the Singer Tract. By then, in the middle of World War II, this last and biggest stretch of wilderness was leased by Chicago Mill and Lumber. The company wanted to sell the land, since there was no labor to cut the wood at the beginning of the war. A man named Richard Pough recognized its value and arranged to buy it as a way to conserve it. He would later found the Nature Conservancy. He had four governors sign on to this project, as well as President Roosevelt. He traveled to Chicago to ink the deal. When the president of Chicago Mill entered the room, he apologized and said the deal was off. "We are just money-grubbers," he explained. He went on to say that they had found some labor. The Chicago Mill learned that German soldiers were being held in Mississippi POW camps and could be used to cut down trees practically for free. The meetings ended, and, despite the intervention of four governors, the last large stand of virgin forest in the Old South was clear-cut by Nazis.

XIII. Once Again, with Feeling

The ivory-bill is a bird we'll be seeing again and again. The story tugs at too much history and too many emotions to be resolved in some neat and tidy way, like a child's story, happily ever after. Here's how powerful a tale it is. Almost immediately after the Cornell announcement and as the certainty of their proof began to falter, the bird flew to the northern panhandle of Florida. There, an Auburn professor and ornithologist named Geoff Hill went to the Choctawhatchee River and the satisfaction came quickly. His assistant Brian Rolek, whom Hill describes as a "novice birder," was the only one to spot the bird.

"Brian had studied the field marks of a perched Ivory-bill before our trip but not those of an Ivory-bill in flight," Hill wrote in *Bird-Watching* magazine. Naturally, he saw the bird in flight and didn't see the white bill, just "large patches of white only on the back (trailing) portion of both the upper and underwing."

After a while, the team was hearing about ivory-bills all over the place. "Despite the small scale of our search, we amassed substantial evidence—including more than 300 sound recordings of *kent* calls and double-knocks—that Ivory-bills were in the forests along the Choctawhatchee River," Hill wrote. And they had thirteen sightings, nearly twice as many as Cornell. Hill notes without irony or embarrassment: "All of the sightings were of flying birds." And his "best sighting" occurred "as I watched an Ivory-bill fly away from me."

It was as if the team had not read any of the counterarguments or accumulated wisdom of the amateur bloggers. How else could you write something like this: "How could we detect birds so dependably for a full year and not get a photograph? My answer is that the woodpeckers do not want people close to them. They invariably detected us before we detected them." No other bird in the world is as successful at avoiding trained bird-watchers as the Arkansas and Florida ivory-bills.

Hill's team often catches sight of the "diagnostic shape, plumage pattern, or flight behavior characteristics of Ivory-billed Woodpeckers," but never any of the definitive field marks. At an American Ornithologists' Union meeting, Rolek presented "a grainy video of a bird that he identified in life as an Ivory-billed Woodpecker."

A grainy video? Well, that rounds out the story, doesn't it? It's like that scene in *Shrek* where all the stock characters of all the children's fairy tales gather at the king's palace, and you find yourself happily picking out the ones you recognize. Oh, there are the dwarfs. There is a troll. It is comforting when you recognize the ones you know are supposed to be there. When I heard that Hill had a blurry video, I felt oddly warmed by the flush of déjà vu. Of course there wasn't enough enthusiasm this time, being so close to the Cornell sightings, to fluff interest in a festival. So donors to Hill's search could only earn a "limited edition collector's pin commemorating the search for the Ivory-billed Woodpecker in the Florida panhandle" for $100 and Hill would throw in a "golf shirt with a specially-designed commemorative logo" for $250.

Although he has only amassed even more of the weak coffee that Nelson's bloggers so smartly conclude doesn't make for a strong brew, Hill nevertheless concludes: "Our evidence suggests that Ivory-billed Woodpeckers may be present in the forests along the Choctawhatchee River and warrants an expanded search of this bottomland forest habitat." He added: "We are going to receive some state and federal funding for the upcoming field season, money that will allow us to have a much larger search team and to deploy many remote cameras."

The money flows, and there's pots of it because the federal government also apparently hasn't kept up with Nelson's blog or read Sibley's articles. The Fish and Wildlife Service had a budget of $27 million to produce a "Recovery Plan" for the ivory-bill and still maintains a website to keep us all updated on the progress: www.fws.gov/ivorybill/. The site boasts that America "has a comprehensive recovery plan ready to implement wherever and whenever it is needed." We can all sleep soundly now. Meanwhile, Cornell has withdrawn its forces and retreated into determined, if not pathetic, defense: "We found one bird," said Fitz grimly, and he hasn't really spoken about it since.

Prior to the Cornell finding, the official status of the bird was "endangered," with no definitive sightings since the 1940s. And that is right back to where we are. The government officially holds that the bird may exist in this habitat and is now committed to preserving the habitat to maintain the bird. In one bizarre case in Arkansas, a judge actually halted a development because the construction work would imperil the ivory-billed woodpecker.

For now, the IBWO officially exists, on paper, and with federal protection to salve our mythic memories. At the very least, the government's bedrock truth will lay the groundwork for a sighting in the future, when a new generation finds its own bookish intellectual to buddy up with some rustic from Mississippi ("You ought to hear him tell stories, seriously, he's *so* funny") and tell once again the tale of the ivory-billed woodpecker. Only to have it unraveled and unstrung by another band of committed amateurs.

The man who led the famous 1968 woodpecker hunt in South Carolina, Alex Sanders, says that he still gets questioned about it: "Over the course of the past thirty-five years, I have often been asked, 'Where is the ivory-billed woodpecker?' I've always answered truthfully, 'I don't know where he is now; but I know where he was when we needed him.' Depending on who is asking, I sometimes add, 'When we need him again, we'll find him.'"

4

A CONFEDERACY OF DABBLERS

I. A Boy's Life, Recombinated

When I was a kid in Charleston, South Carolina, there weren't many things more fun than a secret fort. I built them by assembling sofa cushions in the living room or nailing leftover lumber into the branches of my gingko tree. In one case, still notorious in my family, my friends and I used some stolen spray paint to claim a little place by defacing an out-of-the-way wall belonging to the United States Postal Service (apparently some kind of federal crime).

My friend Parker and I had lots of forts in those days. They were squirreled away atop garages, in the narrow spaces between old houses, or in neglected corners of collapsing warehouses. We gave them cool secret-fort names, depending on who worked near them: Under the Realtor's Nose, Under the Painter's Nose, and the aforementioned, Under the Postman's Nose. Most of what happened there, other than an occasional water-gun fight, was . . . nothing. I'd get a call from

Parker—"Let's meet Under the Old Lady's Nose"—and I'd speed off on my bicycle as fast as possible.

What drew us there was that intoxicating sense of possibility. It's what keeps those places vivid in my mind. It didn't really matter that not long after both of us arrived there on our bikes, we drifted off to do something else. The idea was that in those special places, almost anything could happen. Occasionally something incredible did happen. After we stole the spray paint from Mr. Reynolds, whose backyard abutted the post office, we each spray-painted our futures on the wall. Todd, a future visual artist, painted a naked woman. I annotated it with a thesaurus of Anglo-Saxon obscenities. Parker, the musician, declared his love for a girl we all adored and wrote both his full name and hers right on the wall, making the case pretty easy for the local police to crack.

So when I was recently in Cambridge, Massachusetts, hanging with a couple of amateur biologists, I practically suffered a flashback when Mackenzie Cowell invited me to see the secret meeting place where his crowd of local homebrew geneticists teach the basics of DNA extraction. Under the Recombinant Geneticist's Nose was where, as Cowell suggested, we could extract DNA from "tuna, banana, cow heart."

We parked on a side street not all that far from Harvard Square. The place was an average-looking brownstone. He asked me not to reveal the actual address. (As if. I'm *Jack*, not Parker.) We unlocked the door and went up to the second floor. Three programmers were sitting at desks lined up in front of a kitchen counter. It was lunchtime, and sandwiches were unwrapped and some Second Life action was breaking out on a couple of screens. Awkward hellos were exchanged. One person knew Cowell, but the others didn't really. The place was a coworking arrangement, the kind you see among freelancers, especially programmers, nowadays. One guy rents a spacious apartment and then sublets room access for $400 a month to people who need a quiet place to sit and get lost in hours of furious programming (or play

Second Life while convincing themselves that they are programming furiously).

Only a few weeks before, Cowell had led a meeting of his new Do-It-Yourself Biology group or DIYbio, here at the kitchen counter, and he showed me how it went. From the space where most people kept a few supplies, Cowell pulled out a box—his homemade genetics laboratory—all created from a few easily obtainable supplies. Typically, lab trays are filled with a gel into which is set a lab "comb." In any university lab, this is done with expensive equipment. Here, it was a small Tupperware container jimmied with a cut-up subway fare card. The methylene blue, needed to dye the DNA to see its movement, had been purchased at the local pet shop, where it's sold as an anti-algae chemical for fish tanks. And then there is the glycerol, which is also needed to extract the DNA.

"You can get glycerol from the CVS pharmacy," Cowell said. "They sell it as a suppository." The glycerol comes in squishy tubes. "We were trying to be serious about it, but that was definitely not happening."

Not really all that different from life Under the Grocer's Nose, except: the outcome of Parker and me squirting water at each other wasn't the creation of new life forms. But that is what the latest crew of amateur scientists are, ultimately, up to. Once known by its former noms de plume of genetic engineering, recombinant DNA, or bioengineering, synthetic biology—as it's known today—is fairly new. Polish geneticist Waclaw Szybalski coined the phrase "synthetic biology" in a 1974 research paper. But the modern use of it probably dates to the first International Meeting on Synthetic Biology, in 2004 in Cambridge, Massachusetts.

When you ask anyone in the field what it is, the answer you get will typically involve a metaphor. It's like computers (genes get "programmed") or it's like old-school manufacturing (bacteria will be microscopic "factories" pumping biofuel) or it's like toys (parts will snap together, genes are like LEGOs). The most revealing metaphor, when you first come to it, belongs to Stanford's Professor Drew Endy.

As synthetic biology's most effective evangelist, Endy is boyish-looking, energetic, and smart. He can connect his new science to old ones in a way that makes the near future of engineering DNA sound absolutely inevitable.

Endy tells the story of William Sellers, an engineer who wrote an important paper around the time the Civil War was winding up. Sellers suggested that American engineers abandon the age of hand-forged materials and adopt a standard for all nuts and bolts. He proposed a formula that would create a standard pitch of screw thread conformed to the screw's diameter:

$$P = 0.24 \sqrt{(D + 0.625 - 0.175)}$$

Today Americans still screw, more or less, by the Sellers system. But the key feature of this new screw, Endy argues, was not only the convenience of knowing that every screw was the same size, but here is what was most crucial: Every Sellers nut, when screwed into a Sellers bolt, behaved the same way. "When you pull on the nut," Endy says, "it stays put. It doesn't come flying off of the bolt." It does what it is supposed to do, a feature that engineers like Endy call "reliable functional composition."

This predictability is one of those structural changes to American manufacturing in the nineteenth century that drove its rapid progress. And that is what Endy is trying to do with DNA. He and his colleagues, when they discuss their fresh new science, take up this engineering metaphor. MIT, for instance, maintains a Registry of Standard Biological Parts, a kind of Radio Shack of DNA. Geneticists can order various plasmids or other strings of DNA known to cause, say, glowing in the dark or other biological features. And it works the other way, too: You can register a new DNA strand with a novel functionality—for instance, a "biosynthetic device" that changes the nasty manure-like odor of growing lab bacteria into the sweet satisfying aroma of a banana. This bio-widget or "banana odor biosynthetic system" has been standardized and registered, available in the catalogue as part BBa_J45400.

The idea is that the Registry will become your one-stop shop for DNA parts, so that folks like Cowell and his friends at the coworking space will start playing and creating, advancing the science quickly. Synthetic biology is now under way, not just as a new science but also as a window into what happens when a new enthusiasm lures weekenders to try it on their own, form new clubs, introduce new ideas, and push new terms into the daily lives of the (often nervous) middle class.

The number of standard biological parts doubles every year, and Endy says, "the same thing is happening with the number of teenagers who would like to do genetic engineering; it's doubling every year." This rapid expansion has a lot to do with Endy's salesmanship. Endy predicts a time (soon) when someone will rewrite the DNA of an acorn to include George Jetson–like instructions that direct the future oak to create its own tree house. Or new souped-up ocean coral will suck carbon out of an overloaded Gaia. Apply this concept to the human genome and you're looking at a coming generation who will choose their genetically enhanced superhero powers as one of life's routine decisions, like what college to attend or whom to marry. Endy likes to coin hackerlike jargon that sounds super-hip. It hasn't caught on widely yet, but if you listen carefully on the Stanford campus, maybe you'll hear someone referring to the shifting of a gene from one life form to another as "DNA bashing."

In fact, most of the boosters of synthetic biology are quite skillful at mining these kinds of metaphors. The elder statesman of theoretical physics and a big synthetic biology fan, Freeman Dyson, wrote an influential essay in the *New York Review of Books* addressing the learned class. Like Endy, he imagines that the real breakthrough will occur once professional scientists make enough of the basics available to a new and much larger class of people who will take over the creative function of synthetic biology.

"Now imagine what will happen," Dyson wrote. "There will be do-it-yourself kits for gardeners who will use genetic engineering to breed new varieties of roses and orchids. Also kits for lovers of pigeons and parrots and lizards and snakes to breed new varieties of pets. Breeders of dogs and cats will have their kits too. Domesticated biotechnology, once it gets into the hands of housewives and children, will give us an explosion of diversity of new living creatures, rather than the monoculture crops that the big corporations prefer. New lineages will proliferate to replace those that monoculture farming and deforestation have destroyed. Designing genomes will be a personal thing, a new art form as creative as painting or sculpture."

It's not a brave new world that Dyson envisions, but rather the same old mundane one, just gussied up with the middlebrow creations of housewives and teens. And maybe that's where we're headed, but make no mistake about how we will get there. Dyson and his co-enthusiasts want to put the designer's toolbox of life itself into the hands of the amateur. Presumably, an intelligent designer.

II. The Wild, Wild Test Tube

At a public forum in Cambridge, a crowd of about forty people took their seats in a lecture hall at MIT on a pleasant fall evening. Cowell and his partner Jason Bobe, who have announced the first DIYbio chapter here, welcome everyone. There are a few reps from start-up biotech companies, hoping to catch a rising star. Most of the people here are frustrated programmers who are no longer content with the kind of success one can achieve in the computer domain. Sure, there's money to be made, but where's the glory in creating the latest add-on to Excel or patch for Google's search algorithm? Some apparently think it's time to head to a new frontier—where they are still putting down wood sidewalks over newly trafficked mud.

The key attraction of synthetic biology dominates the night—how cool would it be to engineer life or create it altogether? On some level, hasn't this historically been the greatest wet dream of every scientist, mad or sane, since the beginning of time? Well, yes. So the conversation quickly becomes a question and answer about safety issues. What about making all this knowledge so freely available? Won't some kid resurrect smallpox or weaponize Spanish flu? How does one promote healthy Boy's Club fun for synbio at a time when Americans regularly hear about anthrax attacks, radioactive dirty bombs, and endless airport announcements in tinny android voices to please report any unattended packages? It's a question that haunts the evening.

Over the course of several days I hung out with Bobe and Cowell, they both spent as much time trying to explain to me exactly how they intend to position synbio as they did explaining the science it-self. They very much want it to have that free-flowing joy associated, say, with the young-adult chemistry sets of our imaginations.

Cowell has created a cartoon how-to for basic biology very much in the noble science tone, and their websites are a pleasure to cruise, charged with cautionary principles. Bobe says that he wants one of the main missions of their group to be researching the protocols of garage biology from state to state and to have those guidelines freely available on their website. So if an amateur biologist in Nevada wanted to know whether he could set up a lab in his backyard, he could easily access the current legal requirements.

"At the first meeting, a kid name Mike showed up," Bobe said, referring to the unofficial gathering in the secret fort. Mike proudly showed everybody his online picture. "It's Mike by a desk lamp holding up a test tube," Bobe said. Shot with lots of spooky shadow, Mike's crazed smile and tuft of chin hair makes the whole look very mad scientisty. Another amateur named Julie piped up: "You can't publish that, the FBI will be here any minute!"

It's not exactly an idle speculation. Bobe and the others continually discuss the recent case of a retired seventy-one-year-old chemist named Victor Deeb. He was doing some work in his basement lab in Marlboro, Massachusetts, when an upstairs air conditioner caused a fire to break out on the second floor. When the fire department came and stumbled upon the homemade lab, they summoned the alarm. Even though Deeb had maintained the lab for twenty years without incident—mostly recently working on "a carcinogen-free sealant for the lids of baby-food jars"—the government seized his science equipment.

Officials with the state environmental agency admitted in the local paper that the "chemicals in Mr. Deeb's basement posed no radiological or biological risk, and there was no mercury or poison." Pamela Wilderman, Marlboro's code enforcement officer, summed up her accusation: "I think Mr. Deeb has crossed a line somewhere." But the official wouldn't or couldn't say what the line was.

The case has since turned into a civil rights issue. In answering a fire call, can bureaucrats poke around one's house and decide that it looks like it might be bad, so that all the property has to be impounded? The town's assistant solicitor said it didn't really matter if Deeb's rights had been violated or his livelihood deprived because: "He's a creative person, and I don't think that's something you can shut off."

What?

An earlier generation might have celebrated Victor Deeb as a hero, a charming crank, and a garage inventor trying to come up with the next big thing. Now he is a threat to the "homeland"? But here's the real question on the minds of amateurs: What if Deeb had been a twenty-four-year-old trying to isolate the hemoglobin-producing gene to create bacteria that could pump out an endless supply of artificial human blood (been done, by Berkeley students, already a registered part known as "Bactoblood")?

Or what if Deeb had been "Splicer"—an overseas DIYbio enthusiast who is causing Bobe some ulcerous concern à la Mike? Besides his tangy handle, Splicer's photo icon on the Internet is a baby with nails sprouting from its head. Bobe rolls his eyes at the kind of trouble this sort of teen swagger invites from the unknowing public and small-town safety bureaucrats.

If the professionals like Endy and Dyson are toying with metaphors involving manufacturing and bacterial factories, the amateurs are already at the barricades of this new science. Academics with large funded labs and lots of protocol are not as likely to attract sudden and possibly catastrophic media interest as Bobe and Cowell. They must simultaneously worry about PR on the one hand, while trying to establish a fundamental code of conduct on the other. They want to come up with solid rules of synbio behavior before some incident brings down the fury and ignorance of outsiders. The tricky question is this: Can they figure out the equivalent of the Boy Scouts' rules on campfire etiquette before someone burns down the forest?

Amateurs may dabble in any science, but one of their unacknowledged jobs is dealing with how the common man understands it.

For Bobe, the ready-made metaphor is already out there, both a blessing and a curse: hacking. Now upgraded to "biohacking." As other chapters of DIYbio have immediately sprung up, Bobe confides in me one day about the headlong progress of the "people in San Francisco." He refers to the folks out there in the legendary Silicon Valley as if he were an Eastern banker in 1880 fretting about the rumors one hears about that new town, Dodge City. One of the Bay Area biohackers has somehow managed to get some of the glow-in-the-dark plasmids (literally, the piece of a fish gene that allows it to glow in the dark). Such things are supposed to be difficult to access unless you are a company. The biohacker who's pulled this off apparently hasn't gotten the memo warning about provocative pseudonyms and goes by the handle "clonearmy."

III. Failing Upward

Not far off Fillmore Street in San Francisco, in that stretch that's still mostly Boho coffee joints with a head shop or art gallery or two, is the apartment of clonearmy. No need for secrecy. She's Meredith Patterson, a thirty-something woman pushing five-foot-ten, who favors combat boots and butch leather jackets. She wears the kind of glasses slightly pinched at the tips like cats' eyes to finish off her look with a nice hint of 1950s girl nerd.

On our way to Trader Joe's to pick up some plain yogurt from which to extract some DNA, I noticed a tattoo on her ankle. She pulled her pants up above her boot. "This one's not done yet," she advised. It's a steampunk biomechanical X-ray of her lower tibia and fibula, a series of mechanical cogs, robotic pistons, and bicycle chains. "It's kind of a joke because I have these weird mutant ankles," she said. "I had this thing called an accessory navicular bone." All of her tattoos relate, in some way, to her sense of herself as an off-the-grid scientist: On one arm she has a rose window and sword from her favorite anime story, *Revolutionary Girl Utena.* Down the bicep is the iconic image of Atlas holding up the heavens, most familiar as the paperback cover art of Ayn Rand's novel *Atlas Shrugged.* And keeping the burdened Titan company is the Page of Pentacles, the tarot card figure who signifies the "eternal student," Patterson says, and officially described as "a young man who stands alone in a field full of freshly blossoming flowers . . . unaware of anything around him other than the golden coin which seems to float in his hands."

Patterson does in fact have a sample of the glow-in-the-dark plasmid sealed in a bag in her freezer (next to some frozen chicken wings and a box of Eggos). The gene known as green fluorescent protein or GFP is already famous for many reasons. In 2000 an artist named Eduardo Kac created "GFP Bunny," an albino hare genetically altered into a chimera rabbit that would glow bright green in the presence of ultraviolet light. Since then, the gene has been domesticated—very domesticated. Pet stores now sell GFP-altered zebra fish as GloFish ($7.99 a piece, $6.99 if you buy three—now available in Starfire Red, Electric Green, Sunburst Orange, and Cosmic Blue). The American scientists who isolated this gene won the Nobel Prize in 2008, and GFP is more seriously used as a marker, to track the movement of genes. Patterson's hope is to create "Glo-gurt."

"I thought it would be cool," she said. She imagined how great it would be to go to a rave with glo-sticks you could eat.

While I'm visiting, her goal is to cultivate enough bacteria in her homebrew lab and then to improvise a homemade electroporation device in order to transfer the glow-in-the-dark gene into a bacterium that then can be used to cultivate yogurt according to the regular recipes.

"Electroporation involves exposing a sample of bacteria to a high-voltage, pulsed electrical field," Patterson said. In this case: 2500 volts. (A standard wall socket is 120 volts.) "Essentially," she said, "we're going to Taser them."

Getting the plasmid, it turns out, is no big deal if you're an old Silicon Valley hand. Like nearly every programmer out here, Patterson has a shell company with an address and name. This way, ordering plasmids from Carolina Biological Supply Company in North Carolina was as simple as shopping for a pair of shoes online.

Her lab is on a table right in the front room. The place is what one expects in an apartment shared by a changing number of roommates. I say number, because it's never quite clear to me how many actually live here. The roommate she refers to at one point doesn't show up after several of my visits because she's "at a rave" that appears to be moving into its second lunar orbit. Otherwise, it's all very familiar—a friendly wreck of used furniture, piles of books and boxes, coats, beanbag chairs, and a potted glade of pioneering houseplants clustered desperately at the windows.

Scattered on the table is Patterson's homebrew genetic gear. While Cowell was still worrying about lab-quality pipettes (since they run around $200), Patterson had long ago solved that problem with an online pharmacy selling cheap disposable insulin needles that can measure down to microliters. She originally reengineered an old nine-inch floppy drive motor from a computer she bought on the street for $5 to serve as a centrifuge for spinning vials of liquid containing bacteria.

Patterson's autoclave is a pressure cooker, and the glycol she tells me awkwardly comes from Astroglide, the sex lube. I'm sure there is some brilliant cultural observation to be made about Bay Area amateurs instinctively improvising with sex lube while East Coast biohackers are horsing around with suppositories. It's just that I'm not sure I want to ponder these distinctions long enough to find out what it is.

Patterson's incubator is a Sharper Image tailgater's fridge that can cool or warm.

"Someone was getting rid of one of these for $30; mine now," she said proudly.

Patterson has employed a number of ingenious hacks to get what she needs. She scoured supply house sites regularly for deals. So, for instance, one company offered a free sample of one of five polymerases (very useful enzymes that can copy a DNA strand). But the deal was limited to one shipment per address.

"So it shows up two days later in a Styrofoam cooler full of dry ice pellets. And I am like, wait a second, they just sent me a DNA polymerase and a ton of free dry ice. But they will only send me one type of polymerase and they have five available," Patterson explained, noting that dry ice is much in demand at raves these days. "And I want all of them, so I call up a bunch of my friends and I say, 'Hey, do you want some free dry ice?' All you have to do is order this polymerase stuff," she said, then "give me the polymerase and you can keep the dry ice."

Patterson's evident pleasure in creating this kitchen-top lab and the different ways she has hacked the system is clearly a major part of why she, a computer programmer by day, moonlights as a kitchen biologist. It doesn't matter whether she has socially engineered corporate suppliers, bale-wired some junk she's bought at a street sale, or worked out ingenious substitutes from the local pharmacy (or sex shop), Patterson talks about this part of her work with as much glee as she does the actual genetic engineering she's attempting.

There's a playful quality to all this, an entertaining quality, and in fact, she confesses at one point that she probably owes her interest in all this to an accidental piece of DNA-style performance art she stumbled into. When a famous programmers' conference was getting scheduled—Codecon— she volunteered to put on a little DNA show and the organizers agreed.

She wanted to illuminate the seemingly complex world that most of us imagine when we hear words like "recombinant" and "DNA" and show that it was quite accessible. For instance, extracting DNA from the classic green pea, the famous subject of Gregor Mendel, can be made to sound very scientific and complicated: A professional in a lab might discuss cell disruption to penetrate the membrane, followed by removal of lipids, followed by an isopropanol bath and a protease wash, followed by a centrifuge to yield some stringy DNA in the bottom of a test tube.

Patterson showed up with a box of stuff found in most kitchens or bathrooms. The only thing she lacked was a centrifuge substitute, so she asked the guy in charge to help her find a salad spinner.

"My talk was on a Sunday and there was a party Saturday night,"

Patterson said. "The organizer was going around to everyone he knew to see if they had a salad spinner." By Sunday, though, an Oxo salad spinner with the black push-down button pump had been procured and donated to the Patterson amateur lab.

"I started with dried ground-up peas," she said, "and I put those in a saline buffer." She quickly translates for me: "Regular old saltwater." Then, she continued, "you shake it up a little bit and add some shampoo, which contains a detergent which breaks apart the fatty cell wall. To that you add some meat tenderizer, which contains papain, which is a protease which breaks down the nucleus." So the shampoo gets us inside the cell, and the meat tenderizer gets us inside the nucleus where the DNA resides and releases it from the proteins that accompany it. Then you let it sit for a while until it turns into what Patterson calls a "slurry" of "digested goo." This gunk is put into the salad spinner to separate the solids from the liquids. After pouring off the liquid, one adds rubbing alcohol. DNA likes alcohol about as much as oil likes water. So it tends to bunch together to separate itself from the rest of the liquid. Sticky strings begin to form. This is pure, extracted DNA, ready for bioengineering.

The pleasure of inventing everything yourself—starting from scratch—gives this operation (any amateur operation, for that matter) a kind of buttress against frustration. The tabletop rig that Patterson had cobbled together was so obviously a source of satisfaction that the expected failures of any experiment cycle were easily brushed off as she improvised her way to the next step.

And when things went perfectly, it gave way to moments of intense and obscure beauty. When she was putting some distilled water onto our bacteria samples, she cleaned her hands and carefully removed a single sterilized corked tube. In the other hand, a syringe. With one elegant motion, the long, graceful fingers of one hand drew up some water; with the other she one-handedly pulled the cork. She looked sideways at the open tube so that her slight breathing wouldn't

contaminate her work as she injected the sample with water. She pi-
petted just enough in and re-corked the tube. Twenty times, perfectly, like some tiny private ballet.

There is really no step to this process and no part of this homemade lab that she doesn't know intimately. When something went
wrong, Patterson just stepped back, thought about it for a while,
and dove back in. Part of the freedom and pleasure of the amateur
space derives from the fact that the little lab on the table has no black
boxes on it. There's nothing store-bought whose processes Patterson
doesn't understand. She's built and rebuilt everything sitting here.

When I asked, for instance, about the broth in the tubes, i.e., the
food that will feed our bacteria to grow overnight, she said, "Normally when you are growing lacto, you use MRS broth; MRS stands
for a couple of guys." (De Man, Rogosa, and Sharpe, if you're interested.) "But that stuff is expensive," she said, so she made her own.
"What I did was manage to track down an article Ellicker wrote in
the *Journal of Dairy Science*." The article was written in 1956—talk
about going back to basics.

"I could have solved the problem by throwing money at it," she
said, "but what I've generally found is that old articles tend to have
the cheapest but still effective way of going about anything. This was
back when people didn't have a lot of money to throw at problems
and they were still figuring out things."

Patterson says she doesn't get frustrated too easily, a habit she as-
cribes to her father's constant encouragement when she was a kid. But
it's also the case that amateurs have a different relationship to failure
than professionals. At an office, failure is profoundly frustrating since
it's known to others and embarrassing. Failure and success are binary
modes, up or down, and often tied directly to pay. Did you succeed
or not? Failure can often lead to getting marginalized or pissed off
or fired.

But if the entire rig on your kitchen table is your own creation,
hatched from street castoffs and dairy farmers' lessons dating from

the Eisenhower administration, then failure is just a glitch in the system you've built. Putting your hands in there, e-mailing other amateur scientists for advice, checking out colleagues on your common wiki, fixing what's wrong, and moving one's investigations forward are actually just other ways of being successful. Amateurs are often fixing things, their own devices, so there is this constant reinforcement of feeling smart and competent.

People who study creativity and productivity say that this is a key feature of highly productive pursuits. Most people, when continuously frustrated, will walk away. But if competence is also defined as cunningly figuring out a problem with your lab, then staying with the program becomes a lot easier.

Of course, that staying power can also become a treadmill that keeps an eccentric in his garage for a lifetime, convinced that if he tinkers just a little more he'll eventually find the secret to perpetual motion. No one argues that amateurism is some kind of secret path to success, just that it's a path. And, naturally, if your goal is a little more likely to actually occur in this time/space continuum, then this kind of motivation makes it easier to endure experimental setbacks.

"If you go through many interactions where you feel really incompetent," said Professor Edward Deci, the author of *The Psychology of Self-Determination*, "it has a big impact on you and you feel depressed in no time."

Deci has pioneered the study of what makes people go off and just do something, formally known as "intrinsic motivation" or "self-determination theory," but in this context, let's call it by its common noun, "amateurism." In the workplace, getting people productive and creative in a capitalist sense involves a lot of human resource activity. The effort there is to ensure that everyone is working at his or her skill level and not below it (waste of human capital) or beyond it (the Peter Principle theory that one can be promoted beyond one's skills and become useless).

Outside the world of paid labor, intrinsic motivation becomes a different matter. Whether one is in a literal garage or a symbolic one (a wiki is, arguably, today's figurative garage), research consistently shows that even working alone, one needs a few things to occur: The best amateurs require a sense of opened-ended playfulness—that sense that anything's possible.

Deci cites a study of nursery school children who were asked to draw for fun with some special markers. Afterward, some were given "good player" awards. Later, when the kids were asked to draw again with the markers, something surprising happened.

"The youngsters given awards were less likely to draw at all, and drew worse pictures, than those who were not given the awards," Deci has written. "Why did this happen? Children draw because drawing is fun and because it leads to a result: a picture." But the "good player" reward redefined the pleasure narrowly as authority figure approval. Fun play turned into a form of paid work, the death of amateur passion.

These experiments have been reproduced many times, revealing every time that play is more productive than work. That is, a sense of being on your own and just trying to do this thing (whatever that thing is) can be more productive than if you introduce either money or reward into the equation. Experiments where some kind of meaningless grunt work was asked of people as a *favor* to the experimenter resulted in extremely high productivity returns. The minute those same people were praised and offered money, the productivity rate plunged.

One could argue that such productivity is related to belief in some higher calling—that you are enduring this donkey work because you have faith in the future (noble) rather than for money (labor). Soldiers will recognize this distinction as the same that exists between a citizen serving out of love of country and a mercenary earning a paycheck. The sense of satisfaction from within and the sense of pride flows together to create a motivation that money simply destroys. The word "amateur" comes from the ancient word for "love"—which, when encouraged with money, becomes a profession, a form of the oldest profession. An amateur's love is both public and private, internally motivated but, in order to be productive, outwardly praised. It's a kind of love that hasn't very well spoken its name. It's neither eros nor agape, nothing involving filial bonding or generous charity. It may be the least described love, ultimately personal, charged with the hope that there is a possibility of finding that new thing just over the horizon of the unknown and toting it back across, into the realm of the familiar.

IV. Death Penalty Yogurt

Over the months prior to my seeing Meredith Patterson's lab, she had already been trying to coax the glow gene into her chosen yogurt bacterium, *Lactobacillus acidophilus*. She had tried to use the heat shock method to drive new genes into the cell's nucleus.

"When bacteria get to a certain temperature, they start producing these heat shock proteins which also opens up some holes," she explained. And in that brief moment, the new genes sloshing around nearby can slip in. "In my head, it's like, holy shit, it's hot in here, let's open some windows."

But that hadn't worked at all, so she had moved on to electroporation, 150-millisecond pulses at 2,500 volts—the method we'll be trying on my visit. In my head, I picture the tiny bacteria ballooning like a cartoon character with its finger in a socket—its flagella sticking out like hair—and its microscopic pores bulging open like wide eye sockets, such that the new material can rush in. For us, the question is, how do we administer these shocks to our bacteria. Patterson has already configured the timing mechanism on an Arduino—an easily customized computer board. It will handle the literally split-second timing: The 2,500-volt pulses last only 150 milliseconds each. All we need now is 2,500 volts—the precise amount, I recently learned, once used to carry out the missions of famous twentieth-century electric chairs, the insanely powerful ones from the early days that had nicknames Gruesome Gertie, Yellow Mama, Old Smokey, and Sizzlin' Sally.

To accomplish this, Patterson got hold of a transformer from an old neon sign. It takes in 12 volts and ramps it up to 3,000 volts. So it would make sense that if we fed the transformer 10 volts, it would then kick out 2,500. But Patterson's voltmeter kept telling us something was dodgy here. So she started to connect different transistors to get the right combination to deliver the needed, precise amount of electricity. Patterson maintains a little tool cabinet containing various transistors, but none of them, or any combination of them, would get us to our magic number. The only solution, it was decided, was to jump in the car and drive thirty miles to Fry's, a kind of Home Depot of everything electronic. We did this without hesitation because now the entire mission was stuck in the bottleneck of finding the right transistor mix.

This effort went on for days, I should add. We must have tested the input and outputs of the Arduino board some fifty times. These tests amounted to us sitting on the wooden floor and carefully holding the (insulated) lines in place as we blasted away with, potentially, lethal streams of electricity. One day we spent ten hours trying to configure one wiring set-up after another. Hours of this fiddling passed, but maybe you know this feeling, it was as if no time had passed.

Patterson's cat Alexander continually appeared at the edge of our experiments, poking his nose in at the most inopportune moments. "We named him after Alexander Shulgin," she explained, as if I should immediately recognize the name of the chemist who popularized the drug MDMA, aka ecstasy. "Do not name your cats after chemists; they will want to do chemistry."

As we prepared to run some serious electricity through the Arduino board, Alexander came cantering over and just a millisecond or two before he put his foot on a live wire, I scooped him up and moved him to the other side of our little power grid.

Meanwhile, the tiny amount of lactobacillus that Patterson had extracted from the yogurt and placed in the incubator was growing away. There was one new flaw with that device: Its two-bit thermostat had busted. There no longer was a way to automatically regulate the heat inside, so Patterson would carefully monitor the temperature by checking it on her own. She'd turn the incubator off after a while and wait for it to cool down a few degrees before turning it back on. This way she kept it from overcooking our bugs. We were now several days into constant experimentation, and we spent a lot of time together, staring at transistors, tending the incubator as if it were an old woodstove, sterilizing equipment, waiting for very slow things to happen. Patterson is a smoker, and in moments precisely like these, I allow myself a temporary relapse into a habit I enjoyed back in the Pleistocene era. So we'd take cigarette breaks, standing by her window, often talking. But already, we were comfortable enough to not say a word.

One of those nights we had a brief discussion of flow, the notion developed by Mihály Csíkszentmihályi (pronounced "Me-high Chick-sent-me-high"—perhaps the most fun name to say, ever). This Hungarian-American psychologist holds that there is a very satisfying state of mind that occurs when one is totally absorbed by some action. It may sound as if this is some rare state of being, like a kind of secular nirvana, but it's not. We all experience it pretty frequently. It doesn't require special meditative skills, just the love of doing something so that one gets lost in the labor. One might experience flow while painting a complex landscape or painting the front porch. Or chaperoning an incubator or testing electrical currents on a floor.

54578

77789

Its commonness is why we have so many phrases for this pleasant state of existence: being in the zone, losing ourselves in our work, being on the ball, or in the groove. According to Csíkszentmihályi (say it loud: "Chick-sent-me-high"), this state is marked by a total absorption such that one loses a sense of time and experiences a deep feeling of satisfaction.

"Oh," Patterson said, suddenly recognizing what I was talking about. You mean "codespace"—as programmers call it—"where the world just sort of disappears." She knew it well. "That's a good head space to try new things, especially if there's something I think should work. So I try it and see if it does: 'Oh, that didn't quite work the way it was supposed to. Let's check a few settings and see if this works.' Sweet."

This was also the night that we were scheduled to meet up with some random hackers at a moveable geekfest known as SuperHappyDevHouse. Like Cowell's crowd back in Boston, this is a gathering of mostly programmers who come together at someone's house to exchange ideas and just generally relax. But we were physically incapable of leaving the apartment: The incubator required constant babysitting to keep it from overheating. As we sat in our own groove, occupied by long stretches of work, there appeared a solution, like a bubble slowly popping at the surface of our flow.

"What about one of those light timers you can get to fool burglars?" I asked. Patterson instantly got it. Yes. A light timer. We could program it to turn the incubator off and on. Then we could leave the apartment building. We raced downstairs and drove across the bridge to a late-night Home Depot in San Jose. The new models were perfect for what we were doing and, as Patterson would say, only a few bucks. Digital controls allowed you to customize the on/off experience however bizarrely you wanted—on for five minutes, off for thirty, for instance.

Problem solved. It was just one more jerry-rig for her duct tape and baling-wire lab. And we never did get to SuperHappyDevHouse; since dawn was on the way, we got back into our transistor flow, and there was always one more thing we had to improvise. But for now, there was this intense pleasure. We both stepped back, looking at a light timer plugged into a surge protector with, absurdly, an exhilarating amount of self-satisfaction. Time to light up.

V. The Right to Marry Your Vacuum Cleaner

When I first decided to start hanging around amateur groups to see how they might be different from your average R&D outfit, I originally looked no farther than my backyard. One of the oldest amateur robot clubs in America still meets in Hartford, Connecticut, every month. So I dropped in a few times, hoping to catch a glimpse of amateurs at play and to see how their motivations might be different from the more ordered investigations of academic research aiming for prestige, or private development looking for profits. Meeting in a local high school classroom, most of the members were either enthusiastic teens or adult engineers with a serious robot jones. But it took no time at all to surmise that the enfant terrible of the club was a fourteen-year-old named Nathaniel Barshay, a small boy with a barbershop haircut and a hesitant but inviting smile.

His robots were magnitudes of complexity beyond everyone else's, and everyone else knew it. Most roboticists fiddle with various programs to teach the machine how to walk a line or along a wall. When I first caught up with Barshay, he had purchased some new sensors and was teaching his robot how, in robot terms, to "see." In the course of an afternoon, the crowd looked to him for advice, including the people leading the club. This particular club, the Connecticut Robotics Society, is sort of famous for producing these wunderkinds. Most of the members will tell you how DARPA, the Pentagon's major research arm, occasionally sends a scout to the club to raid them of their best members. Barshay is clearly DARPA-bound, should he choose. When I first chatted with him, we talked about his favorite movies, how he got interested in robots, computer games. Then I asked him what he had done last summer, when he was thirteen years old. And here was his answer: "I taught robotics at Tufts University."

Despite being shy in the way that all young teens are around adults, it didn't take long for Barshay to agree to let me watch him as he prepared to build a robot to enter into the Trinity College Fire Fighting Home Robot Contest (in Hartford). This is one of the oldest competitions, and Barshay had won it before.

The mission is to build a robot—most of these tend to be about the size of a toy truck—that can navigate an unfamiliar maze until it locates a candle flame and then puts it out, usually with an onboard squirt of water. That's a good number of complicated instructions; many robots never get near the candle. But many of the successful solutions were ingenious. It was hard not to be impressed by the kid whose robot was armed with nothing more than a balloon, which, as soon as it neared the flame, burst, and, of course, blew out the candle.

Barshay didn't win that year, but these contests were practically just signposts along the way of his constant tinkering in the basement (literally, his basement). A few months later, Barshay entered another contest. Sponsored by the iRobot Corporation, the competition asked amateurs to invent anything new, as long as you started with a stripped down version of their big commercial seller: the robot vacuum cleaner, the Roomba. In a weekend or two, Barshay installed a number of different sensors (cannibalized from his firefighting robot) and attached a long stick. The idea was to create a walking cane for the blind that would be better than both the traditional stick and guide dog combined. For instance, with Barshay's idea, a blind person could simply ask the stick to take him to, say, the public library, and using information off the Internet and a built-in GPS and Map-

Quest system, the stick would figure out the surest path and then guide the person there.

Many of the other entries in Roomba's contest had a similarly practical cast to them—devices that would water your plants while you were away or take care of other domestic issues for the disabled.

Notice anything? As my hang time with roboticists grew, I kept encountering this. Most of the robots getting hacked together, if they weren't just toys, were extremely *functional*—putting out fires, helping the handicapped . . .

How quickly we seemed to have shot past those early days of BattleBots and other super-futuristic robotic visions. To begin with, how frumpy is it that America's premier robot is a vacuum cleaner? You hear the word "robot," and you're primed to expect science fiction, not a soap opera commercial. Besides the vacuum cleaner, the company's other big seller is exclusively for the Pentagon: "the iRobot 710 Warrior," not to mention the 510 Packbot and the 210 Negotiator (which performs surveillance in lethal areas). If you've got a comic book image of a fighting machine, or the pilotless drones that drop bombs in Afghanistan, think again. The Warrior can locate mines, but it resembles a dentist's extendable light on tiny tank treads. Crucial stuff, don't get me wrong. It's just that when one says "war-fighting robot," the expectation is more Sergeant York and less mechanical ET.

At first I thought this was just human nature, that all robots, like college graduates, begin with grand intentions but slowly settle into the mundane world of vacuum cleaners and office clerks (respectively). That is, until I set up a series of alerts to keep me constantly updated on robot innovations. Robot creativity seems to center on three essential sources—Japan, the United States, and Europe. The cultural differences of the three locations have heavily influenced the kinds of robots produced by both the corporations and the amateurs. America is still the land of Ben Franklin. There has always been a plain-Jane kind of pragmatism to our inventive calling. Franklin is the guy who invented the lightning rod and the bifocals and the public library—all because, on some level, he didn't want his house to burn down while he read his borrowed books well into middle age.

It is largely American imaginations that have turned their robots into not-all-that-glorified appliances. For the aged, we've invented the "intelligent walker" that responds to voice commands ("take me to the kitchen"); for construction workers, a serpentine robot that can climb to dangerous places for inspections; in hospitals, robots run medicines around from room to room while other robots down the hall are performing surgery. Even America's most famous fictional robot, Wall-E, is a trash compactor.

Japanese robot innovations, on the other hand, are so much more about mimicking the human form. They invented the Qrio (Quest for cuRIOsity) that walks about on two legs. It's two feet tall and looks humanoid with a head and a face. In fact, it looks like it walked right out of a sci-fi movie. Its mission, in the usual poorly translated instruction lingo: "Makes life fun, makes you happy." You'll never read even a superbly translated slogan like that on an American robot.

Japan also produced Murata Boy, who can ride bicycles, and Honda's Asimo, the robot that looks like somebody decked out for a moon trip with a backpack and space helmet (not to mention five fingers that articulate). It can run across a room in perfect biped fashion.

Then there was the Aibo, the yapping, flipping robot dog. The word means "pal" in Japanese. By contrast, Boston Dynamics in the United States invented Big Dog, definitely not your pal. The promotional videos on YouTube are haunting. A headless pack animal, the robot looks like a coffin with four legs (each bent at the knee). It ambulates very fast, with the frantic, desperate gait of two guys in a horse suit trying to run without falling over. This robot can walk over most terrain and can get up from falling. When I first saw Big Dog walking, it spooked me in some primal way that I can't describe.

But theorists of robotics can describe it. In fact, there has been a lot of research about how we humans react to artificial-life machines as their appearance or motions get closer on some existential level to real life—to us. We are intrigued by robots for a while. Then, there is a plunge in acceptability as we become repulsed. As the robot more closely approximates lifelikeness, it becomes attractive again.

In robotics circles, this dip of disgust in the spectrum of likeability is called *bukimi no tani*—the "uncanny valley." The various stages down into it and back out have been analyzed and named from the most harmless, "industrial robot," on to "android" and "moving corpse," to "prosthetic hand," then "handicapped person," "bunraku puppet" (life-sized, very lifelike theater puppets manipulated in a creepy way on stage, proving that the Japanese were exploring this valley long before Karel Capek wrote his 1921 play coining the word "robot"), and then on to "unhealthy persons" and, finally, "healthy persons." Maybe it's no surprise, since all humans have a zombie fascination, that the moment robots begin to resemble "moving corpses," we humans get the willies.

Americans seem to avoid it assiduously in our creations. The Japanese imagination, on the other hand, luxuriates in the uncanny valley and has practically colonized the place. One Japanese roboticist, Hiroshi Ishiguro, took it as his challenge to build an exact replica of himself so that it would be difficult to tell him apart from his robot. Staring at pictures of Ishiguro with his arm slung around the shoulder of Geminoid HI-1 definitely triggers a Rod Serling–esque creep-out. You've just crossed over into . . . the Uncanny Valley.

As a result, a lot of robot research in Japan involves skin texture, eye blinking, and the slight fidgets and twitchy movements that define the human physical existence.

An enormous number of robots invented in Japan are young girls around the barely legal age. This is creepy in a different way. At the 2005 World Expo in Tokyo one encountered the Repliee Q1, a pretty girl robot who'd made breakthroughs in blinking, gesturing, and even breathing. Also that year: Cute J-Girl, who looked like an airline stewardess from 1975. The following year, Japan gave us Actroid robot girl, dressed sometimes in black form-fitting vinyl or the *Hello Kitty* look—although she donned a formal kimono for her press conference when she traveled to Washington, DC. In 2009, cybernetic human HRP-4C appeared at a Tokyo fashion show. With a cute Manga-style face above a robot body with unnecessarily perfect form-fitted breasts, she pouted and flirted with reporters. Given her $2 million price tag, she's not yet a major threat to the blow-up plastic doll market.

That same year, the "perfect woman" robot appeared as the creation of a company out of Kobe, Japan. The robot cleans the house and has other talents. According to the website: "You can talk to her about news, traveling, culture and music. Lisa has an IQ of 130. She is even able to satisfy your desires in the bedroom. For this we have cooperated with a renowned sexologist whose expertise has been integrated into Lisa's configuration." Of course Lisa is a hoax, but a revealing one. In the promotional video on the website, Lisa is a human made up in plastic sheen with a stylized hair bob so that she appears extremely "robotlike." In other words, she's entering the uncanny valley from the other slope.

Meanwhile, the Europeans are exploring an entirely different terrain from the Americans or the Japanese. They appear to be culturally drawn to investigating emotional bonds and robots. Their robots hang out in your house and talk to you. European robots are far more likely to venture into the uncanny valley of emotional intelligence; far more likely to cross the fool-a-human threshold known as the Turing Test. As a result, Europeans have become obsessed with robot law. They hold conferences on it regularly, issue manifestos, and seem (perhaps rightly?) absolutely terrified of robot consciousness. Lead paragraphs such as this one appear all the time: "Top robotics expert Professor Noel Sharkey, of the University of Sheffield, has called for international guidelines to be set for the ethical and safe application of robots before it is too late."

The Japanese and the Americans read Isaac Asimov's First Law of Robotics—"A robot may not injure a human or, through inaction, allow a human being to come to harm"—as cool sci-fi writing. Europeans think of Asimov as the future's William Blackstone. If you are worried about "robot rights" and questions of who is culpable when a robot kills a human, then the civil servants of the Old World have a code of law all worked out for you.

The same culture that brought you the 1,700-year-old bureaucracy known as the Vatican, that filled Madrid's Escorial in the sixteenth century with so many reports they are still being studied, that set up the modern bureaucratic labyrinth in Brussels known as the European Union, and that gave the adjective "Byzantine" its meaning—that mind-set has now turned its attention to robots. If you are wondering about inter-human/AI marriage, then a professor at the University of Maastricht in the Netherlands has already written a long thesis on the subject. "My forecast is that around 2050," he announced in 2008, "the state of Massachusetts will be the first jurisdiction to legalize marriages with robots."

Massachusetts? Really? My money's on Japan.

Maybe the great singularity predicted by futurist Ray Kurzweil—the coming together of man and machine—will occur when the three robot cultures build a robot hottie who can fix your car and then sit down to dinner to kvetch about your lack of commitment.

Robot and synbio cultures are amateur pursuits at different points on the development curve. Robot culture is well on its way to maturing, which is to say that the work performed by amateurs now is somewhat marginal (as it is with the once thriving amateur efforts of radio, computers, remote-control airplanes, and rocketry).

Robotics is sort of at the stage that computer hobbyists found themselves at in the late 1980s. That weekend club originally blazed the trail for the desktop computer at a time when many didn't think it was necessary. ("There is no reason anyone would want a computer in their home," said Ken Olsen, the CEO of Digital Equipment in 1977.) Now, of course, those weekenders long ago vanished into the world that amateur computer hobbyists helped invent.

The weekend club, whether a mature robotics one or the embry-
onic club Bobe and Cowell are forming, is a perennial manifestation
of the American amateur culture, arguably dating back to Ben Franklin's early club of men seeking self-improvement. Also known as the
Leather Apron Club, this group was comprised of mostly men like
Franklin, amateur inventors and idea men. It was out of the gatherings of the Leather Apron Club that came many of the ideas credited
to Franklin: the public hospital, the lending library, the first night
watchman, and the volunteer firefighter.

Before computers, weekend clubs obsessed on radio-controlled
model planes and boats, and before that the combustion engine (go-
carts, mostly). And long before that, amateur radio was entirely created by garage broadcasters, before large business interests took over
that world. The suits bullied Congress into writing laws that ran the
amateurs underground, where you can still find a few remnants today.

Hanging out with these groups—both the roboticists and the synthetic biologists—upended for me one of the great myths of amateurism. Americans envision the amateur impulse as another version
of the great rugged individual, the lone ranger. And of course, the
Rockwellian image that stirs in our brain when we say the phrase
"garage inventor" is the eccentric genius (or lunatic) wearing his
workshop apron (Franklin's inheritance) and banging away at some
contraption typically described by the neglected spouse or curious
neighbor as "cockamamie."

But while the image endures, it's merely a kind of interpretation,
a form of art. The truth is that amateurs have always flourished in
the kind of brainstorming, open-sourced, shared debate that Franklin describes in his original writings about the junta. All those weekend club groups are punctuated regularly by various kinds of routine
meet-ups, contests, and conventions.

Franklin corresponded with his friends by handwritten letter, but
that medium gave way to the published proceedings of the various "as-
sociations" that exploded in the nineteenth century, and those gave

way to the club newsletters of the twentieth century. Now we are en-gulfed in an amateurism on steroids: open-source wiki-ism. If the mid-nineteenth and early to mid-twentieth century enjoyed two great cycles of amateur proliferation, then we are arguably well into the third.

VI. Heuristic Performance Art

The killer app that might launch the Boston DIYbio, Bobe told me, is this idea he's been obsessing on for a while, a bioweather map. By enlisting volunteers to regularly sample the same doorknobs or traffic light buttons, he hopes to identify the different bacteria and see pre-cisely where and how they move.

"Is it a cyanobacterium, a proteobacterium, a firmicute?" he asked at the public meeting. He intends to tap into the same kind of enthu-siasm that once had people all over a region setting out rain gauges and then calling in the results to create a map.

Bobe's bioweather map is an old form of collaboration, and the hope is that with their volunteer collaborations and collegiate com-petitions the synbio crowd will soon look about as familiar as the 4H club. The most famous competition is known as iGem, the Interna-tional Genetic Engineered Machine competition. Not unlike the Fire Fighting Robot Contest, iGem invites college student teams from all over the world to strut their DNA at MIT to win the big award. It's folksily known by its retro *Boys' Life* shorthand: the iGem Jamboree.

Those who imagine that college students might come up with attention-grabbing ideas aren't disappointed. One recent competition had a group from Rice University in Texas reacting to all the positive press one hears about red wine. The chemical in wine that reduces

cancer in certain studies is called resveratrol. So the Rice students genetically modified some yeast so that it also produced resveratrol. The
idea was to brew some ale from it so that college students, like their parents, could drink and be healthy at the same time. They call it BioBeer.

Another group, in an earlier competition, solved the problem of
growing E. coli. (Although it shares the same name as the pathologi-
cal kind that causes disease, this bacterium is very safe and typically
serves as the chassis in synthetic construction, so you need a lot of
it.) Typically when it's growing, E. coli releases an odor that has been
described by connoisseurs as resembling, in every respect, shit. So the
team inserted two genes. One changed the growth odor to mint. The
other gene didn't kick in until the bacterium sent out certain signals
that it had stopped growing. When that happened, the lab techs knew
because the E. coli quit smelling like mint and started to scent the
room with banana. Naturally, the MIT bioengineers call it Eau d'ecoli.

Another team invented a new bacterium that should send the
fluoride-in-the-water conspiracy theorists into a tailspin. Since tooth
decay is caused when *Streptococcus mutans* attaches itself to the sides
of our teeth, why not create a bacterium that generates the protein
that causes attachment failure in streptococcus? So they did. Brew it
up in yogurt, and you've got toothpaste you can eat. At last.

Numerous teams have invented different kinds of biosensors, al-
tering bacteria to alert us to the presence of something, say arsenic,
by glowing or sending out a detectable electrical impulse (bactricity,
they call it).

According to Edward Deci, this kind of group dynamic is also
crucial—the group effort of both the specific teams and the larger
iGem convocation. Studies conducted by Deci show that the high-
est rates of productivity require that three basic human needs be
met—group relatedness, a sense of autonomy or that lone ranger
spirit that you're doing it on your own, and the satisfaction of competence, which includes that feeling of flow or a sense of play at the
task. Subtract any one and the creativity and productivity levels drop.

What's most noticeably missing from all those requirements is money. As with the children's drawing study, test after test reveals that what Deci calls "extrinsic motivation" repeatedly drives down levels of both creativity and productivity. Business theorists have spent much of the last thirty years trying to figure out how to translate these lessons into the workplace. Obviously, it's fantastic that amateur passion is such a great motivator, but you can't run an economy on love.

Or, can you, sort of? The key feature of these tests, according to Deci, is to understand what is lost when you introduce money into a relationship that previously had been built on a kind of affection. If you are a person who is doing something out of love or fondness for a friend or a sense of patriotic duty, and suddenly it all changes into an assembly line of expected outputs, what is lost? Let's call it by its very old-fashioned name: freedom.

Given that you can't re-create amateur passion on the job, Deci does draw a distinction between those who encourage self-motivation in the workplace and those who are severely controlling. The latter always drive down not only production rates but also creativity ("creativity" is known in self-determination theory by the painfully not-so-creative term "heuristic performance").

"Effective performance in subordinates and particularly of the heuristic kinds of performance occur when managers are autonomous and supportive instead of controlling," Deci has jargonized. The subtle kind of autonomy Deci talks about—playfulness, freedom—often gets exaggerated and distorted in our pop culture into the image of lone-ranger, cowboy individualism, a can-do, doesn't-suffer-fools-gladly kind of swaggering.

"It can be a little confusing because people think autonomy means separate and independent of others," Deci said, "but we use it to mean self-motivating, to experience a sense of volition and self-initiation."

Deci took me right back to college, where most of us experience this distinction intensely. It's the difference, he said, "between taking a class because you love the subject and taking it because it's required."

The group dynamic often gets crunched into the cliché of the team or collective action. But it's not that labored. It's looser than that. "Human beings need to feel some sense of includedness, relative intimacy, and belonging," Deci said. And, when you integrate into a single effect these three factors—a casual affiliation with a group, a sense of competence at what you're doing, and the sheer joy that you're doing it yourself just 'cause—you enter the magical realm of "intrinsic motivation," the jargon for what's always been called, un-heuristically, amateurism.

VII. Marlboro Time

Around midnight in San Francisco, Patterson and I are on the floor with our fortieth or fiftieth attempt at configuring the 2500-volt transformer so that we can Taser the lactobacillus, get the glow gene in there, and proceed to make Glo-gurt with it. Even here, in this most isolated lab, the group is all around us. Patterson regularly consults old e-mails for advice, downloads one more schematic from another site, consults with a wiki or two. Late in the evening, she calls "Brian," who's a whiz at electrical issues, and they confer for forty-five minutes.

"So, Brian's advice was to turn these around"—she points at two connectors with wires—"and put the load between the power supply and the collector." So we make our adjustments and continue to find problems with the connections. Work like this is mostly just the tedium of getting things right or attempting to, and for long stretches, the only sound is Patterson cheerfully muttering to herself:

"Something lights up, well, hello."

"That's a 15k resister. Again, didn't work."

"I'm wondering if I've misunderstood which pin is which. If I did, that would be stupid."

"Things that do not make sense include . . . what the fuck, yo?"

"Where the hell are you coming from?"

"What the damn hell?"

"Unplug!" she calls out to me, and then stares at the schematic for twenty minutes.

"I would be astonished if they had the wrong drawing."

"Fuck, this shit doesn't even say."

"Plug us in."

"Again, we're not getting dick."

"That's heating up. Unplug that!"

"So we're definitely not going to try that."

We both stare at the tiny board one more time.

"We want red to go here and black to go here, and somebody needs to touch this wire to the base. So if you want to just hold these, I can plug it in. First, make sure you are not touching the lead. Good."

A viscous snapping sound shatters the concentrated silence of the room. Some lights go out, throughout the building. Patterson pulls the plug.

"I think we killed it." A hideous yet familiar metallic smell fills the air. "Time for a cigarette break," she says.

VIII. Salk or Frankenstein?

After Cowell showed me his secret fort in Cambridge, he also wanted to show me his public one. As with Bobe, Cowell has been struggling to navigate just how synthetic biology should present itself to the world—a demonic crew of biohackers blowing stuff up in secret locations? Or a responsible crowd of innovators poking around the front lines of what's known in order to find something new?

For the latter, he's rented a public lab space from a group called NUBlabs. It's a big open warehouse in Cambridge where a bunch of designers of all kinds of things maintain their workstations. Part of it is occupied by a guy importing odd but beautiful bicycles from Europe. He sells that seven-seat circular contraption built by some corporation forward-thinker who preferred to hold his high-level meetings while people got exercise. There are programmers scattered around, and in the corner is Cowell's space. He's thrown together the usual amateur gear for a start-up lab. There's an autoclave off eBay, an old centrifuge he scored, and some pipettes. There are worktables and books and all the other minor gear, but Cowell hasn't invited anyone in yet. He's very much aware that just what happens in the next little while is going to be crucial to how the general public understands what synthetic biology is.

This struggle has been going on for the last few years among the professional crowd. They think of it in different terms. If the kids are worried about how it will look, the grown-ups fret over how it will expand. There are three killer aps—money, altruism, hipness. Drew Endy, for instance, is trying to frame synthetic biology as the next cool science—what computer programming was in the 1980s. His parts registry idea and "gene-bashing" lingo are all sparking the imaginations of young amateurs.

"If you make biology easy to engineer, and you make it accessible, by definition people will learn about it, and write comic strips about it," he's said. Along with Jay Keasling of Berkeley, George Church and Drew Endy constitute the secular trinity of great minds birthing this new field.

Keasling is not writing comic strips. His boosterism takes the form of actually making synthetic biology do something. For instance, he'd like to cure malaria. (Of the three, Keasling is the one most likely to make it to a morning talk show.) The classic malaria treatment involves a substance called artemisinin, which derives from the slow-growing wormwood plant. The idea is to create bacteria that will quickly pump out artemisinin. So far, no luck. But Keasling's bet is that they will succeed soon. And if "curing malaria" is the first thing most people hear about synthetic biology, that's a better start than almost any other kind of headline (such as kids create deadly insect, now rogue).

Meanwhile, George Church occupies an entirely different niche in the synbio ecosystem, both in terms of who he is and what he talks about. Currently at Harvard, Church is a towering six-foot-five, with a lumberjack's beard, a commanding presence, a seductively hyperactive and chatty mind—not to mention a brilliant scientific eccentricity: He suffers from narcolepsy. So the great man can be talking to you and boom, he blinks out for five seconds and then boots right back up. It's the equivalent of Einstein's hair: notice given that you are in the presence of wild and ranging genius.

Church talks up the economic approach, specifically biofuels. He wants to engineer something that makes a lot of money and gets positive attention that way. The obstacle to turning piles of organic material such as switchgrass or other high-sugar plants into easy biofuels is that the sugars in the plant are bound up by cellulose. In order to get it out, the cellulose has to be extracted. What if you could design a bacterium that would chew up cellulose and expel sugar? That would have a worldwide market, much larger and more noticeable than a malarial cure or a comic book.

"Biofuels are the low-hanging fruit of synthetic biology," Church insisted one afternoon in his office. Pharmaceutical cures might earn good press, but the "markets are small relative to fuels, where the markets are huge."

Everyone involved in synthetic biology recognizes on some level that if robotics, say, is a fairly mature pursuit, then synthetic biology is in utero. So they worry constantly about public relations and imagery.

"NASA had the moon shot," Church pondered, as he struggled with how the public comes to understand the complexities of any new scientific discipline. "There was the homebrew computer club, even robotics had a cinematic push." He recognizes that Hollywood prefers to deal in a "dystopic version of biology." He considered the ill effects of *Jurassic Park*, *Gattaca*, or Will Smith's *I Am Legend*, even though the hero of that movie was a geneticist trying to do the right thing.

"There is one isolated non-dystopic movie," Church said, *Lorenzo's Oil*, the story of parents who will stop at nothing to find a new cure for their child's rare affliction. The movie was not exactly a hit. "You can see how hard it is for Hollywood to make a blockbuster out of lipid chemistry," he added.

Later over coffee, Cowell and Bobe can't help but continue this conversation. For amateurs trying to start a DIYbio group, they don't have at their disposal massive funding and can't really talk about engineering trees, curing malaria, or solving a planetary energy problem. Their anxiety is much more local to their group and identity.

"Even the use of the word 'biohacker,'" Bobe suddenly volunteered, "my girlfriend's parents read that word and were terrified."

"Terminology is key," Cowell agreed, and he reminded Bobe of the scientific tragedy that cascaded after the seemingly cool word "cloning" achieved currency at the expense of the less glitzy term "nuclear transfer."

"The word 'hacker' really used to be a badge of distinction—even if they weren't doing anything bad. We need the opposite," Bobe said, trying to come up with a new term. "Hackers are makers. They are scientists."

"Biomaker would be better than biohacker?"

Bobe said there would be resistance, but "we have to change the attitude people have toward hackers."

"The Biomaking Manifesto?"

"Well, you either try to redefine biohacking as a good term or you come up with a different term."

"I think the label is inevitable."

"I'm just trying to be conscientious."

"Initially, 'biohacking' is a good way to describe the ideas. If you go to one of these hobbyist workshops where they are building robots and you say, 'Do you want to come to a biohacking meeting?' they get it."

"Depends on who your audience is. Is it PR for the public?"

"But that doesn't make the term go away."

"Biohacking is cool, if you're young."

"Bio-innovating sounds like a PR term that no eighteen-year-old will call himself."

"Biomaker? Biocreator?"

The question occupied the entire several days I spent hanging out with Cowell and Bobe. Later there was a long discussion about the term "synthetic biology" and how that first word was awkward, suggesting something plastic and unnatural. And there used to be other terms, "bioengineering" and even, briefly, "constructive biology." It's not easy to domesticate an emerging science so that it's cool enough to attract the most renegade thinkers while simultaneously not bringing down the wrath of the FBI. Later, Bobe expressed nothing but jealousy at the way the guys behind *Make* magazine—the new hip *Popular Mechanics* of our time, the DIY monthly that's achieved national success—have pulled it off so beautifully.

"*Make*, which was just a small twist on 'hack,' is really effective," he said.

As Cowell and Bobe attract more and more members, there will be smart, innovative people among them, and there will be people who insist on taking the mad scientist pose. The whole field could turn on a dime, and they know just how Janus-faced the fetal science in fact is—a generation of Jonas Salks over here, Victor Frankensteins over there. They could become a collection of gee-whiz do-gooders right out of the 1950s, or they could become demonized as the fabricators of evil viruses—just as an earlier generation of computer hackers were, only this time the viruses won't be digital.

IX. Yodeling at Bacteria

There is another way to get a plasmid into a bacterium that doesn't require 2500 volts of electricity: "an ultrasound bath," Patterson told me, as she planned yet another approach. This is the same technology that allows us to peer inside a woman's womb and look at a fetus. "Ultrasound is used in labs normally for lysing cells, for ripping them open and getting out the DNA. And it is also used for sterilization—really high amplitude of ultrasound can be used to kill off bacteria.

"When the frequency is in the 40 kilohertz range, you can actually use it for transsection, one of the terms for introducing plasmids into things." (Having failed at frying the bacteria and then Tasering them, we now hoped to yell at them.)

Of course, the issue is how do you get an ultrasound machine?

"This thing ran forty bucks," she said—this thing being a "jewelry cleaner operating at 40 kilohertz." The machine is small and compact, easy to handle. Dozens of them are offered for sale on eBay on any given day. Even as she presses forward in search of Glo-gurt, though, Patterson tells me her interests have recently shifted to something more, well, functional.

She's started a conversation with an Internet pal on the DIYbio list, Jon Kline, about synthesizing a bacterium that would react in the presence of melamine: Recall that in 2008 the substance began showing up in Chinese imports of milk products, eggs, baby food, and pet food and led to numerous deaths of people and animals. Melamine-contaminated milk, alone, sickened some fifty thousand people. The scandal caused a food scare and focused attention on the fact that American agencies were testing for the presence of these lethal chemicals.

Patterson and Kline call their creation the melaminometer.

They have developed two strategies. One is to insert GFP, the same glow plasmid in Patterson's yogurt, and use that as a test for the presence of melamine. One swab on a food sample, and if there's a trace of melamine, then the Q-tip would glow in the dark under a black light. Another approach is to create a bacteria that, in the presence of melamine, would break it down into ammonia and water. Not all that tasty, but it beats getting sick. Maybe they can make it taste like bananas when they get around to melaminometer 2.0.

As Patterson and all her peers come up with new ideas and start trying them out, the question will get to the public sphere as just what are we permitting here? Patterson would argue that this kind of innovation, when it happens slowly and as the result of folksy methods known by 4-H-ers as "animal husbandry," is perfectly acceptable. The "dog," as we currently know him, is a product of the oldest synthetic biology. Thousands of years ago, the occasional wolf brave enough (or tame enough) to approach a human campfire for scraps eventually developed an emotional bond. Dogs seek out alpha dogs to be their leaders and trainers. Early humans quickly figured this out and began the long process of selective breeding that has turned the wolf into all manner of variations of itself—pit bull, collie, Chihuahua. Any major plant humans love to consume—the banana, the ear of corn, the apple, the potato, the tomato, most hot peppers—were all long ago coaxed into becoming the now seemingly fixed bounty of nature we revere. But we made them, using slow-motion synthetic biology.

"Every orchid or rose or lizard or snake is the work of a dedicated and skilled breeder," wrote Freeman Dyson. "There are thousands of people, amateurs and professionals, who devote their lives to this business. Now imagine what will happen when the tools of genetic engineering become accessible to these people."

Of course, that's already happening. Folks like Patterson aren't likely to be deterred from their passion by good press or bad. *Jurassic Park* or *Lorenzo's Oil*—it pretty much doesn't matter. When we spoke late one night about what it was that kept her awake, she talked—lovingly, I should add—about all the bacteria that live on us or in our gut. To her, this was a universe unto itself. And the one she was now committed to explore.

"It's called the human micro-biome," she said, as if referring to some nebula system a hundred thousand light-years away. Amateurs typically gather at every new frontier—colonial America, radio, air flight, the moon, the Internet. Like trendsetters in stores or early adopters with gadgets, amateurs and their fiddling tend to point us toward the next uncharted region. Amateur geneticists are already heading to the next horizon over yonder, the next alluring New World, our bodies, ourselves.

5

MIGHTY WHITE OF YOU:
A COMEDY OF AMATEURS

I. Charlemagne's Heir

I was seventeen years old when I discovered I was the great[48]-grandson of Charlemagne—King of the Franks and Holy Roman Emperor. Where I grew up, it's not unusual to find out such things. The culture of Charleston, South Carolina, is built around the pride associated with a handful of family histories. Like most of my friends downtown, almost without my knowing it, my youth was an unconscious state of perpetual genealogical questing. Might I be the descendent of a signer of the Declaration? Robert E. Lee's messenger? I bugged my mom and aunts and uncles. Who am I really? Might my childhood friends turn out to be third cousins? In Charleston, that last one's almost too easy.

My mother grew exhausted with my pestering and sent me to see Mary Pringle, an ancient cousin and amateur genealogist. Primed with curiosity, I arrived at cousin Mary's elegant antebellum home on a hot summer day. After some iced tea and pleasantries, I was presented with a large, unwieldy sheet of paper, bearing a set of concentric circles. In the center, Mary wrote my name, and in the immediate outer circle, divided in half, she wrote the names of my parents. In the next circle, divided now into fourths, she wrote the names of my four grandparents. We filled it out as far as we could in every direction, and in that area where her family and mine converged—her life's work—a seemingly unbounded wedge flew backward to Scotland and England, until my ancestors were hobnobbing with William Shakespeare and Mary Queen of Scots. "This line," Mary said, pointing to one of the ancient British earls we could claim, "leads in a direct line all the way to Charlemagne."

This revelation was too much past to absorb and too much pride to possess. I wanted to ask her what the Holy Roman Emperor had left me in his will. But Mary's tone was solemn, nearly religious:

"Understand that you are the direct descendent of King Charlemagne," she murmured. The room felt still, as the rest of the universe slowly wheeled about on its gyre—around me, just like on the paper.

I left Mary Pringle's house feeling pretty, well, rooted. It's an important experience for most people—knowing where they come from. And being heir to Charlemagne would serve me just fine on the young gentleman's party circuit. Over the next few years, I became as cunning at hefting this lumbering chunk of self-esteem into passing conversation as a Harvard grad slyly alluding to attending "school in Cambridge."

Roots are important to us—us being all Americans—because they are the source of so much of our national anxiety of not quite belonging. Has any passenger manifest been more fretted over than the *Mayflower*'s? The only use of the Internet by Americans that's competitive with porn, according to several studies, is genealogy. The most significant television miniseries, *Roots*, spawned a wave of pride among African-Americans (and arguably even that hyphenated name) and is partly responsible for the ongoing effort to drain the word "white" of its racist intimations by recasting it as "Irish-American," "Scottish-American," "Italian-American," and the like. For everyone—including Native Americans who itchily remind the rest of the nation that they might also be called First Americans—there is a deep anxiety about rootedness and its claims. When Bill Frist was elevated to majority leader of the Senate in 2003, he had just self-published a book. Its title cries out as much with this anxiety as it does with pride: *Good People Beget Good People: A Genealogy of the Frist Family.*

The truth is, this anxiety can never really be quelled. About three years after I had tea with Mary Pringle, I was in a college calculus class when the teacher made a point about factoring large numbers. He decided to dramatize it by giving an example from the real world, explaining how redundancy affected genealogy in a process called "pedigree collapse." He noted that if you run your line back to A.D. 800, the number of direct ancestors you would have, on average, is 562,949,953,421,312. That's half a quadrillion people, which is more than five thousand times the total number of humans (106 billion) who have ever lived.

How, he asked, could this be? Well, when one goes back in time, the number of ancestors expands arithmetically: 2 grandparents, 4 great-grandparents, 8 great-great-grandparents. But soon enough, one's ancestors assume duplicate places on the family tree. Otherwise, the law of arithmetic progression creates all kinds of crowding problems. The number of ancestors one has by A.D. 1300 is just over 268 million people, or roughly the total population of humans on the planet at that time. Beyond that year, of course, the whole thing starts to collapse inward, and then it rapidly implodes through super-redundancy into the smaller populations that existed then.

The upshot, the teacher explained, is that nearly everyone currently living anywhere on the planet can claim (and he paused for emphasis) "to be the direct descendant of Charlemagne."

The room felt still, if not absurd, as the rest of the universe slowly creaked about me on its gyre, laughing. "The mathematical distinction," the teacher added, "would be to *not* have Charlemagne as a direct ancestor."

When we use the term "rank amateur," the meaning we're aiming at is this level of silliness. Rank amateurism makes delightful, if often insufferable, sense. I'm talking of the kind of insupportable rant your insane uncle unloads at Thanksgiving Day dinner—until someone pierces the bubble of absurdity.

This kind of amateurism is like so many urban legends. There is a surface logic, which is really an anxiety about some current topic (organ transplants, normalizing homosexuality, black people) that becomes a belief centered on some apocryphal anecdote about a missing kidney, gerbilling, or naming a son Nosmo from a half-obscured No Smoking sign. Then one day, someone—often cruelly—reveals that no actual account of any of these stories really exists, suggesting that you were a schmuck/homophobe/racist for believing anything that stupid and there you are. An amateur at *knowing*.

If "amateur" in Europe still generally means an earnest and uncredentialed aspirant—like, say, an amateur astronomer—then one of the fugitive meanings unleashed when the word jumped the pond is this one: complete dolt.

The intellectual slapstick of the rank amateur can practically be broken down into neat categories, because there are a few ongoing scandals that make it easy to chart the rambling topography of getting lost, amateur-style. Few of them are as ripe as the anthropological pursuit of the answer to any of the "first" questions—such as Who was the First Primate, Human, European, American? Amateur anthropologists tend to flock to these unknowable, ultimately meaningless mysteries.

As a result, the well-worn trails of the lost provide a kind of map of amateur waywardness. The quixotic way of the amateur is marked by a number of stations, like the road to Golgotha. Maybe the first one is that no matter how often you learn this lesson, it's easy to fall for the next charlatan's argument coming down the road.

Not long after swearing off the inanity of long-distance genealogy, I read in the *New Yorker* and *Newsweek* and all the top magazines that some serious amateurs had discovered that my great[640]-grandfather was the first man to set foot on the continent of North America some sixteen thousand years ago. Who wouldn't want those bragging rights?

II. The Allegory of the Cave

On a cool leafy hillside above a trickling Cross Creek in remote Pennsylvania, the sun crept through the trees, primordial. Nestled into the slope above, an open rock-shelter seemed just the place where any self-respecting *Homo sapiens* might set down his basketry and spear and light a fire.

Today, there's a parking lot at the hill's base and a set of sturdy stairs that lead to a wooden enclosure built by James Adovasio. He's the Mercyhurt College archaeologist who's been excavating this controversial site since the mid-1970s. Adovasio was guiding a rare tour for a dozen or so amateurs. A brawny variation of Martin Scorsese, he arrived in full archaeological drag: sleeveless flak jacket, boots, work pants, mystical belt buckle.

Inside the shelter today, there's an office, electricity, good lighting, and a suspended boardwalk so that visitors and workers don't stomp over all the evidence. Enormous squared-out holes plunge down into dense earth where tiny round markers dangle like pinned earrings in the stone. It was here that Adovasio found his controversial evidence, stone tools that carbon-date to 16,000 ± 150 years B.C.

This date puts the tools' owners here four millennia before the end of the last ice age, which is around the time the first humans were traditionally believed to have arrived. Adovasio asked us to notice a pencil-thin black line in the stone. No one could really see it. So Adovasio splashed water on it, and the line darkened into little more than a pencil swipe across the rock.

"This is a fire pit," he declared. All of us moved closer to the rail to squint and then decided, as with so much prehistoric archaeology, that we'd just take his expert word for it. He described the scene that once occurred here. Folks sat around the fire and cooked deer and squirrel while snacking on hackberries and nuts. Maybe they battered some rocks into spear points or wove some grasses into primitive baskets. In the chilly rock-shelter, it was easy to look around and imagine this ancient gathering. Typically, the prehistoric picture show that plays on the cave wall of our minds involves cavemen pursuing mastodons with spears. Instead, here we were in their kitchen, where people sat around the fire, eating and talking. Away from the picturesque hunt. Quiet time, culture time, story time.

Now, 16,000 ± 150 years later, we were once again gathered here for story time. But Adovasio was not alone in trying to tell this story. Helping him, sort of, was the fat guy in front of me. He was just one of the crowd, like me, but he had spent much of the tour loudly explaining—allegedly to his long-suffering girlfriend, but really to the confederacy of dunces that was the rest of us—just how much he knew about this place. He wore a fanny pack the size of a car tire cinched above pastel shorts, robin's egg blue socks, and black tennis shoes. His XXL T-shirt declared: KLINGON ASSAULT GROUP.

He had already sneeringly uttered the phrase "politically incorrect" several times to signal that he was no victim of conventional wisdom but a man of daring opinions. He had let everyone in the place know that he very well intended to ask Adovasio the tough questions. So now the time had come: "Professor Adovasio, does working here in the rock-shelter in western Pennsylvania keep you safe from resentments with Native Americans?" He made an interrogative honking noise.

"No," Adovasio insisted, "Native Americans have an intense interest in this site." Adovasio segued quickly into a shaggy dog story about a certain Indian gentleman who was nothing but supportive. I looked at the dozen or so of us, all white folks in their forties and fifties, and none of us seemed a bit mystified about why Native Americans might be resentful. Perhaps that was why Adovasio didn't feel obliged to really address this issue. His work, after all, suggests that the Native Americans were *late* getting here and that before Asians crossed the Bering Strait to settle North America around the commonly agreed time of thirteen thousand years ago, there were other people—from somewhere else—already here. He also knew that even more fresh evidence now suggests that these earliest people, and hence the true First Americans were, in the scientific jargon, "Caucasoid." That is, white people who looked just like the Klingon ± 200 lbs.

III. American Genesis

Our continent's creation story about the Asian hunter-gatherer crossing the Bering Strait is only about a century old and owes its origin to a black cowboy named George McJunkin. He had escaped slavery and fled out west. He taught himself book learning and herded cattle while pondering the world about him. An amateur scientist, McJunkin was said to ride a horse fixed with a big rifle scabbard in which he holstered his telescope.

McJunkin was well read enough to know that some old bones he found in Clovis, New Mexico, in 1908, were extinct animals. Twenty-five years later, experts investigating McJunkin's discoveries found embedded in some of the bones of these ancient bisons a flat, rounded arrowhead with a bit of fluting at the base to assist fastening it to a spear. It would eventually become known as the Clovis point—the oldest spearhead ever found on the continent.

What makes the Clovis point so special is that it is found in massive numbers all across the continent and reliably enough at a level where organic material radiocarbon dates to roughly twelve thousand years ago. How massive? Take Bell County, Texas. The area north of Austin—known as the Gault site—must have been a well-known pit stop among the Clovis tribes. The place has yielded more than a million stone artifacts, more than half of them from the Clovis era.

"The whole idea of archaeology is that there must be enough redundancy in the record," Richard Burger, a professor of anthropology at Yale, told me. Why? Because there is no other way to prove the case in archaeology, no other path to certainty.

"Archaeologists can't do experiments," Burger said. "Unlike lab science, we can't mix carbon and sulfur and conclude that such and such happens. So we have something else that approaches that. We take advantage of redundancy so that the evidence repeats itself in broad patterns. With Clovis, this happens with confidence."

In the last two decades, though, the confident tellers of Clovis Man's story have been challenged by academic renegades devoted to identifying a new "First American." There are at least four major sites (and some minor ones) in the Americas that claim to have found man-made objects dating tens of thousands of years before Clovis time. These theorists argue that while Clovis Man might still have crossed the Bering Strait thirteen thousand years ago, there is evidence that somebody else was already here. Given their natural caution, academics generally stop right there.

In the meantime, though, less credentialed theorists have stepped forward to identify the pre-Clovis somebody. This new theory holds that white people settled this continent first and that Native Americans are just another crowd of later visitors, like Leif Eriksson's Vikings and Christopher Columbus's Spaniards. Most importantly, the way this theory has leached out of cautious academia and into the pop culture as wild-eyed fact suggests that America's neurosis about race has taken up a new and potentially toxic location—deep in the heart of our continent's creation myth. This discovery has happened not on the front page of the newspaper but in the rumor mill at the edge of archaeology, on the covers of pop science magazines, and in the whispers of self-employed anthropologists and unmoored amateurs.

IV. Sesquipedalianismo

For any new story to get told, there has to be an opening, a sudden tectonic jarring of all the conventional wisdom of a discipline, a kind of tilt between an old worldview and a new one. And that's where we are now in the subdiscipline of ancient American archaeology, poised between two views held (as always) by mossbacked conservative traditionalists on the one side and young agitated revolutionaries on the other.

The voice of skepticism and orthodoxy is best embodied by Professor C. Vance Haynes of the University of Arizona. He comes by his skepticism honestly. He once bought into a claim quite similar to Adovasio's, back in the 1950s at a site called Tule Springs in Nevada. He, too, thought the Clovis line had been breached. He was convinced by extensive evidence of "hearths" filled with charcoal and animal bones, revealing a human encampment dating back twenty-eight thousand years. But later, when Haynes conducted precise tests of the charcoal, he realized that it was merely organic matter turning into coal. All of it was wrong. "You begin to see how easy it is to misinterpret things," Haynes said.

Very easy. When you look at the evidence and the fights around it, you can understand why. First, arrowheads are cool things. Every little kid who has ever dug one up knows this. Arrowheads are symmetrical and beautiful objects. Their flutes, their chipped edges, their flared tails have all been studied, categorized, and given handsome names, dozens of them. The Madison point dates from A.D. 1400, the Whitlock much further back, at 400 B.C. Keep going with Haywood points at 5000 B.C. and deeper still to Cascade points at 8000 B.C. (or so) and finally to the oldest, the Clovis point. To hold in your hand a weapon that is five hundred, a thousand, five thousand years old is humbling and, just . . . neato.

The style of these points, as you travel back in time, become noticeably less arrowheady. Instead of tooled edges, it is clear that they were flintknapped—i.e., beat at with another stone. A beveled edge might be replaced by a straight blade. The barbs near the base get more rounded. Those graceful fishtails disappear and then you get a simple stone point with a groove banged out at the bottom, the telltale primitivity signifying Clovis time. Beyond that, it is hard to tell whether the evidence is or is not man-made. In fact, archaeology has a term for naturally occurring objects that appear to be artifacts: geofacts. One archaeologist told me that in the old days, they'd dynamite a cave ceiling and then let naïve students in. When the students returned to class excited by their find of "ancient arrowheads," the teacher would then school them in the ambiguities of geofacts.

So it's easy to understand how much it pains the young cubs of contemporary archaeology when they have to listen to their older colleagues, the establishment, say that the entire array of pre-Clovis evidence is a pile of geofacts.

And not all that big a pile either. While all the evidence of Clovis man would pack a railroad car, according to Vance Hayes, all the good physical evidence of pre–Clovis man "would fit in a foot locker."

The dates are a mixed bag ranging as far back as fifty thousand years ago to more recent sixteen-thousand-year dates. There are no broad patterns, there are no similarities, and there is no redundancy. So when you look at the individual artifacts themselves, it can be pretty underwhelming.

Add to that the messy business of obtaining dates. Rocks cannot be carbon-dated. The organic material they are found nested in can be, though. But that material can be easily contaminated by rain, by burrowing animals, by time. Plus, radiocarbon-dating sounds precise, and the idea of it—that carbon-14 molecules throw off electrons at a metronomically consistent geological pace—is more exact than the reality. Almost since the discovery of radiocarbon dating, scientists have been noting phenomena that cause variations with the regularity of carbon's internal clock—sunspots, stray comets, the 1945 atomic bombs—such that they require applying a "correction factor." Thus, for any ancient evidence to be confirmed, the punk rockers of archaeology have to look for affirmation from their elders, the Lawrence Welk orchestra. Worse, the old fogeys, like Vance Haynes and others, are essentially being asked to confirm a theory that overturns their entire life's work. This combination of murky evidence and professional oedipalism can mean only one thing: academic food fight.

So in prehistoric archaeology there's a lot of dialogue between the conservative traditionalists and the rebel theorists that, boiled down, typically goes like this:

UPSTART ARCHAEOLOGIST: This is a primitive stone tool that's sixteen thousand years old.
EMINENCE GRISE: No, it's not.
UPSTART ARCHAEOLOGIST: Fuck you.

Actually, that's not much of an exaggeration. In Adovasio's book *The First Americans*, he quotes a friend who said, "'If they don't believe the evidence, fuck 'em'—definitely not scientific discourse but not ill considered, either!"

From its opening line—"'Damn,' I said."—Adovasio's book quivers with the fury of a scolded teenager. His own site, the Meadowcroft Rockshelter I visited in southwest Pennsylvania, has been roundly dismissed by elders who note the existence of nearby "coal seams" (yet another factor that throws off C-14 dating) and groundwater seepage. C. Vance Haynes is among those who have wrinkled their noses at Meadowcroft. On page 216 of his book, Adovasio dismisses him as the "grinch of North American archaeology." Anyone who has questioned Adovasio's own site at Meadowcroft is a "gnat." Every page is dipped in upstart snark.

And no love is lost among the rebels themselves. When a Parisian archaeologist discovered an amazing site called Pedra Furada in Brazil, the initial reports were breathtaking. Besides numerous pieces of pre-Clovis evidence, there were cave paintings said to be even older than the images at Lascaux in France or Altamira in Spain. The Pedra Furada drawings depict hot Pleistocene Era group sex. Brazil's tourist bureau developed plans to capitalize on the find. Then Adovasio himself came down as part of an expert panel which, sorrowfully, declared it all wrong. Adovasio wrote that he saw nothing but "almost surely broken rocks that had fallen into the rockshelter," i.e., geofacts. He dismissed the find of "ancient fireplaces" as "nothing more than material blown in from nearby forest fires."

And so it goes. The entire subfield of pre-Clovis is a tiny shark tank where attacks are constant and the chum that keeps bobbing away from them is the unquestionable piece of evidence that convinces all the skeptics that somebody else was here before Clovis.

Of course, the language of this brawl is academic and Latinate, mostly fought with the manly sesquipedalianisms of science jargon. Here, tree rings are "dendrochronological samples." A rock is a "lithic," and a rock that's clearly been flaked by human hands is "an indubitable lithic artifact." Bits of stone chipped off to make a tool are "percussion flakes."

These are the lyrics of the trade, played in the key of the high-science formality. And it's with such swaggering sesquipedalianismo that an entire career of work can be cattily dismissed: "My review has raised doubts about the provenience of virtually every 'compelling,' unambiguous artifact," wrote the archaeologist Stuart Fiedel in 1999 of the most promising pre-Clovis site ever.

The fight over this site—Monte Verde in Chile—is the most notorious in the field. The archaeologist whose work was trashed is Tom Dillehay of the University of Kentucky. He claimed to find fantastic evidence of a pre-Clovis community, a series of huts, one of which was some kind of primitive drugstore since there were traces of pharmaceutical herbs. He found a tent post still staked in the ground with knotted twine from a Juncus tree or, in the jargon, "the indisputably anthropogenic knotted Juncus."

In 1997, a team of specialists, including Vance Haynes, visited the site, examined all of Dillehay's cool evidence, and unanimously approved it. The pre-Clovis line was officially breached. Tom Dillehay was the man. But not for long. Haynes began to waver. Then this Stuart Fiedel, a private-sector archaeologist, wrote a withering dismissal of every single piece of evidence presented.

In his book, Adovasio (who sided with Dillehay on this one) suggested that Fiedel "reserve some space in the State Home for the Terminally Bewildered." Adovasio whacked Fiedel as "a previously little known archaeologist now working for a private salvage archaeology firm" who "has no field experience in Paleo-Indian sites or complex late Pleistocene or Holocene sites" and "has published one rarely used prehistory textbook but otherwise has no apparent credentials."

Archaeology's tribal relations are run by a caste system that goes like this. The Brahmins are the credentialed, tenured professors at known colleges. They publish in peer-reviewed journals. Beneath

them are private sector archaeologists, also known as salvage archaeologists. They might publish in popular journals like *National Geographic.* But their day work is something different altogether. They
determine for, say, a mall developer whether there are any "significant" remains on a piece of real estate slated to become a food court.

"The people in that world earn a good living," said Richard
Burger. "But it is seen as being outside of the intellectual debate
because they are so busy writing reports, they don't really publish
in peer-review journals. Their work is sometimes called 'gray literature.'" Below the salvagers are the rank amateurs and hobbyists who
often spend a weekend out at some site hoping to find a Clovis point
or two to sell on eBay or keep in their special cigar box back home.
Below them all are scum, the scrurrilous amateur critics who write
books such as this one.

Archaeology's caste system is another facet of the discipline that
makes it more amateurish a science than, say, particle physics. How
many weekend astrophysicists could write up a report challenging
Stephen Hawking that would be widely accepted as truth? When
new evidence in, say, particle physics opens up a Kuhnian melee,
the folks who rush into the breach tend to be . . . particle physicists.
(There are exceptions, but take the point.) In prehistoric archaeology, though, with its rather elastic sense of membership ranging from
well-credentialed academics like Adovasio to salvage archaeologists to
slightly bonkers theorists to ranting neo-Nazis—well, all of them can
rush right in. And do.

What underlies the mudslinging use of bloated Latinisms as well
as the compulsion to make a show of tidy whisk brooms and Eu-
clidean grids is the sense, maybe even fear, that archaeology is not a
science at all. There's a lot of play in the radiocarbon-dating, all the
evidence is in dispute, and sure, maybe the elders' caution can easily
be dismissed as a Freudian conflict of interest. But maybe not.

All of this means that the pre-Clovis evidence requires a lot of
interpretation, a fact that makes it very easy for personal desire and

anxiety to seep like groundwater into that drawer full of cobbles and lithics. As one defender of Dillehay confessed in his own report: "I wondered if, by being too close to these stones for too long, I was building an interpretive sand castle."

But the sand castle's been built. From the few lithics, others have begun to tell a new American creation story—about just who pre-Clovis man was, where he came from, how he lived and died.

The sudden appearance of this yarn explains why prehistoric archaeology really isn't as much a science as an object lesson in just how amateurism can get so amateurish. The story that is getting told is a form of improvisational narrative—tribal storytelling. These stories have less to do with what's obvious from the evidence than what some of us, anxious rootless Americans, deeply long to hear. It's time to look closely at the story that's getting told right now about the earliest inhabitants of this continent. I have a little experience in this field. I know how to jerry-rig a narrative using only a couple of wayward factoids to make it sound just right. It's something I was born to do. It's in my royal blood. I am the direct descendant of King Charlemagne.

V. Ladies and Gentlemen, Kennewick Man

For most of the 1990s, the sotto voce chatter about pre-Clovis man and his possible identity was little more than politically naughty buzz out on the edge of archaeology. Insiders talked about spear points, DNA, cordage, and some disputed bones, but it wasn't a story as much as it was narrative tinder, very dry, waiting for a spark.

Which finally flew, one hot summer afternoon in 1996 on the

banks of the Columbia River. Some kids were trying to sneak into a hydroplane race, and as they stomped through the muck of a bank, one of them saw a few old bones and then pieces of a skull. The find was quickly passed on to a local forensic expert, a salvage archaeologist who worked out of a converted rec room in his house. He would become the rhapsode for these bones. Divinely, his name was James Chatters.

Chatters released the radiocarbon dating that put the bones back to 7600 B.C. He also described a Cascade point embedded in the hip. This style of Paleo-Indian arrowhead is a long, thin design that would fit right in with the skeleton's age. So far, so good. Standard ancient skeleton. But then Chatters said something odd, almost nonsensical to those unacquainted with the amateur anthropology rumor mill. He said he didn't believe this skeleton belonged to a Paleo-Indian at all but rather to "a trapper/explorer who'd had difficulties with 'stone-age' peoples during his travels."

In other words, this skeleton was not merely a non-Indian but a non-Indian who had survived well into Clovis time and then been killed by Paleo-Indians. Suddenly, this skeleton was a victim and the find was a crime scene.

Even as the media tried to make sense of this peculiar story, the Indians demanded the bones, charging that they had to be of Native American heritage. This was how these stories typically unfolded.

In 1990, President George H. W. Bush signed the Native American Graves Protection and Repatriation Act. NAGPRA sought to make amends for the grave robbing and bizarre antics of the previous decades. In the nineteenth century, for instance, the Smithsonian wanted Indian skulls to mount on display. So, quite often after a battle, Indian corpses were decapitated and the heads packed in boxes and shipped back to Washington to be "studied." The money was good enough that sometimes Indians would see white men—the emissaries of European civilization—loitering around a burial ground until the crowd left—in order to dig up Grandma and cut off her head. A few centuries' worth of desecration of the Indian body is something mainstream history still avoids mentioning. It's hard for non–Native Americans today to understand the lingering resentment. Try this on: Toward the end of the Civil War in Denver, a group of marauding white men interrupted theatergoers with a mid-show display of fresh Indian scalps—not merely from heads but from women's vaginas as well. The civilized audience whooped with approval.

As Native Americans asserted themselves, beginning in the 1970s, their movement led inexorably to a congressional act aimed at returning all stolen skeletons to the appropriate tribes. Some estimates put the number of skeletons held in museums at holocaust levels: 200,000.

NAGPRA decreed that all Indian human remains that could be culturally identified were to be returned to the appropriate tribe. Dozens of fights with museums erupted, and still go on to this day. Consider the University of California at Berkeley—a place one might suspect is ostentatiously pro return of Native American skeletons. But that would be wrong. Beneath the Hearst Gymnasium swimming pool is a charnel house of "thousands of remains" that Berkeley stubbornly holds on to, fighting all legal efforts to have them restored and reburied.

But these are all fairly recent skeletons—i.e., the last few centuries. Jump back a millennium or two and the skeletons tend not to have been stolen in conflict but discovered at various archaeological sites. These are also being reclaimed and reburied under the NAGPRA law.

In the past, a number of unusual skeletons have been discovered that date long after Clovis but are rumored to possess characteristics of another race of people—different from the Asians who crossed the Bering Strait. These skeletons have long fed the pre-Clovis rumor mill as evidence of some other group of early North Americans who survived the Clovis-era arrival of Paleo-Indians before slowly disappearing. As if to fuel this mill, as soon as such bones are discovered, modern Indians seize them and rebury them. In the

gossipy back alley of amateur American archaeology, they are notorious. They are mourned. Let us name them: the 10,800-year-old
Buhl Woman found in Idaho in 1989, the 7,800-year-old Hour-
glass Cave skeleton found in Colorado, the 7,800-year-old Pelican
Rapids Woman skull and the 8,700-year-old Browns Valley Man,
both found in Minnesota—all reburied.

So, the Native Americans in Washington State immediately sus-
pected this familiar talk about Kennewick's origin was merely a political tactic to end-run the straightforward requirements of NAGPRA.
The scientists, especially when it concerned these ancient skeletons
that they wanted desperately to study, counter-suspected political
correctness run amok. The conspiracy theorists, not surprisingly, saw
a conspiracy. Then, something else happened. The issue quickly got
caught up in energy politics.

At the time of the discovery of Kennewick, the Umatilla Indians
were working with the Clinton administration to dispose of some
outdated chemical weapons (WMD, as we say nowadays). The federal government wanted tribal approval on this difficult matter. And,
by the late 1990s, the Umatilla were also a federally recognized tribe
and had a casino, which meant they had political and financial clout
and couldn't easily be kicked around. So, when they screamed for the
bones, the Clinton administration jumped. Chatters and the group of
scientists who gathered around him calling for an open inquiry into
the skeleton were stunned by what happened.

Bruce Babbitt, the then secretary of the interior, ordered that the
US Army Corps of Engineers seize the bones. In the meantime, to
"stabilize" the site where the bones were found, the Army choppered
in five hundred tons of riprap and buried the bank. The archaeological site was protected by being destroyed.

This wasn't just politics to the scientists, it was medieval obscu-
rantism. This was the equivalent of forcing Galileo to recant and
locking him in his room. Which is how the entire drama would play
out in the courtroom—a fight between Native American Indians try-

ing to respect their elders and secular scientists defending their right
to open inquiry.

But this time, there was one difference, one word that totally
changed the story in the pop-culture telling outside the courtroom.
When Chatters first examined Kennewick in his rec room, he looked
at the skull and then deployed a single word to the media to describe
what he saw: "Caucasoid-like."

The narrative tinder suddenly exploded in flames, and from the
fire arose a new and wild story: A Caucasoid man, who was among
the First Americans, was murdered by genocidal newcomers, Mongoloid invaders coming across Beringia after the last ice age.

Throughout the theories and quarrels of this prehistory, there is
a strange kind of recapitulation going on. Every theory propagated
about the European conquest of the Indians after Christopher Columbus seems to have its doppelganger in the pre-Clovis era. Just
as American Indians were the victims of genocide in the colonial
period, so it seems were the early Caucasoids at the hands of paleo-
Indians. Some theories say that the early Caucasoids were wiped out
by germs, a recapitulation of the account of Indians and smallpox-
infected blankets, which has become a near parable in American history. In this way, the scientists could even claim that the Indians'
attempt to take control of the Kennewick skeleton was simply the
evil twin of nineteenth-century grave robbing, and haven't we all
had enough of that?

To bring the entire fight to a level of absurdity that marks it as a
truly American event, the Asatru Folk Assembly—a neo-Norse movement that claims to represent the "native European" religion—also
claimed Kennewick's bones. The neo-Norsemen argued that they
were the nearest tribe related to Kennewick Man and that under the
law of NAGPRA *they* should be given the bones for reburial. The
court did not give them Kennewick but did allow them to perform
funeral rites over his bones. And so a year after that hydroplane race,
big hairy blond men wearing horns and garish furs performed the

Norse burial ceremony in Washington State for their mourned errant
ancestor.

VI. A Brief History of Caucasians

Does race exist? Of course it does. We see it every day. Guy steals a
purse, and the cop asks, What did he look like? And we all easily say:
He was a six-foot-tall black guy, or a five-and-a-half-foot-tall Asian
man, or a white guy with long red hair. As a set of broad descriptions
of how people look, race exists.

   If you were to look at me, you would easily categorize me as Caucasian. I'm the ruddy sort that burns quickly, with reddish hair now
shading into white. Most people hazarding a guess might say Scots-
Irish, which is what I have always said. Just to be sure, I once sub-
mitted my DNA to see what the incontrovertible scientific evidence
might show. The result was surprising: I carry the DNA marker found
in great abundance among the Fulani Tribe of contemporary Nigeria.

   Sure, maybe the marker is about as significant as my Charlemagne
genes. On the other hand, that very Nigerian coast is the tribal location where many slaves were captured and held in the notorious slave
castles until traders' galleys could transport them to American ports.
The main harbor that received more slaves than any other on the
eastern seaboard was Charleston, South Carolina. My mother's family
has lived there nearly three hundred years. Maybe I have a Thomas
Jefferson problem.

   Since I had my blood work done, my nephew Chance Algar started
poking around the distant family tree, and one Christmas he called me
over to his computer. He showed me my great-great-grandfather—

the man for whom I am named—in the 1860 census. But that man does not turn up on the census roles in 1870. Presumably, he died for the Confederate cause. His widow, Mary, along with their four children moved back in with her parents. In 1870 this older couple is marked on the census as "colored," as are the neighbors on their street. But Mary and her children are marked white, their designation in the previous census. In all likelihood, Mary *and* her parents were of mixed race. But Mary could pass for white. Had the census-taker penciled in a single letter "c" on that form, how different might be the genetic trajectory of my then-toddler great-grandfather. But there it is: the probable origin of my genetic marker. I am one-sixteenth African-American, or in the pseudo-scientific jargon of that time, a mustefino or a hexadecaroon.

Yet it's no longer apparent in the way I now look. I am Caucasian as surely as my Fulani cousins are black: because race is a set of *visual* cues, mainly skin shade but also nose shape, eyelid folds, cheekbone prominence, etc. We hold these vague blueprints of race in our heads because, as primates, one of the great tools of consciousness we possess is observing patterns in nature. It's no surprise that we'd train this talent on ourselves.

The notion of race as an unchanging constant through time is an accepted truth as old as the Bible. When Noah's Flood receded, the three boys Japheth, Shem, and Ham went out into the world to engender, respectively, white people, Semites and all others. This doesn't quite shake out into the latter notions of white, black, and yellow, but you get the idea. The terms are still with us. The early word "Shemitic" settled down to become "semitic." And, among amateur chroniclers writing in the ponderous style of the town historian, it's not hard to find references to the "Hamitic race" as a way of saying "black folks." Japheth never became a common adjective, perhaps because of those unwieldy consonants. More likely, it's because whites appointed themselves the Adamic task of naming the other races. It was not until the Age of Reason that scientists tried to figure out empirically what race meant and how it came to be. The signal year was 1776 with the publication of a book, *On the Natural Variety of Mankind*, by German biologist Frederick Blumenbach.

In his day, Blumenbach's theory had a certain symmetry that made it the very model of good science. These days, his theory seems insane. He argued that Native Americans were the transitional race that eventually led to Asians. (Don't try to work out the geography of this, it will make your head explode.) And another group—which Blumenbach simply conjured from a faraway people, the "Malaysians"—evolved over time to become Africans. (Again, if you're puzzling out the geography, watch your head.)

At the center of all this change was the white race, which was constant. Blumenbach believed darkness was a sign of change from the original. All of mankind had fallen from perfection, but the darker you were, the farther you had fallen. As a result, the best way to locate the original Garden of Eden, according to Blumenbach, was to follow the trail of human . . . beauty. The hotter the women, the hunkier the men, the closer you were to what was left of God's first Paradise. Here's Blumenbach, explaining the etymology of the new word he hoped to coin:

> I have taken the name of this variety from Mount Caucasus, both because its neighborhood, and especially its southern slope, produces the most beautiful race of men, I mean the Georgian.

Blumenbach's theory is totally forgotten today by everybody (except maybe Georgians) but this single word and the oceans of misconceptions that have sprung from it probably are owed to some one trip Blumenbach made to the area where a local girl gave him a lusty wink. The word itself *is* lovely. Say it: *Caucasian*. The word flows off the tongue like a stream trickling out of Eden. Its soothing and genteel murmur poses quite a patrician contrast to the field-labor grunts of the hard *g*'s in Negroid and Mongoloid. Caucasian. When you say it, the exotic isolation of those mountains intimates a biblical narrative. You can almost see it when you say it: the early white forebears walking away from paradise to trek to Europe and begin the difficult task of creating Western Civilization.

Ever since Blumenbach launched this word two and a half centuries ago, the effort to pin down the exact and scientific meaning of race has never ceased and has never settled into any undisputed categories. Even today, the US Census is little more than an explosion of ethnic agony that arrives every ten years like constitutional clockwork.

The number of races has expanded and contracted wildly between Blumenbach and now, depending on the mood of the culture. The basic three have gone through scores of revisions, growing as high as Ernst Haeckel's thirty-four different races in 1873 or Paul Topinard's nineteen in 1885 or Stanley Garn's nine in 1971. Today, we nervously ask if you're white, African-American, Native American, Asian, Hispanic, or of Hawaiian or Pacific Islander descent.

But it wasn't that long ago that the question would have turned upon races only our great-grandfathers would recognize. Let us mourn their passing: the Armenoids, the Assyroids, the Veddoids, the Orientalids, Australoids, the Dalo-Nordic, the Fälish, the Alpines, the Dinarics, the Fenno-Nordic, the Osteuropids, the Lapponoids, the Osterdals, the Cappadocians, the Danubians, the Ladogans, the Trondelagens, and the Pile Dwellers.

In the meantime, science has made its discoveries. The mystery of race has been solved. For the longest time, the answer was stymied by a contradiction. Surely skin tone had something to do with colder climates creating paler shades, but then why weren't Siberians as pale as Swedes, and why were Eskimos as dark as equatorial islanders? The answer was announced, but it's so tedious hardly anyone noticed.

Skin pigmentation changed to regulate the amount of Vitamin D_3 manufactured by the sun just under the skin. This is the theory of Professor Nina Jablonski, a paleoanthropologist with the California

Academy of Sciences. So when the first dark inhabitants moved into Scandinavia, they confronted scant local resources—and almost no external sources for Vitamin D_3. Their kind quickly selected out for paler children whose light skin would manufacture enough Vitamin D_3 to keep them healthy. Meanwhile, Eskimos arrived to the Arctic dark-skinned. The local cuisine of seal and whale is rich in Vitamin D_3, so the skin was never summoned into action. Evolution has one big rule: If there's no pressure on the system to change, then it doesn't bother. So Eskimos remained dark.

When we look at the different races, according to Jablonski's theory, what we're actually seeing is not "superiority" or "good people" or "race." All that we are seeing, the *only* thing we are seeing when we look at skin color, according to the science, is a meandering trail of Vitamin D_3 adaptation rates.

VII. The Mounting Evidence

Science prefers to confirm its newest findings with the newest tools. Fingerprinting is no longer the gold standard of evidence now that DNA testing is the absolute solid proof of guilt or innocence. In anthropology, the cutting-edge techniques come with gleaming names—Optically Stimulated Luminescence, Electron Spin Resonance Dating, and Accelerator Mass Spectrometry. These are the devices that are confirming pre-Clovis dates in ways that make radiocarbon dating look like counting tree rings. By the time we figure out how they are flawed, of course, our prejudices will be so well muddled among the tentative facts that they will be as inextricable as ink from milk.

According to the revolutionaries heralding pre-Clovis, it hardly matters since so much other modern proof is appearing. New lab tests reveal that Native Americans apparently have a signature strand of very old DNA known as Haplogroup X. The only other large population on the earth carrying this genetic marker is Europeans. The suggestion is that there must have been intermarriage before Columbus, possibly before the last ice age. Moreover, now that the Iron Curtain has fallen, archaeologists have been able to do more digging in Siberia, where they expected to find Clovis points or something like them. But they haven't. This absence, as well as the presence of Haplogroup X, has led some people to theorize that while Clovis man might have crossed over thirteen thousand years ago, at the end of the last ice age, he would have encountered someone already here—someone possessed of the X gene as well as the Clovis toolkit.

Who might these people have been and where might they have come from? One prominent theorist with an answer is America's chief archaeologist at the Smithsonian Institution. A big bearded bear of a man, Dennis Stanford could pass as a Norse king from some other time. Stanford has struggled with the mystery of why Clovis points don't show up in Siberia. He notes that they resemble the early work of Solutrean culture. The Solutreans were prehistoric people who lived in modern-day France and Spain some eighteen thousand years ago. They are perhaps most famous for being the possible artists who painted the horses of Lascaux and their own hands on the walls of the Altamira Cave. Stanford argues that their toolkit, which included stone points, looks like a predecessor to the Clovis style.

"There must be fifty or sixty points of comparison," he has said.

He believes that these proto-Europeans must have been intelligent enough to make water craft. Hugging the coast of the glacial crescent of the northern Atlantic, they followed what is called the "kelp highway"—brimming with food—and sailed away to a new land.

Other scientists are providing even more evidence that seems to corroborate these general ideas. Several anthropologists have daringly

revived the argument that examining skull shapes can reveal ethnicity. Pioneered by Douglas Owsley, also now at the Smithsonian, and
his partner Richard Jantz at the University of Tennessee, two scientists who have put together collections of measurements, described
by *Newsweek* as a database of "2,000 or so profiles" that "consists of
some 90 skull measurements, such as distance between the eyes, that
indicate ancestry." They have developed software that allows them
to input a bone's measurements and the output is "ethnicity."

Among their fans and followers, there is talk of some of the peculiar skeletons found over the years. An ancient body, known as
Wizards Beach Man, found at Pyramid Lake, Nevada, in 1978, was
determined to be possibly of "Norse" extraction and to have "no close
resemblance to modern Native Americans." Another skeleton, known
as Spirit Cave Man, was found in Nevada in 1940. His bones date
to 7450 B.C., and when his skull measurements were run through the
database, out spat a finding of "Archaic Caucasoid."

Once again, there's Blumenbach's word. Only this time it's got
that "-oid" ending. What is the difference between Caucasoid and
Caucasian?

"Caucasoid sounds more scientific," said University of North Carolina anthropologist Jonathan Marks, laughing. Otherwise it has no
more meaning or significance than Blumenbach's original. Caucasoid
is a magnificent piece of pure *Star Trek*ery, a word meant to sound all
clinical and precise, even nerdy. But the word is a rhetorical Trojan
Horse. Its surface meaning suggests something scientific, respectable
and learned, when in fact what we really hear is the connotations
lurking inside, long-suppressed intimations of superiority, exception-
alism, and beauty.

VIII. Kennewick: The Biopic

The court fight over Kennewick Man was resolved in favor of the scientists—in part because this is America and who can be against "open inquiry"? In the popular market of ideas, though, the courts also legitimized the story of the Caucasian man who came to this continent as the Authentic First American and whose bones survived the millennia to report the truth. It is the story that has gotten told this last decade about this hundred-century-old man that is arresting in its perversity. It begins with his name. Does anything sound more European, positively British, than Kennewick? Native Americans had dubbed him the "Ancient One." But it didn't take. The mass media, which follows the meandering will of the popular mob, could sense where this story was trending, and so they ran with "Kennewick." Isn't that a suburb of Essex or the other airport in London? Perhaps not so ironically, the origin goes back to a local Indian chief named Konewack, whose Native American name was anglicized to Kennewick after the railroad workers moved in. As if it were a trend, the very year after Kennewick, more ancient bones were found on Prince of Wales Island. This skeleton was quickly declared to be "Prince of Wales Man," making it seem like the Stone Age forebears of the Saxon kings fancied the Pacific Northwest as a dandy vacation spot.

In the few years after Sir Kennewick's discovery, his life was described and depicted in all the leading magazines. One writer on the subject, Sasha Nemecek, confessed that when she looked at the evidence "the misty images of primitive explorers evaporate" and now "I suddenly picture a single artisan spending hours, perhaps days, crafting these stone tools" whose "workmanship is exquisite, even to my untrained eye." For the article, an artist rendered images of what Kennewick and his ilk looked like. He's an average-height white man with round eyes and some sexily tousled long brown hair. He is wearing a pair of long slacks sewn with a fetching seam straight down the leg to his ankles and a big animal coat (with long sleeves)—an outfit that looks like it comes from Ralph Lauren's Flintstone collection. If it weren't for the spear in his hand, you might mistake him for an English professor at Bennington, but in fact he's the "First American."

And his bride has the complex toolkit of her time, not to mention a nice Ann Tayloroid dress and a haircut that presages Jennifer Aniston by nearly ten millennia. She has thoughtfully shaved her legs for the artist, the better to see her lovely Caucasian skin.

Where did these pictures appear? *Scientific American.*

Kennewick was instantaneously described with words that launched him millennia ahead of his primitive enemies, the Paleo-Indians. He was, as Chatters had said from the beginning, probably an individual "trapper/explorer"—two words that, together, suggest that Kennewick was practically an advance scout for Lewis and Clark. And these words imply degrees of complex rational thinking, especially when set beside a horde of "Stone Age peoples." Other articles painted beautiful scenes of Kennewick as the "strongest hunter in his band." Paleo-Indians were still mucking around in "tribes," while Kennewick traveled with a "band," which "usually consisted of immediate and extended family members with several bands ranging over the same general territory."

Family? Absolutely, that's why Kennewick lived "a good life. He had a mate, and two of their four children still were alive. He still could hunt, though he relied on his dog to bring the game down.

And young men in his band still asked his advice, though lately, his sister's mate was showing signs of impatience, always wanting to do things at his time, in his way." Food was important. "To keep up his strength, he and his band dined on rich, lean roasts and steaks." Kennewick is naturally on the Atkins diet. No type II diabetes from obesity for Sir Kennewick.

"It's natural that people of that time would trade with distant bands," the article goes on to say, although, as a caution, it adds, "there's not a lot of physical evidence to prove it." But proof isn't really necessary when you have adverbs such as "likely" to work over: "To protect his feet, Kennewick Man likely trudged the hills and valleys of Eastern Washington and Oregon in sandals made of sagebrush bark."

Within the first few years of his reappearance, Kennewick Man received major, lengthy profiles in nearly every major magazine in North America, from *Newsweek,* the *Economist,* and *Natural History* to the *New Yorker, Maclean's,* and *Discover.* In all of these articles, sourcing is a good place to invisibly move the story in one direction or another. For the confirmation of Kennewick's skull shape, the articles most often cited two people. One was Catherine J. MacMillan, an acquaintance of Chatters and a fellow private-sector archaeologist. Most articles avoid naming the salvage archaeology company she runs, perhaps because it lacks a certain gravitas: the Bone-Apart Agency. The other source is Grover Grantz, who was a professor at Washington State University. He, too, has an unmentioned gravitas problem, as a pioneer of "Sasquatchery" and a man often described as the "only true scientist to throw his hat in the ring"—the ring being the hunt for Bigfoot. Grantz was the physical anthropologist who suggested that believers kill a Sasquatch and bring in the corpse in order to prove his existence. Grantz died in 2002 and donated his skeleton to the Smithsonian to show he had no fear of having the flesh boiled off his bones so that they could be mounted for display.

Kennewick Man "seems to have been a tall, good-looking man, slender and well-proportioned." Blumenbach's notion of superiority as beauty is never really behind us. Also: "Some nearby sites contain large numbers of fine bone needles, indicating that a lot of delicate sewing was going on." Here's a classic case of journalistic nudging. Fine bone needles found in *nearby* sites. Could they have belonged to the marauding hordes of Paleo-Indians? Instead here's the shove: "Kennewick Man may have worn tailored clothing." Dig the "may." But also swish that other word around on your connotative palate. "Tailored." Feel the force, tugging us in a certain direction. Then: "For a person at that time to live so long in relatively good health indicates that he was clever or lucky, or both, or had family and close friends around him." Good health, clever, family, close friends— a veritable claret of connotative complexity.

And these are the elegant accounts which struggle to keep the story contained inside the scientists' own cautious terms. From there, the implications of Kennewick quickly became insinuated in current fashions of political opinion. Here's the *National Review* writing about "the growing suspicion among physical anthropologists, archaeologists, and even geneticists that some of the first people who settled in the New World were Europeans." Note how a tentative resemblance of skull shape, "Caucasoid-like"—always hedged by the scientists—has quickly settled into declarative certainty: "were Europeans." The politically obvious conclusion is also clear, as the writer continues: "An important part of American Indian identity relies on the belief that, in some fundamental way, they were here first. They are indigenous, they are Native, and they make an important moral claim on the national conscience for this very reason. Yet if some population came before them—perhaps a group their own ancestors wiped out through war and disease, in an eerily reversed foreshadowing of the contact Columbus introduced—then a vital piece of their mythologizing suffers a serious blow. This revised history drastically undercuts the posturing occasioned by the 500th anniversary of

Columbus's 1492 voyage." Once you step away from the magazines and books, the story leaches into the poisonous domain of online discussions, where one can easily find comments like this one from shmogie1 on the alt.soc.history board: "Kennewick man is older than any known N/A [Native American] remains, and appears to be much more European than N/A, so your people stole the land from my European ancestors who were here first." And then you finally drift on down to the neo-Nazis, always good for a pithy quote. The extermination of the American Indian, said former Klan Dragon and part-time Nazi Louis Beam, was just "white people" getting revenge.

Most of these accounts conclude with a hushed imagining of how that spear point got into the hip. Because Kennewick Man's skeleton body was found in a riverbed, the writers surmise that he died there, as in this sentence: "He may have perished alone on a fishing trip, far from his family." Cue Samuel Barber's Adagio for Strings.

In these stories, the Indians are typically ignored or they simply move about as a supernumerary horde summoned onstage to throw the Cascade point. They have no friends or family. Might they have also been clever and scored well on their SATs? It's never mentioned, or maybe there just weren't enough bone needles to draw such a conclusion. But the hedge in Kennewick's favor is constant, each detail slightly pushed toward revealing a man who was smart and carried complex tools and had damn sophisticated taste in clothing. He hunted and ate well and had good bone structure. He was surrounded by friends and family, i.e., that intimacy of culture that would lead to the abandonment of nomadism, the invention of agriculture and society, the stable foundation that would lead us inexorably toward Western civilization. Which, in turn, would bring Kennewick's Caucasoid-like descendents back to America to find him and tell his story.

IX. Kennewick's Backstory

The story of a European presence here in America prior to the Indians would be a truly novel tale if it hadn't already been told so many times. The number of theories holding that Native Americans were either latecomers or actually Europeans who'd set aside their history for loincloths is impressive. We—and by we, I mean white people—have been getting Indians wrong from the git-go. Remember where the word "Indian" comes from, for starters. But even the earliest depictions of Indians simply used European bodies and faces with a few feathers added.

Western Europeans were stunned that the New World had so many people already in it. How could these primitives have gotten here first? They must be . . . us! Theories abounded. Some British savants thought Indians were covert Welsh families who'd slipped over on their rafts, the cunning little demons. Others theorized that the Indians were the lost people of Atlantis. There were a whole host of arguments that Indians were Jews. During the colonial era, the chief rabbi of Holland, Menashe ben Israel, theorized that all Native Americans were descendent from the Lost Tribes of Israel, and the theory was confirmed by a 1650 book entitled *Jews in America or the Probabilities That the Americans Be of That Race*. Mormons continue to believe this account of Native American origin, holding that the sons of Lehi sailed to the Americas around the time of Christ and forgot their knowledge of the Torah. They reverted to a state of savagery and their descendents scattered among the plains and throughout the two continents. Thus, all Indians are essentially: Jews Gone Wild.

Most Americans rarely saw images out of books such as the rabbi's. Rather, the most common mass media image was found on the coins in your pocket—and for most of American history, those Indians looked astonishingly European, if not Roman imperial.

In 1914, on a ten-dollar gold coin, it was still possible to see in the face of the Indian the wavy blond Nordic princess of that dream. Then, at last, the famous buffalo nickel appeared on the eve of World War I, the first Indian image that looked like a Native American. It's unlikely Chatters knew the full depth of this history when he asked a local artist to take the Kennewick skull and reconstruct the face.

Well, if only that were what he did. Chatters didn't just hand the skull to someone and ask him to reconstruct the face. Instead, he had an epiphany, as he explained once, right at home: "I turned on the TV, and there was Patrick Stewart—Captain Picard, of *Star Trek*— and I said, 'My God, there he is! Kennewick Man.'" And not long thereafter, the artist's bust appeared on magazine covers across the country as a piece of sculpture that so resembled Picard you found yourself looking to see if he was holding a phaser.

Forensic reconstruction is a very iffy "science." The problem is that the features that we look to for identification are fleshy ones—ears, nose, and eyes—and are the most difficult to know from a skull. By the way, I and every other writer call Kennewick's head a "skull." The implication is that it was found whole. But in fact, it was found in parts. Chatters pieced it together. When other government experts put the pieces together, they built a skull whose dimensional differences from Chatters's version were deemed statistically significant. Again, at every stage of this story, the bits and pieces—in this case, literally—get pushed toward the Caucasoid-like conclusion.

Reconstruction is more art than science or, with its stated success rate of roughly 50 percent, about as good a predictor as a coin toss. Consider what Chatters did: By making Kennewick perfectly resemble one of the most famous pop-culture Brits of our time, he let the visual cues confirm his finding without ever having to once again repeat the term "Caucasoid-like." Add to that the fact that leaving the clay gray-colored made it easier for the brain to fill in the skin tone. Chatters has revealed that he suggested to the artist that he not include the "epicanthic fold" of the Asian eye since leaving that out would be "neutral." Plus, by leaving the sculpture bald, the artist produced a kind of featureless mannequin whom anyone can dress up with the hairstyle, eye color, and skin tone drawn from our deepest racial closet.

Kennewick's skull is always described as "narrow, with a prominent nose, an upper jaw that juts out slightly and a long narrow braincase." This description is often phrased this way: dolichocranic and slightly prognathous, marked by a lack of an inferior zygomatic projection.

Such sesquipedalianismo. Yet here's the problem with looking at those vague features and declaring them "Caucasoid": We don't really know what people's skulls looked like ten thousand years ago. We only have a few, like the pre-Clovis points, so it's reckless to draw any conclusions. Skull shapes, like skin color, can change much more quickly than we think, especially if there's been traumatic environmental change.

Franz Boas, the legendary anthropologist from the turn of the last century, is most famous for debunking a lot of skull science in his time by proving that the skulls of immigrant children from all parts of the world more closely resemble one another than they do their parents'. Rapid dietary shifts can cause major structural changes in skeletons—just ask the average Japanese citizen who has shot up four and a half inches in height in a single generation, or the average American man who has packed on an extra twenty-five pounds since 1960. The truth is that there exists no coherent history of skull shapes back through time, so to say a ten-thousand-year-old skull resembles a modern white guy skull is to compare apples with raisins.

In time, Chatters tried to calm the storm over his own remarks. He had repeatedly said things like this: Kennewick Man "could also pass for my father-in-law, who happens to be Scandinavian." Then one day he was suddenly insisting: "Nobody's talking about white here." His contradictions are maddening. At one point, Chatters explained: "I referred to the remains as Caucasoid-like. . . . I did not state, nor did I intend to imply, once the skeleton's age became known, that he was a member of a European group." Afterward, he offered writer Elaine Dewar a coy aside: "I say you can say European. Who can prove you wrong?"

He insisted that he meant that the skull simply didn't resemble the classic "Mongoloid" features of Asia. He said Kennewick could have been Polynesian or even ancient Japanese. It turns out that those vague Caucasoid features are also found in the Ainu people of prehistoric Japan, as well as other places outside Europe.

Don't be confused here. The scientists themselves who fling around words like "Caucasoid" are the very ones who also admit that the "Caucasian" skull is found everywhere. That's right. *Everywhere.* This Caucasian skull shape—they will admit—is found all over the planet. For example, another ancient skull always brought up alongside Kennewick's is a female skull found in Mexico. Nicknamed Luzia, the skull was analyzed in a report that found a resemblance to skulls seen among early Australians, bones found in China's Zhoukoudian Upper Cave, and a set of African remains knowns as Taforalt 9.

So we've narrowed the source of this Caucasian skull to Australia, China, and Africa. Huh? Another study, of an ancient skeleton known as Spirit Cave Man, narrowed down his skull shape origin to: Asian/Pacific, the Zulu of Africa, the Ainu of Japan, the Norse, or the Zalawar of Hungary. Just to add to the confusion, in 2009, an ancient skeleton one thousand years old and identified as "Incan," was dug up in . . . Norway.

What conclusion can be drawn from finding Caucasian skulls in Asia? Or finding African skulls in Brazil? Or finding Polynesian skulls at the continental divide? Is it that these "groups" traveled a lot thousands of years ago, or that skull shapes change radically and quickly over time? Of course, it's the latter, and some anthropologists have known it for some time. In the early twentieth century, Harvard anthropologist Earnest Hooton documented the wide variety of skull shapes he found among ancient Native Americans. (That's right. This early scientist who spoke the uncomfortable truth about race was named Earnest Hooton.) "He studied Native American skulls from pre-contact all the way to the eighteenth century and he sorted them into cranial racial categories," said Jonathan Marks. "He called them 'pseudo-Australoid' and 'pseudo-Negroid' and 'pseudo-Mediterranean' because they had those features. He was smart enough *not* to say, Well, I guess these people encountered a stray Australian aborigine on his way to Colorado. Clearly he recognized that there was considerably more diversity in early Indian skulls than he was used to seeing. And that's the point in all this: Once you've started to racialize those variations, you've already given your answer."

What this suggests may not be that Africans and Mongoloids and Europeans were storming the American shores ten thousand years ago as much as that in any one group at any one time, you will find all kind of anomalies. In fact, among many nineteenth-century images of Native Americans, you can easily find lots of paintings and even photographs of Indians whose skull shape is precisely that of Captain Picard with his "Caucasoid" and dolichocranic good looks. The famous image of Chief Whirling Thunder (Google it) looks more eerily like Jean-Luc Picard than Kennewick does.

The Center for the Study of the First Americans, at Texas A&M University, is a clearinghouse for pro-Caucasian theories of early America. The center publishes a manly newsletter, *Mammoth Trumpet*. There one can find a set of arguments that inspire a kind of sorrow and pity. The director, Dr. Robson Bonnichsen (like so many of these academics: the look of a Norse king with a big bushy beard), commonly says things like this: "We're getting some hints from people working with genetic data that these earliest populations might have some shared genetic characteristics with latter-day European populations." Maybe he doesn't know that he's the direct heir to King Charlemagne?

What makes the claim all the more paltry is that once you start reading about the European connection to pre-Clovis man here in America, you can't help but notice that the same essential story is getting told in other, separate fields—such as the story of when the first European evolved or when early ape creatures crossed over the line leading to humans. All of them make claims that have the contours of the same fight—the revolutionaries challenging the traditionalists, all of them finding a way to shoehorn Europeans into a story, with hints of superiority and beauty. In so many of these fights, you can find the same kinds of amateurs making the same mistakes, arriving always at the same conclusion: that European development and civilization are somehow separate from the proletarian evolution of the rest of the human race.

For instance, the current theory about the beginning of mankind—the Out of Africa theory—states that an early pre-human, *Homo erectus*, evolved into *Homo sapiens*, who then left Africa some one hundred thousand years ago and eventually evolved into the modern peoples of the world. But there is a small contingent of rebel theorists—the "multiregionalists"—who hold that it was *Homo erectus* who spread out to various locations, in each of which he developed into a particular transitional hominid. In Asia: Peking Man. In south Asia: Java Man. And in Europe: Neanderthal Man. Each of these specimens would eventually evolve simultaneously into *Homo sapiens*.

According to the rebels, there was some gene mixing at the margins of these separately developing species, to keep the general hominid ability to reproduce together. It's a serviceable theory that manages to keep all mankind barely in the same species while creating an intellectual space for racial differences and European uniqueness. It is the "separate but equal" theory of physical anthropology.

As theories go, however, multiregionalism can be pretty slippery. For the longest time DNA tests revealed that Neanderthal Man made no direct genetic contribution to modern man. But recently researchers in Europe—several of them sporting Viking beards—discovered that there was a genetic connection. Multiregionalists labor mightily to keep Neanderthal Man in the picture, arguing that there had to have been some sex among the different humans and that the evidence is with us. One of the arguments is that my big nose (as well as those great beaks on Jews and Arabs) is telling evidence of Neanderthal genes. That's the theory of Dr. Colin Groves, whose very dolichocranic skull sports the requisite Nordic beard.

Remember how Neanderthal Man used to look—the ruthless brute of comic books, the near knuckle-dragger who exited around the time of the Last Glacial Maximum? Well, he's had a complete makeover. Frank Frazetta's neckless, club-swinging primates are now key players in the unique European formation of modern-day Caucasians, so they've put down their bludgeons and picked up some complex tools. One DNA study suggested that Neanderthal Man had red hair, practically Scandinavian. He's gotten a haircut, Botoxed the beetling brow, and in the museums the Neanderthal models have replaced their murderous scowl with a pensive, more Rodinesque expression. One current display in Europe includes a cute Neanderthal boy with big eyes and the Broadway musical hair of a Dickensian street urchin. Like his dad, he's had his Neander-snout bobbed into something that could easily develop into a tastefully trim WASP nose, and he holds a questioning expression that instinctively makes you quietly pray that he gets that ring to the volcano or it'll spell doom for Middle Earth.

There are so many of these Euro-centric theories where the key moment of development that "makes us human" somehow occurred in France or Germany that I began to collect them, like baseball cards. Those cave paintings in Lascaux and Altamira are often held up as the threshold event revealing "abstract" thought, which made us truly human.

My personal favorite, this week, takes us all the way back to the apes. A primate specialist in Toronto named David Begun holds that he has found "the last common ancestor to the great apes"—i.e., the notorious missing link. Where?

In Europe. His theory is that African apes crossed into Europe, picked up those civilizing traits that would eventually lead to human-ness, and then slipped back to the Dark Continent just under the deadline for their Out of Africa journey. A few years back, another ape, excavated near Barcelona, Spain, was heralded as further proof of Begun's theory. The researchers remained tight-lipped about what it all meant, but popular outlets found ways to get the point across, such as this sentence in a CBS News report: "The researchers sidestepped a controversy raging through the field by not claiming their find moves great ape evolution—and the emergence of humans—from Africa to Europe."

X. Kennewick's True Origins

Every once in a while, one of the science magazines will ask me-chanical engineers to consider the not-so-intelligent design of the human body. This chestnut of an article usually tells us that with a little more webbing in the toes we'd be great swimmers or that with slightly fleshier Yoda ears we'd be able to hear whispers a block away. These pieces usually make some reference to the naughty ob-servation that only a third-rate architect would run "a toxic waste line through a recreation area." We also learn that the spine is really a bit of jerry-rigging for an upright primate. A tube of flexible car-tilage would result in far fewer deaths and better protection for the core piping of the central nervous system. Add to the list that our knee joints aren't much to speak of, that our vision is actually fairly limited, and that our hips are oddly narrow (making child-birth nightmarish). If our shanks were longer, we wouldn't be writh-ing hobblers when we ran. Instead we'd resemble gazelles or, more likely, ostriches. Still, we'd be awesomely fast. But it never worked out that way. The body—with its Rice Krispies knees, stumpy tibia, and dainty ears—has merely gotten us by all these eons. So, here we are, like it or not, with a chassis that's . . . just fine, as is. We wish we didn't have to spend half our culture's resources on patching its grotty design, but what can you do already?

Our brain is like this too. Its perceptions are just as flawed in understanding the world as our body is in navigating it. Our species has a hard time wrapping its brain around this fact because we've devoted the last five thousand or so years of written history to con-vincing ourselves, through intense repetition, that we are the very best there is, the Xerox copy of an omnipotent deity. We are made in His image because nearly every Scripture and Holy Writ on earth includes that claim.

We can't shake the idea that the brain is special, the center of self and the storehouse of being. We want it to be constant, Gibraltar-ian, immortal. But just as we have come to terms with the idea that the human body is not the fixed, instantaneous creation of a celestial architect (or that the universe is not a massively static amphitheater), the same can also be said of our glorious brain.

Evolutionary science has shown us that the brain is a patched-up jalopy—an improvised, makeshift do-over. The brain is reliable enough to get you to the next place, but when you finally look under the hood, it's a little shocking to find a collection of barely successful workarounds and ad-hoc fixes using what appear to be the cerebral equivalent of baling twine, chewing gum, duct tape, and haywire. The reptilian stub got a big makeover during the mammalian period, with an overlay of the new limbic portion of the brain, and then later the more humany stuff known as the neocortal got plopped on top of that—each a series of fixes and patches of the previous networks. For instance, two parts of the brain that evolved with *Homo habilis* (literally, "handy man" because he was the first tool-making hominid) were the Broca's and Wernicke's areas, both crucial in putting things together to make tools. These parts of the brain evolved about two million years ago. Then, about one hundred thousand years ago, scientists now theorize, these tool-making portions of the brain were hot-wired and hijacked to form the centers of the complex human language you speak every day. That's how evolution works; parts get re-adapted for new uses ("exapted," in the jargon), or useless bits lying around ("spandrels," in that same jargon) suddenly get appropriated to new uses. Ancient chewing bones in the upper jaws of reptiles got taken over a good while back and now serve at the scaffolding of the middle ear—the incus, malleus, and stapes—that allows us to hear.

Evolution did not set us on a trajectory toward the *perfect* brain, the best possible brain, or even, arguably, a decent brain. Rather, we got the amateur version, the unendingly fiddled-with version, a flawed instrument just good enough to get us through to reproductive age. After that achievement, evolution occurs (or not) without a central mission, which might explain the onset of loopy eccentricity in middle-aged aunts and uncles.

Had that evolution failed, we would have gone the way of the Neanderthal or the Australopithecus, visible only in the fossil record. But the brain shambled its way through to right now. And so we live. Scientists studying the early brain have determined that on the savannahs of Africa, we developed thousands of shortcuts in the brain to gain a quick and usually accurate depiction of reality. Our ability to make snap judgments was very handy—evolutionarily. We oversimplify the world we see—and take shortcuts in the viewing of it—in order to make quick sense of it. These shortcuts are called "heuristics," and nowadays they can make navigating our way through a modern world, dominated by rational choice, quite dicey.

Take a quick one that we all hear our parents say when we're kids: "Know what you are looking for." It's easy to project how helpful that would have been a hundred thousand years ago, when the difficulty of getting food was such that being sidetracked even momentarily could rapidly become total failure or death. But today, when that primitive tic rears its ancient bias, it more likely means we miss all kinds of new opportunities. In fact, many of these ancient heuristics have survived the eons to form a kind of distortion field through which we perceive the universe. And it's only by looking at Kennewick through such a mirror that one can see anything like a wandering Caucasoid.

Take the most basic notion known as the fundamental attribution error: We are ourselves looking out at the world. That sounds fine, but it has serious and often unavoidable repercussions. When it comes to our own actions, we easily comprehend the state of affairs around us—the situation—because we are trapped in our bodies moving through time. But when we watch other people, we don't see their situation; rather, we see their bodies as discrete actors in the world. So we are much more likely to ascribe menacing personal motives to another's actions ("That guy who didn't do his homework is lazy"), while we are very understanding when judging ourselves ("I didn't do mine because of a family crisis"), sometimes extremely understanding ("My dog ate my homework").

I once hung out with an abortion doctor in the Dakotas as he went about his rounds. He told me that pro-life women are no less likely to have abortions than pro-choice women. He said he sometimes found the protesters in one town showing up as patients in the next town (and after the abortion they would go right back to hurling insults at him on the street). But when queried, the pro-life woman would explain away her own choice to abort, saying that her circumstances were unique and one needed to understand the pressures she was under. The other women having abortions? They were baby killers.

Experiments confirm this tendency in every human endeavor. According to Tom Gilovich, the author of *How We Know What Isn't So*, 25 percent of "college students believe they are in the top 1% in terms of their ability to get along with others." It's everybody else who's the asshole. According to the *Journal of the American Medical Association*, 85 percent of medical students believe politicians are behaving unethically when they accept gifts from lobbyists. But only about half as many medical students—46 percent—think it's unacceptable for doctors to receive similar goodies from drug companies. We can trust our kind, sort of, but definitely not the other kind. There are hundreds of studies yielding the same type of statistic (another medical study found that young doctors believe that 84 percent of their colleagues might be corrupted by pharmaceutical companies' freebies, but only 16 percent thought they *personally* were vulnerable).

We can excuse ourselves, literally, because we see so many legitimate excuses in front of us. Other people? Liars, baby killers, thieves. So are the Native Americans politically correct tools of the federal government? Are the scientists opportunistic liars relying on hokum to make an end run around the law? If you're on the other side, absolutely.

We naturally and easily create a world of order out of events that if examined more closely have other causes or, often, no discernible causes at all. Our ability to craft meaning out of non-meaning is impressive and no doubt has been fairly useful these last two hundred thousand years. But our view of reality, like everything, is not necessarily the best possible view, or even the "real" view—just the one that got us through to right now. The fact is that we see the world from inside this distortion field, and the more researchers study it, the more we learn just how twisted and tenacious it is.

These perceptual flaws now have many names, are being studied continuously, and have generated mountains of papers. The taxonomy of our flawed selves is an explosive and growing field and beginning to penetrate the world outside the lab. Many people have heard of the confirmation bias—the tendency to sort through evidence to confirm what we already know. That one has practically entered the common culture. Most days, it would appear that the Internet is little more than an exhausting orgy of confirmation bias.

There is a kingdom of graduate students and their notable mentors devising experiments to further understand dozens of fabulously named quirks: the Von Restorff Effect, the Status Quo Bias, Loss Aversion, the Semmelweis Reflex, the Déformation professionnelle, the Clustering Illusion, the Hawthorne Effect, the Ludic Fallacy, the Ostrich Effect, the Reminiscence Bump, Subjective Validation, the Texas Sharpshooter Fallacy, the Barnum Effect, Illusory Superiority, the Just-World Phenomenon, the Lake Wobegon Effect, the Outgroup Homogeneity Bias, the Availability Heuristic or the Informational Cascade.

One of the most important biases is called anchoring, the cognitive bias that tends to make most of us always lean toward the first notion we were exposed to. Scientists have discovered that we "anchor and adjust" our beliefs. In other words, we can never really cut off our relationship to that first big impression.

The most famous experiment is simple yet mind-boggling. Say I get people to spin a wheel imprinted with two numbers—15 and 65—and it lands on 15. Then I ask a completely unrelated question—How many African nations are members of the United Nations? Most will cluster their answers around the number in the spin. Crazy, but true. That line you heard from your mom about "always make a good first impression" is not only true but a kind of classic heuristic—i.e., a short nuggetlike axiom that long ago worked well for us but nowadays can lead us into a forest of nonsense. The anchoring tendency is so strong that business schools teach it as a fundamental exercise in negotiation theory. Always be the first to state a number in a salary negotiation. Why? Because the final number will, more often than not, cluster around the first number uttered.

With Kennewick, the anchor was that first racial utterance, a work of periphrastic art: "Caucasoid-like." We can discuss Kennewick all day long, but every conversation veers back to some aspect of this issue—whether he is or is not Caucasoid-like.

Humans are wired to see things even when they aren't there. This accounts for so many routine sightings of the Virgin Mary and Jesus and even Michael Jackson on toast, in the bark of trees, or in a photo of spaghetti. These sightings might sound ridiculous, but they are great examples of how the brain fills in the story we want to tell (or picture we want to see). Brain scientists will tell you that the medium for such appearances must always be grainy—like toast, tree bark, or a photo of smeared spaghetti sauce. A blurred medium will activate the portion of the brain that fills out a pattern into whatever the brain wants to see confirmed. In fact, often if you can't see the image, then squinting helps. Depriving the eye of the true specifics of the image allows the brain to fill in the image with its preconceptions, and there it is (like the blurry images of Bigfoot and the ivory-billed woodpecker). Has anyone ever wondered why, in a world where my local ice-cream parlor can print a high-pixel resolution image of my daughter's face into the icing of a chocolate cake, the Creator hasn't updated his tree bark appearances past the daguerreotype phase?

In the Kennewick controversy, this tendency to see Jesus in toast, technically known as pareidolia, is what explains the Solutrean Hypothesis. Only the theory's most devoted zealots see similarities between the Solutrean laurel leaf arrowhead and the Clovis point. Only those who most desire it can see in these few bits of stone an entire land-based culture that could have turned into sailors without any evidence; maritime *Homo sapiens* who left the countryside of Europe and managed to adapt overnight to Inuit-style living, camping on ice and fishing along the kelp highway. Even though the Solutreans disappeared some four thousand years *before* the appearance of Clovis, and even though they left no redundant evidence behind, if you look at these dissimilar stone tools, you can see their entire voyage right there in the flutes of the Clovis points.

But only if you squint.

The language used to describe Kennewick is thoroughly infected with many of these biases. One of the most powerful is called the self-esteem bias. That is, we more eagerly see things that flatter us than those that don't. Putting together a skull and nudging it a few millimeters here and there to make it more possible to see a "European" shape is a perfect example of the self-esteem bias on the part of white researchers.

Since there were a number of different ways to assemble the skull and one of them trended closer toward confirming what these researchers deeply wanted to see in the skull, the skilled scientist would certainly set up an experiment to work around this obvious tendency. If Chatters had sent precise molds of the skull to five different anthropologists and asked them to "assemble" it without telling them the age or the location of the finding and then asked them to explain what one might surmise from the skull—*then* you would have had an experiment and possibly a clear-eyed view of the skull. Instead putting it together yourself and then declaring that it just so happens to confirm what it is you so deeply long to see would make any cognitive scientist throw up her hands in despair.

The Kennewick court case itself is a classic example of another bias known as the Endowment Effect. Our ability to unconsciously create value for an object we are holding (or wish to hold) is impressive. A famous experiment demonstrating this effect involved giving free coffee mugs to people and selling them to other people. Later, when asked to sell them, people who had paid money for the mugs insisted on higher prices. People who were given the mugs didn't care so much.

Because everyone was struggling to retain control of the skull and bones, they not only had to be valuable, but that also tended to make people believe they had to be valuable in other ways. Of course the skeleton had to be unique proof of a European presence prior to paleo-Indians. Why else were the Indians fighting so hard to take possession of it?

Priming is the other cognitive bias that overwhelmed the popular media in this story from the beginning. For instance, if I asked you to think about your grandfather's death and then asked you to categorize words as "negative" or "positive" as I read off "happy," "singing," and "crying," you would more quickly categorize the word "crying" as negative because I had already primed your mind to be on the alert for negative things. This happens in all kinds of ways. But few of them are as textbook perfect as handing a reconstruction artist a skull with the explicit observation that you think the skull bears an uncanny resemblance to Patrick Stewart of *Star Trek*.

Two other errors make the case for Kennewick look absolutely solid. The Texas Sharpshooter Fallacy takes its name from someone shooting up the side of a barn before drawing a circle around the most clustered shots and then bragging about his bull's-eye aim. For Kennewick, it's roughly like finding a bone needle leagues away from the skeleton and concluding that the "explorer/trapper" must have worn "tailored" pants.

Most people believe that we are born into a world of illusion but grow out of it as adults. When we are kids, sure, we might believe the explanations of the *Just So Stories*, or that little men live in TV sets, or that tiny fairies dwell in a realm beneath the toadstools. But then a time comes when we matriculate to a view of the world that's more sophisticated. Culturally, we mark this coming of age in certain ways—the revelation of Santa Claus or the outing of the tooth fairy.

And then we are welcomed into the Cartesian world of adulthood, where we foolishly think we have entered a realm of logic and rational choice, a place where individuals make reasoned judgments about the world around them. What scientists are showing us is that while the common adult view of reality might be more empirically precise than a five-year-old's—it's not as precise as we want to believe. Academics have a name for the sloppy habits most adults have in their way of knowing the world, their epistemology. They call it a "makes sense epistemology." That is, most of us, once we determine a cause for something that "makes sense," rarely take the next step of a scientist—expose that idea to a test of some kind to see if we're off.

Academics have numerous ways of trying to look around our flawed biases. Regression analysis is a form of statistics that uses large collections of data regarding many individuals' actions to reveal the true movement of our hive, rather than relying on the august sentiments of elders. Now the Internet has organically developed several ways that group dynamics are performing a similar function.

The wiki—a technological platform that allows for a collective narrative to be written—has revealed all kinds of new or faster truths. It, too, has been derided as an assault on the very book of elder wisdom (*Encyclopedia Britannica*). Another more recent invention is the betting market. It turns out that creating a place where people with inside knowledge about events can win money by betting on that knowledge (think of the Iowa Electronic Markets, Intrade, NewsFutures) is another brilliant way to see past our prejudices and reveal the kinds of knowledge typically kept out of view. The attempt by the Bush administration to create a terrorism market—where terrorists could make money by revealing the most likely next targets—was canceled when people were offended by the possibility of rewarding terrorists in any way, even though the end result might be advance warning of another hit.

The oldest method to shake us out of our conceived universe is laughter. Needless to say, this has been studied! Solemnity and gravitas, while looking great on the face of an ancient professor, turn out to be a form of intellectual prison. Let's go to the experiment: Give someone a corkboard on a wall, a box of thumbtacks, and a candle—then tell them to fasten the candle to the board. Overwhelmingly, most people will try to tack the candle to the board or light the candle and use hot wax to affix it. But neither works. Now show a similar group a Laurel and Hardy movie before the assignment, and creativity increases. Many of them will empty the tack box, pin the box to the board, and put the candle in it.

Other studies have confirmed just how solemnity (and its partner, overconfidence) in one's knowledge is deeply related to being correct in one's views. But it's an inverse relationship. The more confident one is in one's views, the more likely one is to be flat wrong. An in-depth survey of pundits on television charted two elements of their presentation—their accuracy in prediction and the display of confidence in their opinions. Perhaps it will come as no surprise that survival in the pundit mosh pit on television is linked directly to the pundit's level of blowhardiness. The more absolutely certain a pundit was in couching a view, however, the more likely that opinion was found to be wrong. All pundits, in this way, bear a strong resemblance to Michael Gary Scott of *The Office*. Yet, all that said, the bubble of television information thrives on the "confidence bias"— our own flawed preference for blustery self-assurance in the present tense rather than spot-on accuracy down the road.

All these cognitive biases, from the fundamental attribution error to the confidence bias, come together at the end of this story in what's known as an informational cascade. Typically the term describes how the same choice repeated by others just bandwagons without anyone pausing to make an independent judgment. In the Kennewick cascade, though, there were tiny tweaks all along the way—from the assembly of the skull to the detonation of the word-esque substance "Caucasoid-like" to the numerous stories about Kennewick's "family" fleeing the savage "hordes." The accumulation of errors gathered and increased, forming a cascade of faux evidence that for many, many people constituted a perfect proof.

Despite all the distortion involved in trying to see the world for what it is and in creating new ideas that are real enough to be repeated by others, there do emerge a set of rules from the best amateur pursuits. First, start at the beginning. All the assumptions of even the best experts are infected with their own prejudices and biases. If you are Steven Jobs in a garage in Cupertino in 1976, then you don't need to know or listen to the wisdom of, say, IBM chief Watson, who once cockily said: "I think there is a world market for about five computers."

Second, enter your literal or metaphorical garage in a sense of play. It almost doesn't bear saying: The garage is a place of play, both when we are kids and as middle-aged grown-ups desperate to escape the bills and solemnity and tedium of "the house." The garage is an outpost of joy, love, and freedom, which is why it long ago achieved mythic status as the fountainhead of amateur American creativity. But it's that playful, supple state of mind that's key. Why else do corporations spend so much time putting their executives on six-person bicycles or sending them off on retreats to smash the tedium of familiar thinking? Getting people into a state of playfulness is almost impossible. Amateurs enjoy the luxury of starting there.

Finally, there has to be an outside world of peers that you connect to who can keep you from getting sidetracked by your own or your culture's biases. Scientists operating at the professional level do this through peer review. Amateurs can accomplish the same by joining weekend hobbyist groups, like the old robot clubs, where folks show off their latest creations and get critiques from friendly peers who want to make it better. Or perhaps you join a newsletter or subscribe to *Make* magazine or sign on with a DIY group or contribute along with others to a wiki devoted to your pursuit.

However one gets all the way back to the beginning of an idea, banishes crushing solemnity, and creates a small-scale community to keep it honest, you have to get there. Otherwise, you may find yourself looking at the *Rashomon* shape of a skull and seeing an itinerant European wandering the estuaries of the Pacific Northwest.

XI. A Caucasian Homecoming

The question of just when we became human gets answered in our popular press all the time. Was it when we assembled the first rudimentary tool kit or grunted out the few phonemes of complex language? Was it when we made those paintings in Altamira and Lascaux, or when we left off being knuckle-dragging ape-like critters and stood up? Was the aquatic ape somehow involved? It's one of those lines that doesn't exist as a moment in time, but as an idea it does exist, and various scientists routinely make claims. Not long ago, a British scholar named Jonathan Kingdon laid out a new theory—about why we stood up—in his book *Lowly Origin*.

"Standing up" has been a particularly fertile field for this kind of musing, with theories ranging from cooling off to intimidating other species or freeing the hands. I'd always heard that we abandoned squatting because we wanted to see over the top of the grass on the African savannahs. One early 1980s theory was that standing evolved for "phallic display directed at females." (Were this the case, every creature in nature, down to the ameoba, would stand, and the great outdoors would be a very animated place.)

Kingdon plods through a different argument. It's dense and slow. Standing up, he says, probably had a lot to do with getting food and happened in undramatic stages, first by straightening the back while squatting and later extending the legs—all of this happening over vast swaths of time in tiny incremental stages. As theories go, that's not nearly as fun as "seeing over the grass," but it has the ring of truth to it, a ring that, let's face it, never will endear such an idea to writers of newsweekly cover lines or green-lighters of movies of the week. Which is also why you've never heard of Jonathan Kingdon.

Scientists like to invoke Occam's Razor, the principle that the simplest explanation is often the most truthful. The principle was born during the Age of Reason when logical thought was trying to cut through the intellectual encrustation accrued after millennia of seeing nature through both Holy Scripture and the blowhardiness of intellectuals trying to impress one another with their sesquipedalianismo.

These days we have a different, almost opposite problem. Pop thinkers tend to oversimplify in a way meant to attract attention. The first time I ever got a whiff of this was when I was a teenager reading Desmond Morris's book *The Naked Ape*. Morris theorized that the reason human females had big breasts (as opposed to the tiny sagging dugs of other primates) was because we had discovered love. In doing so, we switched from copulating doggie style to the more romantic missionary position. But all those millennia of looking at the round globes of the female's buttocks from behind had also developed into the image stimulus required for the maintenance of erections during intercourse. Morris argued that the male still needed large rounded visual cues so, according to the rules of Darwin, we were rewarded with great big hooters.

Even as a kid, I remember thinking, Excellent, but really? Morris's simplicity makes monstrous assumptions that just so happen to yield a theory pre-edited for the short, punchy demands of modern mass media. A hook, if you will. (Not that it didn't work: Thirty years after reading that book, the only detail I can remember is the boob theory.) Morris's theory has little to do with truth and everything to do with selling books. Perhaps it's time to set aside Occam's Razor and pick up Morris's Razor, which shuns any theory that might excite a cable television producer while simultaneously elevating the plodding theory that makes a kind of dull, honest sense.

Apply Morris's Razor to Kennewick Man and here's what you

might get: Chances are Adovasio and his colleagues are right about the basic assertion of an ancient arrival of *Homo sapiens* to this continent. For instance, the archaeological record in Australia is redundant with proof that aboriginals arrived there at least fifty thousand years ago. That journey would have required boating some eighty miles, many believe. So there's nothing extraordinary about there possibly being multiple entries to the American continent, with at least one crew, probably Asians like the Ainu, lugging their haplogroup X into North America some twenty to thirty thousand years ago, giving them plenty of time to leave some pre-Clovis fossils.

Sure.

That's one story, a very Kingdon-like theory, all very probable but not a very good cable special or science magazine cover story. The Morris Razor, though, discards the other bits where the First American is of an ancient tribe (that just happens to physically resemble the very scientists making the claim) whose sad end came after a genocidal campaign between superior but outnumbered Caucasoids and hordes of Mongoloid "Stone Age peoples." This epic extrapolation is drawn from one single Cascade point, a leap about as likely as a Martian anthropologist staring at a scrap of gray wool, an Enfield bullet, and a dinged canteen and then successfully imagining the states' rights debate of the Civil War.

The same Martian anthropologist might also quarrel with the view that the Kennewick battle is a latter-day clash between science and religion—the Indians with their childishly mythic stories of origin and the scientists with their lithics and their scientific dates, 8700 ± 50 years. In an editorial a while back, the *Seattle Times* captured half the fight perfectly. Kennewick had "held onto his secrets for more than 9,000 years and now, finally, scientists will get a chance to be his voice."

Why assume the scientists' narrative in this case is closer to the empirical truth? In fact, if you know the history of archaeology, you know that there are times when one can find more objective, hard factual truth in the local oral narratives than in the scientists' analysis. This may well be one of those times. The Indians make the argument that their creationist stories are the truth that they believe in. Every culture had its founding stories. Those myths can sometimes be decoded to reveal the nuggets of ancient journalistic truth that set them in play, just as Helge Ingstad's devotion to finding the truth buried in the Viking sagas eventually led to the confirming archaeological digs at L'Anse aux Meadows in Newfoundland.

There are several Indian creation stories about coming out of ice. The Paiute tell one that ends this way:

> Ice had formed ahead of them, and it reached all the way to the sky. The people could not cross it. . . . A Raven flew up and struck the ice and cracked it. Coyote said, "These small people can't get across the ice." Another Raven flew up again and cracked the ice again. Coyote said, "Try again, try again." Raven flew up again and broke the ice. The people ran across.

Many Native American origin accounts involve coming out of ice, which certainly fits into all the theories of America's human origins. So why aren't these stories studied the way Ingstad examined his own sagas? Why is the benefit of the doubt given to the scientists' story? It's quite possible that every objective fact that went into the telling of this new "scientific" pre-Clovis story is not true at all—only a factoidlike projection of racial anxiety—and are more "mythic" than the creation story the Indians are telling.

Part of the problem of reading either of these stories is that we no longer have a capacity to appreciate the real power of myth. Most of us are reared to think of myth as an anthology of dead stories of some long-ago culture: Edith Hamilton making bedtime stories out of Greek myths; Richard Wagner making art out of Norse myth; fundamentalist Christians making trouble out of Scripture.

When we read ancient stories or Holy Writ or founding epics, we forget that the original audience who heard these accounts did not differentiate between mythic and factual storytelling. Nor did these stories have authors, as we conceive them. Stories arose from the collective culture, accrued a kind of truth over time. For that reason alone, they were sacred and had real power to move people. Belief is what keeps any tribe together.

Today we've split storytelling into two modes—fiction and nonfiction. And we've split our reading that way as well.

The idea of the lone author writing truth has completely vanquished the other side of storytelling—the collectively conjured account. I think we still have these stories, but we just don't recognize them for what they are. Tiny anxieties show up as urban legends. In the late 1980s when the queasily mortal idea of organ donation was infiltrating the social mainstream, suddenly one heard an author-less story of a man waking up in a Times Square flat after a night of partying to find a stitched wound on his lower back and his kidney missing.

Enduring myth can be based on fact, as in Ingstad's case. But often the collective account needs no factual basis, just a mild apprehension that the world is not quite what it seems. No one has ever found a razor blade in an apple at Halloween, nor has any doctor treated anyone for gerbilling. Bill Gates is not giving away computers, and the sewers of New York are gator-free. The story of the Ancient European One is this kind of story, toggling back and forth between the world of fiction and nonfiction, authored by a few curious facts and the collective anxiety of the majority.

Because we no longer read mythological stories, we no longer appreciate their immense power. We find ourselves stunned at how something so many deeply long to be true will simply assemble itself into fact right before our eyes. The scientists who eventually won control of Kennewick's bones have been studying them now for ten years. What have they learned? Well, they don't like to talk about it much. The only new idea that has been made public is an analysis of levels of mineral deposits in the bones, suggesting Kennewick was buried intentionally. Great.

More recently, Chatters has reverted to his incoherent ways, happily agreeing that the anachronistic word "European" aptly describes the skeleton. I've heard him celebrate "Solutrean Pride" and cheerfully joke with racist radio hosts who sneeringly refer to Native Americans as "Berengians" and guffaw at declaring February to be "Solutrean History Month." The scientists have discovered almost nothing of Kennewick, but the growing band of amateurs they set loose have conjured a new and powerful creation myth. And if they profoundly long to believe that men of Caucasoid extraction toured here sixteen thousand years ago in Savile Row suits, ate gourmet cuisine, and explored the Pacific Northwest with their intact pre-Christianized families until the marauding horde of war-whooping Mongoloid injuns came descending pell-mell from their tribal haunts to drive Cascade points into European hips until they fell, one after another, in the earliest and most pitiful campaign of ethnic cleansing, then that is what science will painstakingly prove, that is what the high courts will evenhandedly affirm, and that is what in time ever more amateurs will happily come to believe.

6

EYEING HEAVEN

I. The Pasture at the End of the Universe

In the crane shot of this moment, from high above the walnut trees in a large backyard in rural Oregon, the camera would come in on a ninety-two-year-old hippie, with long, snowy hair neatly tied off in a perfect ponytail, lightly bobbing up and down on tiptoes all around a workbench—capering, really, like a geriatric satyr. Seated at that workbench is his student, me, sweating in a T-shirt and scrubbing what looks like a two-layer cake made of opaque glass.

"No, NO, NO!" he screams. "Straight up and down! Along the sides!" His voice is so attenuated with age it registers as an old woman's. You might think he is in a true fit of pique, except that it's impossible to miss the sly grin occasionally cracking through his chiseled face. Fit and svelte, with an elfin body, the old man has on Air Max Nikes with a nicely creased pair of khakis tucked into high white athletic socks. Despite the warm summer air, he wears a billowing

North Face jacket. He reminds me constantly that I am embarking on serious work—the figuring of a telescope lens—a piece of work that will, in the end, require that my range of error be "one-one-thousandth the width of Saran Wrap." His name is John Dobson, and he is probably the most famous and successful amateur anything. A former monk of the Ramakrishna Order in the Vedanta Monastery in San Francisco, Dobson was kicked out some sixty years ago for not devoting enough time to his commitment but also because he realized that his cosmological desire in life was not to contemplate the universe but to teach others how to look at it—with really cheap, really big, easily made telescopes.

At the time he started, in the mid-1950s, the only kind of telescope one could get readily was the store-bought model often advertised in the back of magazines and comic books. It stood on an aluminum tripod and was a tube a little thicker than a paper-towel roll. The mirror—the key piece of any telescope—might be two inches in diameter. If you were lucky and your daddy rich, you might get one that was four inches. The piece of glass I am beginning to shape—"Straight up and down! Straight up and down!"—is fourteen inches in diameter. (It's the difference between seeing a big fat moon in your eyepiece and seeing the granular texture inside a crater on that moon.)

Before Dobson came along, if you wanted a bigger telescope, it was possible to build it yourself. The classic text was Jean Texereau's *How to Make a Telescope*, published in English in 1957. Here's the chapter summary covering what I'm doing right now:

2. MAKING THE MAIN MIRROR

2.1. Form of the Main Mirror in the Newtonian Telescope

2.2. Working of Optical Surfaces & Theories Concerning Polishing

2.3. The Mirror Blank and Tool

So I'll take the yelling.

Half a century ago, when the world first began to notice the corner of Haight and Ashbury streets, Dobson made the classic amateur move. He took a technological process that years of expert exclusivity had led everyone to assume was abstruse and esoteric, and he made it simple and available. (Although he did it, not on Haight, but a little farther north, near the Presidio, at the corner of Broderick and Jackson.) Where serious astronomers insisted on certain types of glass and procedures and mounts, Dobson figured out that with a cheap piece of porthole glass, some sand, a large cardboard tube, and an eyepiece unscrewed from a pair of used binoculars at the Salvation Army, he could jimmy together a telescope that rivaled those found in major universities. In the intervening half century, Dobson has inspired generations of uncredentialed enthusiasts to prowl the heavens.

While it's worth stating the obvious—that the university professors of astronomy and the big guns at NASA, the European Space Agency, and increasingly the Chinese National Space Agency are the primary leaders in astronomical exploration—there is a Dobsonian army of amateurs out there, and their current work is changing once again the nature of the backyard telescope and even some of the cutting edge issues regarding outer space.

The essence of a good telescope mirror hasn't really changed since Galileo shaped an objective lens out of glass and formed the kind of telescope (refractor, to get technical) once called a spyglass and now associated with pirates. During the Enlightenment it also became popular to grind a concave curve into a piece of glass and then silver-coat it into a mirror (a reflector) that could focus the image and throw it to an eyepiece and then to your eyeball. The trick was to scoop out this chunk of glass to form a parabolic dimple and do it precisely. Dobson began with the simple idea that if you rub one blank piece of glass, as flat and round as a layer of cake, onto another with certain repetitive motions ("straight up and down" and "along the sides, you're going to ruin this thing!"), one piece of glass will develop an indentation, which will eventually become your mirror. The other piece will develop a bulge and become what is known as your "tool."

This work is advanced by tossing some sand in there to scour the glass. When Dobson started doing this, he got regular sand and sifted it himself into various sizes using different gauges of window screens. Now he's upgraded to buying Carborundum, a fine black grit that comes in extremely precise gauges—80 Carborundum is sifted through a screen that has eighty tiny holes per inch. A teaspoon of Carborundum sprinkled on the glass with a little cool water is like setting thousands of little blades to work with each stroke. As the mirror gets closer and closer to the final shape, the gauge of Carborundum increases to, say, 900. This is why when Dobson refers to error margins measured in fractions of Saran Wrap thickness, he means it.

When I plunked the top piece of glass onto the other and he heard a glassy click, Dobson freaked.

"No, NO, NO," shouted my guru, back in his normal rant state. "Slide it on, don't drop it." He bobbled off, huffing and muttering like a querulous grandmother. I hurled myself, carefully, back into my work. Getting this mirror into shape would take about three days of sweat equity. I applied the grit and started pushing the heavy glass up and down. It made a monstrous noise, so I often could barely make out Dobson's reedy voice as he changed tempo to one of merry commentary. "Carborundum is star dust. We're using star dust to look at star dust," he said, in one of his many Zen koan–like notes. Carborundum is silicon carbide, he explained, manufactured naturally in the Orion nebula.

"We get ours at a closer outlet," he chirped. Dobson speaks in a singsong voice when he's in commentary mode. It's a prophet's voice. "Star dust, we are," he actually said to me. Our pop culture has made it mandatory that all gurus affect a singular style, but I see now that this is based on reality. Dobson shifts in and out of several modes, like pull-stops on a mood organ: cosmic paradoxes, corny jokes, and fake volcanic rage—the standard rhetorical strategies of most gurus, I suspect, from Plato to Yoda.

These bubbly koans and rehearsed rages constitute an evolved efficiency born of five decades of telescope making. He knows where all the common mistakes are made, and he's fine-tuned the tactics of teaching others to avoid them into an obscure art form. He talked to me constantly throughout my work, filling my head with deep-space factoids while simultaneously flogging me like a galley master. It was really hard work, and I would have to do it. The result in the end would have been a near miracle in every other century: to look through my own keyhole at the outer reaches of the known universe.

The decibel volume of the grit started to die down, and the stuff began to cream into a kind of gray slurry. I rinsed off the mirror and the tool. I grabbed my small cup of black Carborundum and applied a fresh sprinkling across the glass with a dab of water. Again the volume cranked up as Dobson gamboled off, puckishly prancing in a distant part of a backyard that was more like a field. Way out at the edge, he held up some green that he'd plucked from the ground.

"Do you know what this is?" he howled above the Carborundum's abrasive roar. I suggested dandelion, and instantly I could see his disbelief that I would guess something that ridiculous. He put it in his mouth. Apparently, it was edible. He shouted something, another witheringly amicable put-down. He turned his back to me and picked some more green from the yard and continued on the prowl for a half hour. I had signed on for almost a week of this—never suspecting that my nonagenarian telescope guru was someone whose idea of lunch involved grazing.

II. The Big Surrender

One afternoon, when I was a sophomore in college, I bumped into a friend at the library. He told me that there was going to be a big lecture by a prominent professor flown in from California. It was a talk intended to coax undeclared students into science and had a wry title like "The Outer Limits of the Universe: A Tour."

"Let's get stoned," my friend cackled, "and go." If you've seen the movie *2001: A Space Odyssey*, then you know that for a certain generation, the universe was marketed to the bourgeoisie mostly as a cool light show, a slightly more mind-blowing version of the strobe-light spectacular that had become routine at Deep Purple concerts. Instead of music, there were mind-bending facts or dimensions of scale that were, to our feeble brains, entertainingly incomprehensible. When an astronomer says that a solar system is sixty trillion miles away or that it would take the Apollo spacecraft traveling to a certain galaxy a billion billion billion lifetimes to get there, what precisely is getting conveyed that's any more precise than a six-year-old's "gajillion"? Maybe it *is* best to be stoned for such lectures.

That night, we took our seats and the professor did not disappoint. He had lots of amazing slides of spiral galaxies, psychedelic nebulae, and re-creations of exploding stars. At one point, with the lights dim and some wild image on the enormous screen, he started talking about quasars, those extremely distant and extremely powerful sources of light.

"Here," he said, flashing up a single tiny dot of light in a field of woolly stars, "is the quasar that is the farthest out object we have ever seen with a telescope. It is, literally, the edge of the known universe." He let that sink in.

"And how far away is it? Consider that light travels at 186,000 miles per second. That means that in a single second, light can circle the earth seven times. We call that distance a light-second." He let that sink in.

He changed the slide to something a little trippier, but still, there was that far-off quasar: "A light-second is a measure of distance for astronomers, not time. A light-minute is the distance light travels in one minute. The sun is a bit more than eight light-minutes away from the earth."

Another image appeared. The room was caught in a lovely haze (or maybe a lot of people prepared for the talk the same way I had). "We also have a light-day. We can talk about a light-week. And we have the light-year, the most well-known interstellar measurement of distance. Try to imagine that distance. Light traveling 186,000 miles per second for an entire year. Proxima Centauri is the closest star outside our solar system, and it is just over four light-years away. Imagine that distance. Light zinging through space for more than four years."

He paused again, letting his incremental description build and set. Then he pointed to the quasar dot in the image. "This quasar is 130 million light-*centuries* away from earth."

Poof! If the other people in the room weren't stoned, they were now. And it was true then—and is still true—that conjuring this effect is the essence of good space writing. Can you jar loose that childlike sense of wonder? That has always been the lure of a good telescope. It's not hard to do when you bring your eye down to that lens—when you see Saturn as if it were a distant mountain range. In the same way that the big surrender of a giant movie theater practically locates us in that most intimate space of the beautiful actors on the screen, a good telescope creates a kind of proximity, reeling in these remote locations such that it seems as if we have traveled out to their vicinity. Every time I squint into an eyepiece, I still feel that—let's call it a collegiate sense of awe—and the fresh sensation of being out of body, off the earth, up in space.

Astronomers have a term of art called "seeing." It's meant to describe the conditions in which one can break free of visual obstacles—earth's atmospheric turbulence, varying temperatures, and even wind speeds—and get a real good eyeful of what we came for: mind-boggling frontier, outer-limit space. "The seeing is good tonight," an astronomer will say. What they are trying to see is really not all that different from what people have attempted to see since the dawn of astronomy—as far into the distance as possible, with the hope of understanding, of finding something new.

It's the lure of astronomy but it's also why this field has drawn a steady pilgrimage of self-taught sky-buffs for the last half millennium. Here is the original proof of wonder and the primal motive of the amateur: the seeing, the seeing for oneself.

The amateurs have come and continue to come. If one thinks of organized sports as the most mature pro-am relationship, then astronomy probably occupies second place. It's crowded with different kinds of amateurs: the phalanx of volunteers willing to perform the donkey work of astronomy—to confirm and reconfirm the location of variable stars, or hunt for supernovae, or scour the barely discernible blinks and wobbles of faraway stars suggestive of an exoplanet. And there are other kinds, the ambitious amateurs struggling to crack the ranks of pro with the DIY observations that they manage to have published, as well as a few truly innovative thinkers, devising new theories or creating new equipment.

The amateurs come for another, simple reason. Ever since Galileo, the gear one needs can be put together at home with a few accessible items and a little elbow grease (actually, now that I know, massive amounts of elbow grease). As a result, it didn't take me long to find another set of innovators, literally in their garages, trying to cast new telescope mirrors. They noticed that the average Dobsonian is, say, twelve to fourteen inches in diameter. And the professional telescopes at the other end of the spectrum are simply monstrous: The Large Binocular Telescope in Arizona today has a mirror wide enough that Shamu the whale could easily stretch out on it. So the latest crowd of self-made opportunists are populating a new niche—the world of astronomy that aspires to mirrors a bit larger than, say, a hula hoop. And with that size come entire geographies of sky-gazing that are largely ignored.

Their innovations are ingenious—involving recycled glass, TV wall mounts, and parts from Radio Shack. Among these, I found one amateur astronomer in particular who has been studying the most recent discoveries of certain far-off planets and has ginned up one of the most provocative ideas to speed our success in making contact with extraterrestrials.

III. The Last Hippie

The second night I spent with Dobson in Oregon, every muscle in my upper arms and across my back ached fiercely, so we decided to call it a day in the late afternoon. The sun had angled down far enough that we could feel no guilt about goofing off a bit. We hosed down our bench, covered my lens with a towel, and stepped inside.

Our host, Garth, had made oxtail stew. Dobson was off getting ready for dinner in his room. Garth and I talked recipes until we got around to Dobson.

"He comes through once or so a year," he told me. "He'll arrange a lens-grinding class somewhere and then sleep at a friend's house." It's a simple system and one that Dobson has been using for forty years. He has friends, essentially, everywhere. He's never patented anything, and he takes a decent cut of the class fees for his organization. "Sidewalk Astronomers"—named to distinguish the very public aspect of Dobson's mission and to pose a contrast to the elite and solitary nature of what preceded him, "backyard astronomy"—now has chapters all over the world. Dobson is not only one of the very original hippies, he may be the only one who never got sidetracked by fame, drugs, or wealth.

He may have quit the monastery, but the ascetic life to which he committed himself as a young man, he continues to live. He sleeps on people's floors and lives mainly off what he makes teaching a class. Dobson is one of a great type in this country—known over the years as colonial frontiersman, cowboy, hobo, hippie, RV roamer. Among these drifters, though, one finds a subset who are uniquely American. When one thinks about the ponytailed John Dobson flitting about the wide-open skies of America, teaching the secret of building a telescope, it's hard not to recall his spiritual kinsmen—Johnny Appleseed, John Harvey Kellogg, Charles Atlas. There exists a type of self-invented American obsessive who becomes seized by the genius of a single idea—apples, grains, fitness—and devotes the rest of his life to an itinerant evangelism.

John Chapman elevated his pseudonym, Johnny Appleseed, into a name both legendary and majestic. Likewise the stargazing hippie has become a monumental noun: "I am building a Dobsonian." The word is used to describe an entire phylum of telescopes now. It's a word that resonates with "Newtonian" and carries, perhaps unfairly, that level of gravitas.

When Dobson abandoned monastic prayer for telescope prosely-tizing, he attracted a few disciples. Eventually they obtained a school bus and traveled around the way Johnny Appleseed did, moving from town to town, leaving homemade telescopes in their wake. It's im-portant to remember that, at the time, anyone with a passion to gaze at the stars beyond a late night meditation was limited to those store-bought two-inchers. Then, here comes to town the crazy hippie with his pile of cheap porthole glass, a cardboard tube, and some sand. He would set up one of his cardboard telescopes on a street corner and invite views with a patter that was half carnival barker and half Upanishad. "Would you like to walk on the moon?" he might say. (Dobson told me: "Always approach the girls; they'll listen and then drag their reluctant boyfriends along.") Afterward he would make the case for attending one of his telescope classes. Suddenly, you could spend a few days laboring away with like-minded people and, when it was over, own a twelve-inch telescope. Imagine you had grown up walking around your town, dreaming one day of owning a really nice bicycle, and then along came a guy who offered to help you hand-build a working Formula 1 dragster.

Dobson would pull into parks, attract his followers, and set up all-night star parties. Once, upon his entering a national park, a guard tried to turn him away, saying that the sky was not part of the park. Yes, the cavorting guru replied, but "the park is part of the sky." These gatherings date back several centuries, actually, but their current popularity owes a great deal to Dobson. The annual Stella-fane star party in Vermont attracts more than three thousand people every summer. The homemade telescope enthusiasts who congregate at star parties dwell in what is colloquially known as the Valley of the Dobs.

After dinner in Oregon, the old man escorted me outside. Garth's Dobsonian was set up next to the street. The really nice thing about a Dobsonian is that the entire cardboard gizmo is set on a gimbal made of plywood. It both rocks up and down and swivels left and right easily (spinning typically on a slick vinyl LP bought, as mine was, at a garage sale for a dime). The two simple motions mean that you can just point the telescope anywhere you want with great ease and start focusing. After fiddling with the eyepiece, Dobson stepped back.

There was the moon's surface up close. The craters were scattered atop a smooth, dusty plateau, creating a landscape that, at this level of intimacy, seemed familiar—reminiscent of a time-lapse photo of the aftermath of a drop splashing in a bowl of milk. I could imagine myself walking on that moon dust, the notoriously powdery regolith that makes the surface feel like a treeless prairie after a dust storm.

I could hear Dobson and Garth almost laughing at my cries of joy, the pleasure of good "seeing." I was reminded that at the Sistine Chapel, there are guards whose job entails quieting the crowds' groans because often in the inevitable crescendo, this ambient sound becomes increasingly obscene. But the sounds in Rome are people observing man-made beauty and art, experiencing awe.

We don't really have a good vocabulary for what was happening when I peered closely at those craters, which is the precise opposite of the Sistine sensation, the inverse of wonder. What's happening inside the tiny space of that eyepiece is understanding, a kind of knowing, a bite of the apple. The mysterious object in the night sky becomes instantly intimate. You can familiarize yourself with the place. Walk around it a bit. Get to know it. Imagine yourself running the dusty plains or leaping into a milk-drop crater. These are not so much groans of wonder as yips of orientation.

Ah, I see where I am now.

When I pulled back, Dobson spun the telescope toward Saturn. We talked a bit about the Cassini Division, the black line that's sometimes visible there. Dobson focused the telescope, as he has tens of thousands of times.

"Here," he said, in one of his rare koan-free moments, "I want you to see this." It didn't take much time at all, and it was the precise effect Dobson has been arranging on street corners for decades. In a few seconds, I was leaping across the Cassini line, a line as wide as the continental United States. It was an incredible sensation: Saturn was no longer a planet, but a place.

IV. The Cosmos, Updated

If you had one million pictures of one million galaxies and you wanted to organize them in folders by type, how would you go about it? If you spent fifteen minutes on each image—trying to decide what kind of galaxy it was, spiral or elliptical, and whether it contained any notable irregularities and novelties—then, given an eight-hour workday with no vacation time, it would take an average lifetime and then some—eighty-six years. So you think, maybe, I'll hire a staff. But even with a crew of ten, nine years seems a long time for such grueling, mind-numbing work.

What would really work a lot better? A staff of 230,000.

In the late '00s, when scientists set up a website called Galaxy Zoo and invited amateur astronomers from all over the world to sign in and classify images, that is what happened.

Communities formed around some of these efforts. One of them created a fellowship around a couple of peculiar galaxies that were pretty small and oddly colored, like little emeralds in the distant sky. They became known playfully as the Green Peas. The amateurs who spotted them in the images called themselves the Peas Corps and their online thread where they discussed their observations was slugged, "Give peas a chance."

In time, they realized that they had found something new. In the grade-school textbooks, for the longest time, galaxies came in two classical types, spiral and elliptical. But the old sober idiom is giving way to new terms as discoveries increasingly familiarize us with a universe that now has newer and more names: irregular, ring, ventricular, starburst, and now, the Peas Corps has contributed its own goofball name, as so often happens in a profession distinguished by amateurism. "Green Pea galaxy" is now the term of art used to describe an intense kelly green star factory that has one-one-thousandth the mass of our Milky Way but is pumping out ten stars for our every one.

The dark sky has always been every culture's final frontier and its first palimpsest. Professional astronomers may consider themselves the primary authors of it, but every culture writes and rewrites all over it, thinking, theorizing, seeing, dreaming. The metaphors have changed radically. The universe is such a different place now from the languid Kubrickian void of the previous generation. That serene expanse of totally cool collegiate space that might be a speck under the fingernail of a giant is, today, a much more knowable, mapable, named, and landmarked cosmic jungle. We now live in a wild and violent place where normal stars are occasionally consumed by stellar zombies; where a cosmic drive-by can cause "resident stripping," furiously yanking the guts from a dwarf galaxy, resulting in a billion-mile slough of stellar litter; where a patch of darkness might suddenly reveal the wreckage of a "vampire star"; where entire galaxies of four hundred billion stars can collide with another of comparable size in a "galactic smashup" or where dozens of them can pile up because a monstrous "cannibal galaxy" appears driven to consume its neighbors; where our own Milky Way is now known to be on a 300,000-miles-per-hour collision course with our neighbor galaxy Andromeda, which will result in a new galaxy already nicknamed—Milkomeda—that will unavoidably come into existence in about four billion years.

All of this violence happens in a universe of incomparable extremes—one that is, when resting, just under 3°K and, at its most violent, churns temperatures of 100,000,000°K. The current general theory of the universe literally holds that 96 percent of all material stuff—dark matter and dark energy—cannot refract light, so it's invisible. Dark matter is there but we cannot see it. Of all the matter in the universe, the remaining 4 percent is called baryonic matter because the baryon is the heavy bit in an atomic nucleus and is considered (this week) basic to the construction of all visible matter. These intermittent flecks of visible stuff bunch up—a process known ponderously as "baryonic acoustic oscillation." Whatever forms those clumpings eventually take—stars, planets, rocky asteroids and comets, gassy nebulae, our bodies—the sum total of it all is still, essentially, only 4 percent of the matter in the universe, the only visible stuff out there, and all of it is composed of space lint.

The universe, then, as we see it, is but a few shards of exploding flotsam and collapsing jetsam bobbing along in a vast and expanding ocean of ghostly motes. Occasionally amid the violent jets of plasma and colliding galaxies and rogue black holes, a spurt of stellar dust will gather in the tug of a medium star and for hundreds of millions of years begin to clump together into little dust bunnies until these smack together into "planetary embryos" and then condense into planets, which cool as tiny greenhouses nursing elements other than the universe's tedious streams of hydrogen.

We think of the earth or our gas giants such as Jupiter as the only models for what a planet might look like, for obvious reasons, but recent discoveries suggest that exoplanets might be dominated by different elements, so that on distant planets we might find plateaus marked by lakes of methane, or oceans of ammonia, or rainstorms that extrude droplets of molten rock.

But perhaps as rarely, a planet might form around the dominance of carbon, and there, in an isolated tiny fold at the edge of a spur off a spiral arm of a galaxy, the necessary insulation of improbable distances and statistically arcane geographies might cool the entire system to a temperature somewhat on the more habitable side of 100,000,000°K. In that wan blemish of the time-space continuum, earthlike conditions form and then, equally unlikely, give rise to life and then, perhaps extremely less likely, conscious life. Some have examined these stunning odds and concluded that the purpose of the universe is not merely to rarely burp up a fleck of life, but that intelligent life is destined to dominate the universe. This theory is known as the Anthropic Principle—this idea that the purpose of the universe is to birth life like us and permit us to be fruitful and multiply. This theory has its dissidents, among them Martin Gardner, who before his death argued that the universe is not plagued by intentions and purpose. Gardner gave his idea a scientific name, the Completely Ridiculous Anthropic Principle, the acronym for which the audience would figure out on their way out the door.

Every day, it seems, the universe is revealed to be a new place, with novel fields of study, such as "celestial mechanics," and new forms of hypothetical energy: "quintessence." Recently astronomers collected dust grains pelting our upper atmosphere probably from a star called "Beta Pictoris" some sixty light-years away and which may be the source of the origin of life here—jibing with the old but still surreal theory of panspermia. This dust is not to be confused with an even more exquisite dust called "Ultra Primitive Material"—a trail of which we happened to pass through in 2003, alleged to be the original dust that became our solar system and was preserved, bound up in cometary ice. And this is not to be confused with pre-solar grains—even older, dustier dust. When the clergyman says that "of dust we are made and to dust we shall return," he has little idea just how cosmically true it is. His language is metaphorical, grand, even sentimental, but the world that is rapidly coming into focus is not. Dust to dust, only the blip in between is the universe.

V. Snuggling Comets

The heroic story we all hear in high school about Galileo is that he was the guy who proved the Copernican notion that the earth was not the fixed center of the universe. The other part of the lore is the cautionary tale. The Inquisition put him on trial because he discussed these proofs in a book entitled *Dialogue Concerning the Two Chief World Systems*. Four cacophonous centuries later, those two worldviews are still bickering.

In the end, Galileo was ordered to back off his view that the earth was not motionless and the fixed center of the universe. Which he did; wearing the white robes of a penitent, he asserted that the earth did not move. When the members of the Inquisition left his chambers for the last time, it is said Galileo hissed, "*Eppur si muove*" ("And yet it moves").

Despite the confession, Galileo confirmed the Copernican Revolution, shifting us out of a geocentric universe and into a heliocentric one. With his proof, he legitimized one more mechanical explanation of the world. Once again, the conventional thinking provided by mystical authority (the Church) or traditional wisdom (Ptolemy and Aristotle) was grudgingly set aside, and Galileo became one of the iconic names of those who inaugurated the Renaissance. Not bad, for a monk.

But there is also the gritty vernacular version of the story that might not be as heroic, but reveals the long history of improvisational astronomy. Galileo mastered the telescope not so much to jump-start the Enlightenment but to make some fast money. He was a monk, and, like any respectable celibate of that time, he also had three illegitimate children and was desperate to provide for them.

He jumped on the idea of telescope-building when he first heard of the devices coming out of the Netherlands. Those items had a magnification power of 3X. (The plastic spyglasses that are now included free with any Halloween pirate costume are more powerful.) The concept was quite simple. In a long tube that we would still recognize as a telescope, the far end would hold a convex piece of glass. The idea had grown out of the fiddling lots of people had been doing with lenses.

In the late 1200s, a new killer app from Italy had entered the popular culture—reading glasses. They had replaced the "reading stone," a magnifier placed directly onto a manuscript. The new idea was to put the magnifier directly onto one's face—at first a radical, awkward, and unlikely notion. Soon, a new class of entrepreneur—spectacle-mongers (an actual phrase, once upon a time)—mastered the technique of shaping glass into smaller, manageable, and vaguely familiar shapes. (The word "lens" comes from the word "lentils.") The new invention had widespread repercussions. By restoring the precise vision of adults around the presbyopian age of forty, eyeglasses are responsible for adding another span of productivity and creativity to the natural human career. It wouldn't be hard to argue that eyeglasses were responsible for the Renaissance and gin up one of those books like *The Potato: How the Humble Spud Rescued the Western World*; or *Cod: A Biography of the Fish That Changed the World*; or *Tulipmania: The Story of the World's Most Coveted Flower and the Extraordinary Passions It Aroused*. Call it: *Eyeglasses: How Spectacles Saw a New World and Brought Forth the Enlightenment*.

Galileo quickly became adept at the difficult labor of grinding lenses himself and eventually bootstrapped his 3X telescope into 8X and then 20X. He initially went to the Venetian Senate to sell these earliest telescopes as powerful military tools. Think of Galileo as the first modern defense contractor. Eventually Galileo also turned his hopeful moneymaker to the sky and observed moons circling Jupiter, confirming that not everything orbited the earth. And he recorded the phases of Venus, which only made sense if that planet orbited the sun.

Seeing just a little farther on than the last guy—always the motive and the goal of astronomy—often was, and still is, enough to refurbish whole neighborhoods of the cosmos and sometimes restructure the entire universe. Isaac Newton invented the "Newtonian" by using a mirror to reflect the light and then throw it off to the side—with another mirror, the "secondary"—and into the eyepiece. William Herschel made minor improvements in refining the parabolic shape of his mirrors and discovered Uranus.

After the switch from lenses (curved on two sides) to mirrors (only one side to shape), other telescope improvements led to Charles Messier in France discovering so many things he put a number of them in his Messier catalogue, still the primary "bird list" for any greenhorn astronomer.

No one has run the exact numbers, but it's safe to say that much of the sky has been identified and named by self-motivated pioneers. Even today, when amateurism is supposed to be dead, lay astronomers range from Cindy Foote, a wife in Utah who's confirmed the discovery of two exoplanets, to a number of eccentric talents such as Robert Evan, who is a Christian minister in Australia, and Koichi Itagaki, who runs a bean confectionary company in Japan. They both possess an ability to look at a night sky, then come back later and notice if any tiny change in the light has occurred. With this amazing visual memory, they've discovered, respectively, forty-two and fifty supernovas.

With such a constant army of novices stomping around the galaxies, monitoring asteroids and NEOs (near earth objects), coining homemade names, becoming storm chasers on Jupiter, providing popular boosterism for the next NASA-launched probe—the universe is a different place entirely than it was not that long ago. We have, strangely, come to know this place. Things are named. Ever farther and more curious bodies are seen. Bizarre physics are being understood. The nearby earthlike exoplanet Gliese 581c (118 trillion miles away) has already earned a vernacular nickname, even though the scientific authorities refuse to recognize it: Ymir, named for the Frost Giant in Norse mythology known as the gravel-yeller. Slowly and in inches, perhaps, we're taming this place with understanding.

Comets were once considered messengers of evil or, as Rene Descartes thought, alien visitors spying on us. The seventeenth-century French poet Guillaume de Salluste Du Bartas wrote that the appearance of a comet signaled different, but always horrible, meanings to all classes of people: "To Princes, Death! To Kingdoms, many Crosses; To all Estates, inevitable Losses! To Herdsmen, Rot; to Plowmen, hapless Seasons; To Sailors, Storms; To Cities, Civil Treasons."

Today, the menacing Hermes of space is as domesticated as an obese house cat. The arrival of a comet is now an occasion for parties out in a farmer's pasture. When Hale-Bopp arrived, some friends and I carted a telescope to a meadow on the edge of town. We drank beer all night long and laughed in our folding chairs at our absurdly gargantuan universe, carrying on as if we were sitting in a backyard 13 billion light-years wide. It felt oddly cozy.

And that is what has changed since, say, Neil Armstrong walked on the moon. All these large-scale structural discoveries, as well as so many massive cartographic projects to locate and categorize literally millions of galaxies and stars, have made the universe a little more, you know, doable.

The proliferation of amateur stargazers has mucked up the sky in a good way, with dilettantish hands. The old constellations—the ones most of us grew up learning in our backyards—turn out to be inept guideposts to finding anything in the sky. So they are slowly going through a makeover. Our lives don't involve a lot of dealings with water bearers (Aquarius), queens (Cassiopeia), lions (Leo), or—for most folks—chained ladies (Andromeda). Such characters, or at least their stories, were commonplace in the day-to-day chatter of a long-ago time.

A number of amateurs have thrown out new names for different shapes that make it a lot easier to aim one's telescope on a dark night. You might not have heard of the Coathanger or the Mercedes-Benz, but you can probably guess what they look like in the sky. Amateurs know these DIY constellations as "asterisms." Naming something is a claim of familiarity, even ownership, and has been ever since Adam took up the task of naming the animals and assuming dominion over "everything that creeps on the earth." In a way that he could never have anticipated, Dobson himself is very much responsible for a kind of *coup d'univers*.

So far, credentialed astronomers and amateurs together have discovered more than five hundred planets outside our solar system—exoplanets. The professionals tried to keep the new names very sober and scientific-sounding. Officially they all bear Dewey decimal designations in the style of Bach's Opus K551 (known to non-musicologists as the Jupiter Symphony) or Brahms's First Symphony in C Minor, Op. 68 (aka Beethoven's Tenth). The same happened with exoplanets. Scientists know the first exoplanet discovered in 1995 as "51 Pegasi b," but the madding crowd insists upon sticking with Greek mythology, and informally they have named it for the ancient slayer of monsters Bellerophon. One exoplanet I am particularly interested in is formally known as HD 209458b. But the online hoi polloi have already dubbed it Osiris. The world of exoplanets, like a lot of the sky, just won't hold still for proper scientists, anymore than any Wild West's frontier town waited for the Chamber of Commerce.

The terminology of space tends toward terms like ESO 137–001 (the name of a galaxy in the Abell 3627 cluster) precisely because it's easier to order the world that way and because it feels so sciencey. But the other tendency in astronomy is playful, half-cocked, improvisational, at times childlike. The Cartwheel Galaxy, as well as the Cigar, the Sombrero, the Pinwheel, the Sunflower, and the Tadpole galaxies—all officially recognized now—could have been named by Bart Simpson.

The reigning theory of the origin of the universe is called the Big Bang—a phrase that originated as a schoolyard taunt and was meant as a put-down when "this big bang idea" was first sneeringly uttered in 1949 on a BBC broadcast by Frederick Hoyle, then the most prominent defender of the now abandoned "steady state" theory. And the Big Bang is now met with complementary theories hypothesizing the universe's end that quickly were characterized as the Big Chill, the Big Crunch, and the Big Rip.

A new technical expression that came into usage recently describes a gassy formation in deep space. I am not making this up, the formal term is: blob. It's real scientific jargon, just ask any astronomer at a university or a ten-year-old boy in a mud puddle. And the dopey, amicable terminology has a way of amplifying this effect, of making a place that is largely incomprehensible seem, on some abstract level, possibly familiar.

Take the big rocks loitering out past Neptune. If you aim your telescope properly, you can make out the really large ones, such as 68410 Nichols, 4659 Roddenberry, and 7307 Takei, named for, respectively, the communications officer Lieutenant Uhura aboard the *Starship Enterprise*, played by the hot actress Nichelle Nichols; *Star Trek*'s brilliant creator, Gene Roddenberry; and the spaceship's helmsman Lieutenant Sulu, played by George Takei. Nothing quite scales our solar system down to the intimacy of a shag-carpeted ranch home quite like naming its secondary features after characters we came to know as sexually emerging teenagers.

And these aren't slangy nicknames like some of the asterisms, but rather the official ones, declared and recorded by a delicious bureaucracy known as the International Astronomical Union's Committee on Small Body Nomenclature.

"I am now a heavenly body," Takei said upon hearing of the honor, winking knowingly at the rest of the universe

VI. Innovation, P. T. Barnum–style

Attend any star party, call any astronomer, or chat online, and you will hear of groups of amateurs trying to pull off some kind of serious astronomy in their spare time. The Galaxy Zoo—hundreds of thousands of amateur astronomers scanning the universe—has published some twenty scholarly papers.

One crowd I began to hear about—centered on a mobile home park in a remote stretch of central California—appeared intent on sparking a second Dobsonian revolution. Somewhere out there, amid the dry scrub, was a guy leading a small army of amateurs. They were attempting to create new amateur equipment that would inch them closer to all kinds of professional science, some of it abetting the search for habitable planets, including alien life.

"He has his eyes on one- to two-meter telescopes," said Bill Hudson, a telescope manufacturer in Utah. On the Internet, his group was known as the "alt-az initiative"—a shorthand term referring to the Dobsonian mount they hoped to use on their telescopes. The idea made sense: Between the commonplace telescope (with a mirror the size of a large dinner plate) and those mountaintop mammoths in Hawaii or Chile one reads about (where the mirrors could occupy half a football field) was a world of amateur pursuits for those with mirrors roughly the size of car hoods. Here was the main obstacle:

A professional telescope in that mid-range size can run around $20 million.

But what if a team of garage obsessives could fiddle their way to a Galilean leap, crafting a Dobsonian version—cheap, portable, and big—from various bits and parts that cost only a few thousand dollars? I wanted to know what kind of discoveries might flow from such an advance, this time arming a worldwide platoon of eager astronomers with mirrors nearly as powerful as Mount Palomar's. And, since this work was currently under way, here's what really got me to buy my Jet Blue ticket to California: Would I be able to see, up close, what the reality of a true innovative breakthrough looked like? Would I witness an amateur discovery in real time?

That would depend on whether I could find the Rinconada Trailer Park. The leader of this group, Russ Genet, lived there, and he warned me that there were a couple of curves in the road where reality and the MapQuest printout didn't quite sync. "If you see a gas station on your right, you've gone too far"—and, whoosh, was that a gas station? Frustration inaugurated my trip to the odd trailer park and quickly developed into a leitmotif. Looking innovation square in the face turns out to be like spotting a shooting star, fairly gone by the time you see it.

My imaginative idea of a village of inventors at work in their sheds was belied by my visit. The Rinconada Trailer Park, for instance, had, besides Genet, only one other tenant, the landlord himself—giving the visit a Hitchcockian air. When I parked my rental in a spacious area, I was told I had to move it since the patch of grass I was on apparently qualified as the owner's "parking space." I was shown my sleeping quarters, a tiny, cozy travel trailer that, given its quaint size, made me feel like I had snacked on Alice's famous "EAT ME" cake.

Genet's a big man, with a white leprechaun's chin strap for a beard. He's full of smiles and zealous gestures. He is generous with his laugh—a room-engulfing yuk. He's a skillful carpenter who clearly enjoys jimmying anything at hand. The room he added on to his wide-load is an impressive piece of DIY construction and carpentry. We sat out in front of his house on a warm sunny day with sandwiches and iced tea—my first day behind the barricades of the coming revolution aborning in Genet's mobile home.

He was happy to show me a one-meter mirror that had just arrived. Crated up in rough-hewn timber, it sat under a cover in front of his house. Was it homemade? I eagerly inquired. No, he said casually, a company sent it to him. Basically, he had conned the CEO out of it. Genet was going to use it to see if he could put together a portable system that would fit into his Jeep. Granted, portability was part of the goal, but that part didn't sound too innovationy. No Discovery Channel special here. It was time, I thought, to move on to some of the elements of the telescope and figure out where the great leaps forward were going to take place.

Modern telescopes may still be fairly DIYable, but they are a lot more complicated than the mere lagniappe Galileo invented. The traditional parts that allow you to see—the mirror, the casing, the eyepiece—are still the primary pieces. But today, if you are going to track a star across the sky, you will need a camera, a motor to slowly move it across the sky at night, an encoder that gives the telescope the instructions to stay on target, and a frame made out of material sturdy enough to take a good gust of wind. The slightest shift down here on earth, of course, produces light-years of error out there in the cosmos.

Genet and I struck up a conversation for a moment about encoders. This seemed like an obvious place where a smart thinker could create a great innovation. An encoder solves a basic problem but also creates new ones. If your telescope is fairly heavy and you instruct the motor to turn, then there will be some undesired movement in the system. Like anything, it will wobble as it comes to a standstill. "If you have a really accurate encoder," Genet explained, "then electronic finesse can make up for mechanical grossness." He described the current need: an encoder that can figure out precisely which rate of speed to drive the telescope so that when it does slow down, it will come to rest precisely where it should be. Through several glasses of tea, Genet laid out the basic physics of stiffness and backlash, gear reduction and motor speed. All this real-world messiness, he explained, could be eliminated by some cunning programming at the encoder level.

I was anxious. How have the amateurs been using their bail wire, duct tape, and itchy curiosity to solve this nuanced problem?

"We're looking at the Heidenhain, one of the largest encoder makers on the planet," Genet said cheerfully. "They've come out with a thirty-three-million-tick-per-revolution encoder for $500. Absolutely amazing."

So wait. A half afternoon of movement physics, a yellow pad crammed with notes, and a gallon of iced tea, and the answer is: buy it from the largest telescope company in the world? Maybe I hadn't explained to Genet my purpose for visiting the two-man mobile home park—evidence of an amateur revolution.

For any reporter, there's a pleasure in delving into a specialty—like telescope making. It's akin to traveling to a foreign country. The language is weird, the views are uncommon, but the company is always stimulating. The fun typically involves finding some way to carry back from this outpost of human endeavor a sense of the specialist's zeal and understanding. The hope is to translate some of that into language that a non–telescope maker, even someone with no interest in astronomy, can enjoy as stories.

A little while later, we were talking about direct drive motors. Maybe, here, I thought, I will see the moment of aha!—the lightbulb illuminating overhead. Then, suddenly, Genet described an occasion when one of his collaborators was making this very kind of breakthrough. Most direct-drive motors are composed of magnets set in a circle around a coil of wire—a radial flux motor. One of the original alt-az fiddlers, David Rowe, figured out a way to locate the magnet right on the coil. There was a loss of energy efficiency, but it permitted the motor to respond more accurately.

Closer, I thought. This mild innovation had promise. Had Rowe created a new kind of motor? Would patents be involved? Was it possible for me to understand what the precise mechanics at work here were? And maybe how this innovation came to him, and could we pinpoint just where the imaginative impulse took flight?

Well, um, no. The reality is that this kind of direct-drive motor is not new. (I switched from iced tea to coffee before considering a shift to whiskey.) What Rowe brought to the problem was to turn to an older motor that was easy to come by, if somewhat lousy in energy use.

By late afternoon, I felt hot flashes shooting up my back. Genet and I were walking through some beautiful nearby woods, taking a hike by a nice lake. He began to describe his team, which does meet every year or so but mostly exists in Google groups and Yahoo listservs. His online operation largely involved Genet encouraging other people whose ideas have promise but haven't come close to paying off. His research process is built around e-mail exchanges with isolated people whose efforts vaguely intersect with his own. A professor in South Carolina named Terry Richardson is a lifelong sky obsessive who has the idea of spinning epoxy glue. The centrifugal force of a viscous liquid creates the parabolic shape needed for a telescope. The idea is to spin the glue in a heated environment and then slowly cool it down so that it hardens in precisely the shape needed. So far, the results have been encouraging but haven't delivered a decent mirror. Another team member has created a vacuum chamber covered with a thin skin of Mylar. Pull the vacuum in a certain way and the Mylar bows inwardly to create a temporary mirror. Also, cool idea, but not quite workable in terms of actually seeing something.

The innovations are small but steady. Another contributor's brushless drive improvements were new and had already been adopted by other telescope makers, but still not the Discovery Channel special—*Amateur Star Trek: To Home Depot and Beyond!*—I was looking for. I left California, as so many do, heartbroken.

Once I returned home, Genet looped me into his e-mail and I experienced the Internet effort up close. There is an unemployed NASA scientist in Florida, named Andrew Arigema, who has been experimenting with different types of glass structures to solve this revolution's most fundamental problem: A mirror that is, say, fifty inches in diameter will probably weigh more than a thousand pounds and therefore defeat the hope for portable, and probably cheap. Was there some way to create a good mirror that was big and sturdy but didn't weigh half a ton?

Over the course of months of online chats and more and more nonstop e-mails, Genet focused on a small side team he had created. Arigema would cast mirrors in Florida (by heating them up and shaping them, "slumping" the glass) and ship them to a key member of the group in Oregon, David Davis, who polished them to parabolic perfection and then tested them to see if they captured light well. Essentially, Genet had created, with FedEx's help, a far-flung testing laboratory.

The e-mail exchanges are often technical and arcane. A dozen e-mails might be devoted to detailed discussions of cutter speeds and feed rates. But then there might surface a very specific solution—could the weight problem be solved by making a very thin mirror out of good glass but then figuring out how to glue some lightweight backing to provide good structure? Even the bonding agent became a lively debate—centering around muffler sealant. Another one turned on mount technologies that relied on the mechanics found in those wall TV swivel units in a motel.

From time to time, in this e-mail ocean of aracana, a thin reed of an idea would bob to the surface and you could feel everybody getting their amateur revolution on. The cheap backing to a thin mirror, it was discovered one day, could be made out of a kind of foam glass marketed as Earthstone. It was light enough that it could float in water and sturdy enough that Arigema took one of his experimental foam glass mirrors to their annual meeting and proudly dropped it on the floor. It bounced. This particular foam glass is sold as a grill cleaner, but its central ingredient is recycled beer bottles. The Earthstone company is located next to a dump in Arizona and actually uses the landfill's natural off-gas of methane to power its plant. The idea then is leaning toward making telescopes out of a slumped glass tabletop backed by recycled bottles.

After watching all this happen up close, I realized how little Genet had to do with any innovation. He admits he's not much of an inventor himself but rather is the guy who, when he first hears about the possibility of, say, recycled beer bottles, calls the CEO and cons him into some "samples" for Arigema. With almost no money to work with, the team relies on Genet's P. T. Barnum skills to provide free materials and occasional funding.

As the organizer, Genet maintains an unrelentingly cheerful attitude. His e-mails arrive in flurries. There is no beat-down by a participating business type about how "this is not how research is done," or sour thought about how this might not work out, that isn't met by his "yup, yup, but what about?" enthusiasm. Genet will pass along a note with his own interstitial comments beaming from inside the text in bright blue or green or yellow fonts, signifying each pass of a commentor. And there are times in the subtle tones of an e-mail—especially one coming from someone who has done real-world R&D—where the reader can sense a participant slightly annoyed with what he or she perceives as the Pollyannaish views of an unsinkable booster like Russ Genet.

This slight agitation with Genet's can-do-ism prompted a flush of déjà vu for me because one gets this same vibe from people who seem, by and large, fed up with John Dobson. Timothy Ferris's classic amateur astronomy text, *Seeing in the Dark*, aggressively ignores Dobson in favor of long interviews with people who are fairly irrelevant—such as a married couple who runs a campground in Arizona where one can bunk for a week in super-dark country. Even in Genet's e-mail exchange, at one point, Dobson's name came up and one writer couldn't resist a little dig about how "it would be too easy to sound like you're making a hero out of Dobson, and there's already been enough of that."

Having spent some time with Dobson, I know how much of a pain he can be. Like anyone who achieves a certain fame in one area, he thinks it permits him to sound off about anything and expect the same acclaim. So Dobson will climb aboard any nearby hobby horse—the structure of the universe is one of his favorites—and he can sound entirely insufferable. He breezily disses the Big Bang and openly mocks Stephen Hawking—all of which marks him in the world of establishment science as a crank.

It's easy to work up a decent dislike of Dobson, the man. But it's also true that those who attack him resent his outsized fame (and that monumental adjective, Dobsonian). What one often hears is: Oh, his telescope wasn't really that much of an innovation. He just figured out a cheap way to grind a lens. Or that he devised a smart box made out of inexpensive plywood and vinyl records that created an ingenious mount, but, really, nothing new, so what? And here's where it gets interesting: That's true. If you deconstruct Dobson's actual achievement, what you have is a clever box, a cheap way to grind a lens, and a streamlined set of instructions that won't make you insane. Broken down, the great Dobsonian breakthrough looks like a collection of minor and marginal improvements.

It's not long before I see that Genet's group is on the same flight path. If Andrew completes his foam glass mirror weighing a few pounds, and the other folks experimenting with lightweight construction devise a super-strong, wind-resistant frame, and if you throw in a cheap motor and an off-the-shelf encoder, you will have something that can be cobbled together for a few thousand dollars. You will also have a recapitulation of the Dobsonian revolution—and one that doesn't look at all the ways innovation happens in the *Harvard Business Review*.

Innovation is supposed to happen in one of two ways. There is the Great Galilean Aha!—the instantaneous, practically divine revelation—and the Edisonian Grind, the slow-motion epiphany involving the unending effort of the inventor who lives in the lab struggling through trial and error until he arrives at the answer. Put another way, the two schools of innovation are inspiration and perspiration. In the movies, great leaps forward get depicted as either an inspiring lightbulb moment ("Hey, wait a minute," says our hero, "what if I mix this with that—why then . . .") or images connoting hard work—a series of fast cuts showing our protagonist racing through thousands of versions of his obsession, maybe some calendar pages flapping by.

But amateurs show that there is another path to innovation that doesn't yet have a movie shorthand—the collaborative, marginal effort that culminates in a Great New Thing. Maybe that's why Dobson has his intellectual detractors. One won't find his achievement used as a case study in an airport paperback about entrepreneurial innovation, because Dobson also provided charm and charisma. Dobson traveled the country in his big yellow bus for years. He taught lens-crafting classes, creating an army of amateur astronomers who've pushed open the window of our universe one more crack or two. Add to that a lot of small, not so impressive tweaks and you have a thing known as the Dobsonian revolution, not merely a cheap lens or plywood mount.

Genet also wallows in his role as circus barker, the guy who can't stop e-mailing and introducing people. He is always looking for another, marginal innovation that will continue to add to the cause. He knows that if he can introduce a David Davis to an Andrew Arigema—a union of an Oregon lens grinder and a Florida slumper—then he may well get his forty-pound, one-meter mirror inside a year. He knows that if he keeps the guys who are devising smart motors in touch with the epoxy glue folks, then maybe something will work out (but probably not, so on to the next e-mail and random chance).

In the time I have known him, Genet has introduced me by e-mail to some two dozen people, hoping that I might get some idea or new thread of inquiry. Almost all of the time, it doesn't pay off, but Genet is never demoralized. He keeps up with the efforts of his far-strung research team. He scours the Internet looking for new materials and ideas. Then he puts them in front of his people to see if they might fly. Oh, look, here's some guy making super-lightweight, super-strong foam glass from recycled beer bottles in Arizona. So Russ calls up George Morandin, the CEO of Earthstone. Genet excites him with some all-American patter about redefining the universe and the ultimate act of recycling. "Garbage in, galaxies out," Genet said to me on the phone one day, a line I suspect George Morandin heard just before agreeing to ship at his own expense a planeload of large foam glass samples to Arigema in Florida.

Amateur R&D has less in common with Archimedes and Galileo or Edison and Jobs than it does with Zeno, the Greek metaphysician whose famous paradox observed that if you walk half the way down a gangplank and then half the remaining distance each time, you never get to the end. This is how Russ's group proceeds, moving ever closer to the line but perhaps never actually getting there. But often getting closer is close enough.

Unlike a businessman (or Thomas Edison), they aren't interested in marketability, only workability. With telescopes, you only have to get far enough to see something just a bit better or more focused. One subgroup of Genet's crew no longer even lusts for a telescope that can focus on an image. They are obsessed with just pulling in as much light as possible so they can analyze it. These folks refer to their cruder version of a telescope as a "lightbucket."

They literally just want lots of photons from a specific location. Being in focus is not relevant since they want to analyze the light to find out all kinds of things that will elevate their work to, essentially, what the professionals are doing. In other words, what Genet and his crew are proposing now is the contemporary equivalent of old-fashioned—call it nineteenth-century—amateur astronomy. These are individuals who intend to contribute specific findings to the giant pile of professional knowledge. Most of the time when you hear people laud amateur astronomy, they are talking about the amazing contributions that can come from hundreds of people attacking a problem all at once, like the discovery of Green Pea galaxies. But this is different. What Genet is proposing is that those ten thousand people now build a cheap telescope nearly as powerful as those found in universities and then pursue their own individual science projects.

In those fractional advances lie galaxies to discover, new laws of the universe, and if one of the amateurs I talked to is right, maybe even a smart new way to harness this lightbucket brigade to grasp the current Holy Grail of astronomy: contact with extraterrestrials.

VII. A Recycled Universe

John Dobson is lying on a blanket on the top of a hill in Vermont—couchant is the heraldic term—surrounded by a half-dozen young beautiful girls and one jealous boy. He is explaining the whole universe to them—half with jokes, half with iconoclastic science.

"Momentum," he explains, in his notorious style, "is how heavy you are multiplied by what the hell you are doing."

The annual Vermont star party, which is where Dobson is holding court, is called Stellafane. Such revelries are held all over the world, and a great deal of their popularity can be traced to this one itinerant telescope maker, John Dobson. At this gathering, campers and RVs are parked in little neighborhoods scattered throughout hundreds of acres of pastures and isolated meadows. Thousands of astronomers are here for a long weekend of stargazing and late-night thoughts on, literally, the entire universe.

By night, the amateurs wander about, illuminating their way with low-intensity, deep-red-spectrum, flat-beam flashlights. The night eye can adapt to darkness in five or so minutes but has to start all over once it gets hit with the daytime-like rays of a standard flashlight. The truly hard-core take no chances and wander about sporting red night-vision goggles like apocalyptic warriors, or covering their "seeing" eye with a patch like midnight pirates, so that the rods and cones in the eye can maintain shift-to-dark sensitivity. When the time comes to look, they flip up their patch, enjoy the feathered detail of, say, Flocculent Spiral Galaxy NGC 4414, and then pop it back down to shelter their eye like a candle in the wind. One lady cooking burgers beneath her Winnebago awning called the gathering "Geekstock." True, not a lot of drugs here. The high that everyone seeks at Stellafane is quite literal.

Dobson is often a guest at these star parties, and if he's there, you will no doubt wander into the orbit of his cosmology. I've heard it now three or four times. I don't entirely grasp the nuances of some of his scientific claims. I'm not sure anyone does, or that it matters. Even for the pros, cosmology is the greatest guessing game ever. The facts are precious few and extremely frail. Most of them are derived from highly contentious methods of painstakingly extracted and extremely sensitive data gleaned from a dim smudge of ancient light. Not a lot to go on, in other words. That said, and even though John Dobson is a man who made telescopes out of plywood and porthole glass and therefore is about as qualified to talk cosmology as my plumber is qualified to discuss the effect of climate change on the Gulf Stream, well, still, Dobson makes a case for a really cool cosmos.

At the edge of the universe, Dobson explains with a knowing tone in his voice, gravitational energy converts to radiation. Now, maybe you understand that last clause in the physics sense, maybe you don't understand it at all in the experiential sense. In other words, even though you know each word, and even strung together as a sentence, they combine to form a kind of sense, it's not a kind of sense that relates to anything you, a civilian, have ever actually experienced, and so the words arrive in your ears as a kind of playful poetry. I might even understand the entire sentence, but the whole meaning doesn't quite snag a hook in my brain. But what carries you along is the way Dobson says it, with an inflection and metric rhythm that makes any other view seem absolutely dopey. When Dobson goes into his full-on cosmology, I often hear what he says as free verse, the astronomical equivalent of reading Allen Ginsberg's *Howl* or Ezra Pound's *Cantos*, both of which you'll recall were always lauded by your grooviest college professor as works that you should allow to flow over you. Dobson's cosmology is best experienced that way, the way Ginsberg chanted his works, as free-verse poetry practically sung. Does this conversion predict the current temperature of deep space? Well:

> It turns out
> that *radiation*
>   running through low mass particles
> gets *thermalized*
>   at three degrees Kelvin!

He performed the next sentence in a single two-burst strophe that beautifully suggested that we can only pity the other side:

> The amount that we get in my model corresponds to what
> we measure.

Then he switched into full-throated astro-diva, actually singing the next sentence so that even if you didn't understand the astrophysics, you could not resist joining in the general ridicule that you would definitely wallow in if, in fact, you were totally confident in his theory:

> and the amount predicted
> by the Big Bang
> is two orders of magnitude
> over what we see!

Dobson is rejecting the Big Bang theory, the fundamental metaphor of official acceptable cosmology. He is proclaiming an entirely different metaphor—a recycling universe. Dobson's cosmos is a giant Mobius strip that feeds back on itself and re-creates itself—half self-resurrecting phoenix, half tail-consuming ouroboros. That's how he sees the universe—as a kind of particle doughnut in which the trajectory of the outer surface flings matter back toward the center.

In the course of his exclamations, Dobson happily slaughters nearly every cosmic sacred cow there is. Dark matter—the single most crucial strut holding up our current understanding of the universe? A total "fudge"!

> And they have to patch
> the dark matter
> with dark energy.
> It's just patches
> on top of patches
> on top of patches
> on top of patches.

But here's the thing: That is basically true. The universe may not be turtles all the way down, but it is Band-Aids all the way down. The reason scientists have posited that some 96 percent of the matter and energy is invisible to us is because their equations predict that we need that much matter and energy to exist in order for their equations to work. Not only must these particles exist, but they must do so in such massive intergalactic profusion that most matter must resemble diaphanous webs draped like delicate Halloween gossamer from black hole to black hole. And yet the theory of dark matter is so tenuous that it has become a kind of tradition among science journalists, when writing about the subject, to find the scientist who will admit that the entire notion might be a nauseating typo in the equations, one that has led them all down a gut-wrenching intellectual cul-de-sac for half a century.

"I have been looking for dark-matter particles for more than 15 years. I'm 42," Juan Collar of the University of Chicago admitted to the *New York Times*. "So most of my colleagues, my age, we are kind of going through a midlife crisis."

What gets exposed in these discussions is the key feature of all thinking about the universe. Whether we are sitting in the Department of Astrophysics at Cambridge or under the night sky of Stellafane, we're all amateurs once we get out here. Even the alleged facts that a genius like Stephen Hawking is working with are highly provisional. As I wrote these sentences, for instance, I received an e-mail alert about a new study out of the University of Durham in England that "suggests that the conventional wisdom about the content of the Universe may be wrong."

The item goes on to report that the "scientists find evidence that the errors in its data may be much larger than previously thought, which in turn makes the standard model of the Universe open to question." The release states a possibility that must strike terror in the hearts of scientists the world over, that these calculations "could imply that dark matter and dark energy are not present after all."

Imagine a small-town manager of a Gap outlet getting a memo from the London School of Economics explaining that some new research reveals that capitalism doesn't actually work. Just FYI.

So we might well live in a recycling universe. And the firm evidence of it might arrive next week in a tweet from Arizona State University.

VIII. The Oldest Cosmic Wiki

Even though a reincarnating universe could be argued, Dobson often goes one leap more: "Let's go back about four to five thousand years. There were some physicists that built their physics into their language and left it there for all to see. Their name for the universe was *jarot*, 'the changing.'" Dobson tells you that Hindu theology foretold the whole story five millennia ago.

In the world of astrophysics, if you add a pinch of theology, you've jumped the shark. Most scientists stiffen and walk away. And yet Dobson is merely trying to do what everyone obsessed with the outer edge of the universe is trying to do: tell the story. The fact that he has chosen to reach into our cultural past for the narrative elements of his story is, frankly, one more reason why Dobson finds himself marooned on a blanket with a handful of twenty-five-year-old ingénues and one beta male waiting for the cosmic silverback to take a nap so he can make his opportunistic move.

The fact is, religion is no longer invited to any of science's jamborees. Part of the reason is because organized religion has ransacked their ancient stories looking for something that resembles a scientific fact. And all that the creation scientists and intelligent designers have been able to come up with is variations of the old God of Gaps argument. Where is God today, according to some ministers? Hiding out in our DNA code, the new genetic Kaballah. This kind of thinking never ends. Fundamentalists have overworked this argument for so long that most scientists are just exhausted with it. And they've walked away, shunning in practical ways the need for any story at all.

When Dobson riffles through the glossary of Hindu 101 and finds evidence of an ancient recycling universe, he's no different from the nice liberal Episcopalian minister who argues that the Big Bang, quantum entanglement, and entropy can all be found in the Bible as creation, miracle, and sin. And all of them are missing what Galileo's real discovery was—not the moons of Jupiter, but the elements of a new story to describe our place in the universe. He literally moved us out of the center of God's loving estate and into the suburbs of a moderately sized star—a change of location that would require an entirely novel account of the universe's origins, or cosmogony.

The Bible is a Bronze Age attempt by society's most learned men to cobble together a working cosmogony. Looked at that way, maybe the Bible deserves a different kind of reading. Even the philosopher Daniel Dennett, one of the most popular of the current atheists, has acknowledged that from an evolutionary perspective, the Bible has to be the most competent Darwinian text in history. If literary works were species, the Bible would be the coelacanth, the horseshoe crab, or the dung beetle of cosmogonies. That alone should make the book worthy of study. These stories—however musty and dull they might sound now to fresh skeptics in graduate school—have adapted and survived while Greek mythology, the Viking Eddas, Sumaria's Gilgamesh, the Mayan Popol Vuh, Shinto's Kojiki, and Ancient Egypt's Pert Em Hru (Book of the Dead), along with thousands of other Scriptures, have been marginalized or have perished.

When Richard Dawkins says that Christians are all atheists with respect to the Roman gods or the Viking pantheon and that Christians just need to go one atheism further, one question he might want to ask as a scientist is: What accounts for this one stubborn bit of cultural mythology hanging on so well? What is the panda's thumb of the Bible?

The much rewritten and retranslated Bible is the longest-running, most successful cultural wiki of amateur cosmic theory in Western history. And science has at least one thing to learn from the Bible: how to tell a story. In the current wave of debates between religionists and atheists, the most favored approach by the scientists is a form of reductionist ridicule. For instance, Stephen Hawking has famously scoffed at our cosmic irrelevance, saying that humans are nothing more than "chemical scum on a moderate-sized planet, orbiting round a very average star in the outer suburb of one among a hundred billion galaxies." That idea sounded a lot more profound when I first heard it from the guy in my dorm with the bong.

This rhetorical tactic of attempting to awaken the somnolent masses by trashing revered ideals is an old one. Marcus Aurelius, who helped establish the philosophical school of the Stoics, was fond of dismissing a good meal as nothing more than "dead fish." Aurelius's definition of sex was "the rubbing together of pieces of gut, followed by the spasmodic secretion of a little bit of slime." (Sadly, Mrs. Aurelius's meditations did not survive.) Another skeptic snarked that Christianity is the belief that a "cosmic Jewish zombie who was his own father can make you live forever if you symbolically flash and telepathically tell him you accept him as your master, so that you can remove an evil force from your soul that is present in humanity because a rib-woman was convinced by a talking snake to eat from a magical tree."

There's something kick-ass in these tweaks, but there's also a smarty-pants quality to all this, one that perhaps culminated in a 2003 op-ed piece by Daniel Dennett. He proposed that modern educated skeptics should begin to refer to themselves as "brights." Thankfully, for everyone, that movement died before it was born. On a radio broadcast, I heard the skeptic and scientist PZ Myers refer to the Bible as little more than "poetry." I don't disagree with him. It was the withering contempt for "poetry" that made me realize once again how feeble a grasp some skeptics have of how to communicate outside the amen choruses at academic conferences and Ted Talks. One misses the point—and it's a really big point—by calling religion, as one skeptic recently did, a "a spandrel piggybacking on adaptations such as the orgasm."

A spandrel is the nonfunctional space above a weight-bearing arch. But it's also the place where, say, Michelangelo did most of his work in the Sistine Chapel. That is the problem with this point of view. It scorns the part of life most people care about: the poetry, the spandrels, the baroque cultures we shape—the stories we tell.

If Stephen Hawking visited Notre Dame Cathedral tomorrow and declared that what he saw was nothing more than "a stone-based structure whose horizontal distribution of off-vault compression directed lines of pressure-thrust to load-bearing piers," I am not sure most people would consider him a genius. They'd think he was a putz.

IX. E.T.'s Area Code

Funny, because as so many, like Dobson, scour the ancient tales looking for a story that might resonate today, the elements of a grand science narrative—new discoveries—arrive daily. Hang out long enough with amateur astronomers and eventually the conversation steers toward exoplanets and extraterrestrial life. It's no secret among the Russ Genet enthusiasts that one of the goals of the one-meter telescope crowd is to find new exoplanets and perhaps figure out which has life on it and how to communicate with that life. It's only a matter of very little time before one of these earth-sized exoplanets is theorized to contain some kind of life and, in being so theorized, refocuses the thoughts of our cosmogony in a way not seen since Galileo moved us all to the solar suburbs.

The discovery of intelligent life in space, of course, would change everything, rewrite all of our assumptions and create not just a new story about the cosmos but a proliferation of them. We don't have the slightest idea how that story will get told or the manifold ways it will rewrite our world, but we are anxious for it. Every day more and more exoplanets are added to the great list of known places where life might exist. A number of different NASA-launched space telescopes are downloading petabytes of unexamined data. Algorithms have already been developed to sift this growing mountain of data into piles that amateurs will be invited to poke through in hopes of finding gems of possibility. Eventually, some hope to spot the exoplanet whose light signature implies a slight elevation in the atmosphere of carbon dioxide, methane, and water vapor—indicating possibly that something there is breathing.

Only a few years ago, the obsession of the mainstream media was asteroids and NEOs that might strike earth. Those are still sources of excitement, but the shift in pop culture toward fascination with exoplanets is under way, although the topic remains to go mega-public. That may be because exoplanets don't blow anything up or because Will Smith hasn't made a movie about them yet.

Among professional astronomers, there may well be more intellectual interest in, say, the questions of dark matter, and possibly some quiet resentment that the exoplanet types so easily garner widespread pop culture coverage anytime there is a hint that a newly discovered planet might have some kind of life on it. (Plus, the kind of people who get overexcited by such discussions also include crackpots, oddball theorists, and those who swim in oceans of woo.)

To go to a Stellafane gathering and just listen to the telescope hounds discuss the variety and complexity of theories is to get the sense of what it must have been like at the Court of Ferdinand and Isabella after Columbus returned and the discussions grappled with the notion of a possible New World. There exists a kind of orthodoxy about these delicate issues—represented by the official organization

SETI—run by high-profile, mainstream astronomers and partly funded by the digital generation's most out-there philanthropist Paul Allen. (The digital revolution has provided our age with new Medicis and Borgias—the software billionaires devoting their treasure to building a space elevator, or downloading the brain into a computer program, or promoting immortality via the lecture circuit of Ray Kurzweil.)

When I first started contacting amateur astronomers, I kept hearing about this one guy who had a unique system for contacting aliens. Russ Genet had mentioned him, and a telescope manufacturer in Utah had told me about him too.

There are numerous methods already employed to try to scour the universe for broadcast signals from outer space aliens. The systematic way we've done this has been to sweep the sky looking for patterned signals among radio waves. Jim Edwards, a radar developer who often works with the Pentagon, has been involved in the signal corps and he's brought to this issue the start-from-the-beginning thinking so indicative of the amateur's faith.

His theory is reminiscent of the mid-nineteenth-century search for the Northwest Passage. The ships would sail far north of the Hudson Bay to the Barrow Strait, where there was no regular human traffic. In the vast expanses of shore, the sea captains would look for conspicuous spits of land that were noticeable from a distance. There on the flat shore, they would pile rocks into an unnatural—i.e., obviously man-made—cairn, and in the rocks they might put a note saying little more than "We were here" and the date. In the accounts of nineteenth-century voyages, the captains describe how they'd hug the coast, looking for noticeable land features, hoping to see the unnatural rock pile, inside of which would often be a bottle with a note, maybe a small flag. In the famous search for the lost explorer John Franklin, Lieutenant William Hobson sailed along the northwestern coast of King William Island to a place named Victory Point, where he spotted a pile of rocks. In it he found a note written on an old bureaucratic admiralty form that read simply, "All well," and the date "May 28, 1847." Many of these cairns became landmarks. Sailors would know where they were and would check them in their passages through a strait to see if any other traffic had sailed by recently.

Over a beer in a local hamburger joint in Redondo Beach, Edwards said he started by assuming that alien life forms far more advanced than us don't exist. "If anybody out there were vastly ahead of us," he said, "we'd pick them up on our car radio." So Edwards presumes that any alien life that is intelligent and is trying to communicate with us is probably as advanced as we are, more or less. To think like them means we only have to think like us.

Or like an Antarctic explorer. If you enter a massive bay, and you are looking for a message from a previous explorer, where to look? Well, first, as you scan the horizon, look for the unusual, eye-catching land formation.

For Edwards, the "odd spit of land" in space appears the moment when a giant like Jupiter passes in front of a sun. From our perspective it is a very noticeable event. It turns out many solar systems have gas giants like Jupiter (whether they have habitable planets or hot Venus-like planets is another question). But it appears that the natural history of planetary formation often resembles our own—with small hot planets in tight orbit, then habitable planets in what astronomers call the Goldilocks zone, and finally the big outer planets like Neptune, Jupiter, and Saturn.

The existence of these gas giants is how we know that exoplanets exist. They are the easiest for us to see because when they pass in front of their star (from our perspective), they block some light, causing the star to dim—and to dim on a fixed schedule—i.e., planetary orbit.

Both professional and amateur astronomers focus on a star, and if they notice a periodic dip in the light's intensity, then they know there is a high likelihood that something is moving in front of that sun to block the light. This was one of the main methods used to detect many of the nearly six-hundred-plus exoplanets discovered to date.

For now we can't photograph these exoplanets (at least not well; some very fuzzy dots have been produced by NASA). The way astronomers find them is to set a telescope to monitor a star's light and plot the data of the light's intensity on a graph. It looks mostly like a flat line running from left to right. But when the big planet moves in front of the sun, that line (moving from left to right) dips down, plateaus at the bottom of a trough, runs flat for a while (as the planet continues to pass in front of the sun), and then rises back up to its original intensity when the exoplanet moves on with the rest of its orbit. It forms a shape like a cup on a graph with a very flat bottom. For amateur astronomers, confirming the existence of an exoplanet with their own telescopes spitting out a flat-cup graph is a big thrill. Discovering it in the first place and adding an exoplanet to the great list of them is the dream.

Edwards's assumption is that if intelligent life elsewhere is roughly as intelligent as us, then they will see that moment of transit, that dip in the graph as an unusual place (the jutting spit of land, the sheer seaside cliff wall) on which to build an interstellar cairn and hoist a flag. So let's assume there's a star that's one hundred light-years away and has intelligent life on an orbiting planet. If those aliens can see our sun, they can figure out when their gas giant transits in front of their sun from our perspective. That's a brief moment—it differs for each exoplanet—but let's say it's five hours long and it happens, oh, once every two years. Edwards argues a life as intelligent as ourselves might pulse a laser flash in an artificial pattern during the transit as a kind of beacon. And he explains how our most intelligent astronomers and theirs would most likely use an H-alpha filter, like "super dark welder's goggles," to screen out competing light and reveal the intelligently designed optical signal.

Those aliens would only fire off their flare when their massive Jupiter-like planet was dimming their star from our perspective. Similarly, if we were trying to signal our location here, we would fire off our laser when our Jupiter was dimming our sun in relation to that one star system. Instead of looking for signals from all stars at all times, we could dramatically limit the search to just these few hours per star.

"So we have this sweet spot where both parties know not only where to look but when to look," Edwards said. "I think that's cool." If a host of amateurs built Russ Genet–like light buckets, then amateurs could crowd-source the search for beacons the way the Peas Corps scoured millions of galaxies and plucked out certain peculiar examples.

Professionals "can't do things that take a long time or risk taking a chance not getting a good payback on their time with the scope," Edwards said. Often they must be employed on tasks with a high likelihood of success—the kind of projects that win grant proposals. "Amateur astronomers do these kinds of experiments all the time," Edwards said. "This is their stock in trade: They get to do all the things that the professionals don't get to do."

So far, the SETI program has come up with nothing. The truth is, our increasingly familiar thirteen-billion-light-century-wide backyard is still a very large place. And yet, the SETI folks are said to keep a bottle of champagne in constant refrigeration. Anticipation has already led to the formation of a rather presumptuously titled committee—the "SETI Post-Detection Taskgroup."

Their mission? To "prepare, reflect on, manage, advise, and consult in preparation for and upon the discovery of a putative signal of extraterrestrial intelligent (ETI) origin." They have already written the Declaration of Principles Following the Detection of Extraterrestrial Intelligence.

The general thinking is that such a finding would radically reorient human civilization. Sure. And there is something silly in the SETI protocols, but reading them, one gets the sense that the tone is practically a placeholder for the kind of world-changing effect such a discovery would have. The atheist/theist squabble of today would shift dramatically. The discovery of other life would not end organized religion. Probably nothing could. But the weight of authority would shift dramatically closer to the scientists. Their work, however seemingly fatuous now (Google the "Drake equation"), would be seen as far more predictive than the millennia of clergy who flattered us with claims that we are God's unique creation.

That is why the amateurs have gathered, tellingly, at the edges of astronomy. From the massive arguments about atheism, to the technical debates about how to craft a hula hoop–sized mirror, to Edwards's late-night thoughts on transgalactic communication—the amateurs have come. From our earliest stirrings, we have always thought that maybe some of those blinking stars were distant beings trying to send us a signal, and now it turns out that that piece of scriptural conjecture might have been instinctively correct.

When Jim Edwards contemplates the night sky, he sees in his mind a bowl of stars whose transit hours are blinking on and off continuously throughout the night—a heaven filled with Gatsby lights, beckoning us for a closer look. Physical contact with others—what are called third-kind encounters—might be only the stuff of movies for now. And even second-kind encounters—back and forth communications—are still far off. But for now Edwards is longing only for an encounter of the first kind, the simple beacon. "Basically, each star is a blinking light and the only thing that you are communicating is that you are there," he said. "All you are saying is, I am here."

7

THE PURSUIT OF HAPPINESS

I. Girl, Interrupted

Claude-Anne Kirshen, who would grow up to become one of America's more innovative scholars, was a beautiful, smart seventeen-year-old in Brussels in 1940. She'd taken the vocational test that would set her on a path to becoming a high school teacher. She had a yellow Citroen car, a handsome boyfriend named René, and a new job just a few doors down from the house of Jacques Brel, the internationally famous songwriter.

"So that was my outlook at the moment," she told me one night over dinner. "Final exams were to be in June as always, and I was sure that I had already won the teaching competition and I was sure I would get this job." Then, a slight hitch.

"Hitler invaded in May," she noted. Suddenly young Kirshen felt that every solid thing she knew to be true had become unmoored. "The Nazis took the country in ten minutes."

From her balcony, she watched the bombs drop. And then a few metaphorical ones fell. She had taken a long walk with her brother and told him of a Spanish novel she had read. "I said that the Jews, they seemed awful, and he took a breath and said, 'You know that our grandfather was Jewish. . . .'" Then she learned that both her mother's parents were Jewish and that the reason her father could not practice law in Romania in those days was *because* he was Jewish. Overnight, she was a Jew. "It hit me like a bomb, I had to start re-thinking everything," she said. "Who was Jewish? Who was not? One girl, Irene Rosenfeld—she is still alive and living in this country—she said to me, 'We should be friends, we should stick together,' and I said, 'Why?'—*She* knew." Claude-Anne's parents had decided long ago to suppress their religious background and now, as she was about to turn eighteen, she discovered she was precisely the enemy Adolf Hitler intended to pursue and destroy.

"I was a total innocent and an idiot," she said. Her boyfriend, she discovered, was "very anti-Semitic." When she told him that she was Jewish, she was stunned to learn that he knew too. And, "it was the usual story: 'I hate the Jews, but not in your case.'"

Her brother sent news that he had moved the family's funds to America and suggested that they flee to France. Claude-Anne's mother was not merely a Jewish woman somewhat in denial, but insisted upon keeping up with her bridge games in Brussels in the hopes that the life of leisure she once led would return. But pretty quickly the unavoidable became obvious. They loaded up their clothes, an Irish nanny, and their dog, and headed for France. The decision was to go to Bordeaux. A family friend got them as far as the French border, after which a series of cabs got them from one town to the next. Claude-Anne's new life as a Jew really began the day she and her mother pulled into a small hotel in France.

"So we were in France and we went to a hotel," she said. "The woman saw our luggage, our nanny, my mother and me, and the dog. She asked if we wanted accommodations out back or a choice of rooms and just as we were about to go up, a whole family entered the hotel and the woman's face changed. The hotel keeper immediately said, 'We are booked up.' They pleaded and said they had children and they could stay anywhere, they would stay in the lobby. She said, 'We are all full.' They asked if she could call another hotel that might have space. 'No,' she said, 'all the hotels I know are booked up.' After they left, she turned to us and she said, 'It's a good thing that God gave them a nose to be recognized by.' And that was my first brush with French anti-Semitism and it was really a blow."

They were in France for a year, often on the move. In the town of Argenton-sur-Creuse, she took the dog out for a walk one day. She had met an American there, who accompanied her down by the river. "His name was Roode, a Dutch name. And he begins by telling me the schools he went to. I understood that's how Americans introduced themselves—what schools did you go to? His school was something that sounded like a brothel to me: Groton.

"So we walked and we got along with his dismal French and my English and, at a certain point, there was a river and a little peasant's house and a man opens the door and says that there is going to be an attack, a bombing. 'Come into the house and take shelter,' and the American said, 'Those French are hysterical.' And I thought, 'How can *hysterical* apply to a man?' We took three more steps and the bomb exploded in front of me. The first one had fallen in the water. I had heard a big noise, a big splash. I was about to explain to Roode that you don't use the word *hysterical* for a man and then a second bomb exploded. I felt the leash go, a burning in my hand, and the dog ran away. I saw blood on the dog and I slowly sank to the ground. I was bleeding and the American was beside me. It was shrapnel. It had entered my leg under the knee and went out the side. Went right through me. It didn't fracture any bone. And to this day, I have these two scars on my legs and the exit scar is the worst, like a hole. I used to charge ten cents to see the scars on my knee."

The people in the house took her in, but she was bleeding profusely. "Then the door opens and there enters a soldier of the Foreign Legion—tall, blond, and strong. I remember there was a song by Edith Piaf and it went, *'Il était jeune, il était beau, Mon legionnaire!'*" She remembered how odd it was that so many of the soldiers in the French Foreign Legion were young Germans. He scooped her up in his arms. When he stopped a motorist to get her to the hospital, the French driver declined, saying he didn't want any blood in his car. "Then freeing one of his hands, he pulls out his revolver and said in perfect French, *'Je te fais sauter la cervelle'*—I will blow your brains out. They put us in the car—that did it."

She wound up lost in a hospital hallway until her mother—accompanied by the dog, who had walked home—got her out of there. They fled to America, where she got a job in New York as a translator, working for the war effort. She eventually met an academic, an Italian professor of the Middle Ages, whose Spanish surname derived from a long-ago suppression of the Jews: Roberto Sabatini Lopez. Soon enough, he got an appointment at Yale University. By the end of the war, they moved to New Haven, where the local professors' wives explained to her the rest of her life—maintain a nice home and advance her husband's career. It was that much-earlier time. Feminism was a generation away.

"I was desperately frustrated. There was nothing to do but be a housewife. And Roberto was paid $3,700 year. It was 1946.

"Apartments were hard to find because veterans were coming back and they got priority. The guy took us around and said, 'If you don't take this one, you are on your own.' We opened the door, and wallpaper detached and flew onto my face—909 Howard Avenue—and I said, 'How come this wallpaper is free?' He said that the owner was in jail because he killed his wife. The man said, 'Don't take it if you don't want, but it is the only apartment.'" Soon, she'd bought some paint and struggled to fix up the place.

"I got a visit from the Yale welcoming committee one day. We didn't have a telephone and so, all of a sudden, two or three well-dressed women walked up, and the place smelled of cabbage and these elegant ladies said, 'How are you?' and we hadn't even unpacked. I was miserable. I had never painted a wall. I was barefooted when they arrived and the paint had dripped all on me. I was a sight."

So, Claude-Anne Lopez, once on track to be a schoolteacher in Brussels, was now an all-American housewife. Her future in 1946 was a kind of prison—one of petits fours, cocktails, and a lot of small talk, in a dump on Howard Avenue, a depressing little street near the New Haven train yards.

II. The Sound of T. Rex Clapping

Fraudulence always seems to lie at the heart of amateur pursuits. Maybe you don't have the right credentials, or background, or something else—other people's presumptions—keeps you from doing what you want, so you just pretend. It's a kind of prison break. The culture around you won't let you *out* of where you are or *into* where you want to go. So, you pretend to be someone else, and make your move.

I first realized how liberating it was to pretend to be something you're not when I infiltrated a secret weekend convocation of geniuses. Every so often the MacArthur Foundation flies all the previous fellowship winners to an undisclosed location for an unpublicized meeting of talks and socializing. A friend who was a winner from a while back told me about it, and so I figured the best way to go (on a magazine assignment) was to pretend to be one of them.

As I moved among this crowd at receptions and late-night parties at the Hotel Nikko in Chicago, I was surprised and gratified at how easy it was to pass myself off as a genius. I never did get caught, unless you count getting spotted in the bar one night by an acquaintance, Stanley Crouch (genius, '93):

CROUCH: Wait a minute. I don't think you are a genius.
ME: Argue with my momma, smarty pants.

During this long and boozy weekend, I discovered that the group broke into two natural constituencies: those who were highly credentialed and believed they clearly deserved this honor and those self-invented types who felt like they'd had an incredible stroke of luck. For three days, I watched the collision of the institutionally credentialed and the improvisational outsider. It turns out they don't get along that well, and their differences are conspicuous. The pros had a drink and went to bed; the amateurs stayed up all night and got drunk. Amateurs prefer wonder to certainty, invention to knowledge, freedom to security, beer to wine. The credentialed pros at the MacArthur conclave solemnly accepted their new celebrity as Fellows. The amateurs wore the title "genius" like a funny hat at a New Year's Eve party.

The thrill I felt being undercover in the Nikko, I discovered, is a common sensation among amateurs. They feel like frauds, like fakes, like someone might discover that they are not who they pretend to be. *Now* they were being honored, but once, a while back, they simply assumed a role for which they were never credentialed.

The paleontologist Jack Horner is one of those. A college dropout, he taught himself an entire discipline, in this case paleontology, and just became one of the country's greatest dinosaur theorists. He looks like an American rebel. He's a long drink of water in jeans and a work shirt—a handsome hippie with a Ben Franklin mane. When he talks, he walks—bobbing back and forth in front of the room like a slacker looking for his bong. It's an ironic tic, since his work is anything but laid back. At the genius convention, he gave a talk one morning about his most radical idea. Horner is the guy who overthrew the single most accepted dinosaur fact in history: that Tyrannosaurus rex was a vicious predator.

Watching Horner in action, you realize you are seeing something deeply American. He's part evangelical, part stand-up comic. Horner's talk was packed with his groundbreaking ideas but carried the dopey title "Would Tyrannosaurus Rex Really Eat a Lawyer?" The room was crowded with other geniuses and their kids. Horner started off by asking if anyone could remember where they saw T. rex eat a lawyer. Of course, all the kids knew.

"*Jurassic Park!*" they screamed.

"How many people think T. rex would eat a lawyer?" he asked. The room became a forest of upraised hands. "I wish you were right," he said, to uncomfortable laughter. Horner began loping back and forth. He casually shook loose some old assumptions. He brought up Henry Fairfield Osborn, the most famous paleontologist of the early twentieth century. Osborn made it onto the cover of *Time* magazine. The Museum of Natural History in New York is dedicated to him. He was a man of great repute whose hint at archness was summed up in his rakish fedora, a symbol so potent it survived into our time . . . on Indiana Jones's head. Osborn is the quintessential American expert.

"Now, here was a man who liked himself more than dinosaurs," Horner said. He was "one of those guys who believed that if he said something, everyone should believe it." Having softened up his audience's faith in authority and conventional wisdom, Horner plowed into arguments that were like set pieces of T. rex schtick—ideas with punch lines.

"What about those cute little hands?" Horner asked. They were useless, and could never do any work for a predator stalking dinner.

"T. rex couldn't even clap," Horner said. An easy laughter took hold of the crowd. Horner explained that T. rex, with his muscular legs, couldn't sprint—a fatal flaw for a hunter. His body posture, the bones now revealed, was not so much an upright Godzilla on the attack as a horizontal turkey on the lam. Horner duck-walked in front of his lectern, to the delight of the kids. He told us that T. rex's eyes were beady and weak, also a poor adaptation for a hunter. And yet, said Horner, almost conjuring a lightbulb over each of our heads, T. rex's massive olfactory cavities in his brain suggested the most exquisite sense of smell in the history of nasal evolution. He would have been able to smell dead flesh some twenty-five miles away.

Suddenly, we understood where he was headed. We could imagine it. We could see it: No longer Godzilla, Tyrannosaurus rex scampered on two legs, his back parallel to the ground, flitting (like thunder) from corpse to corpse: an enormous buzzard.

"So, would T. rex eat a lawyer?" Horner concluded. "If the lawyer's *alive*, I'm afraid he would not eat him. The question is, can you tell if a lawyer's alive?"

The room burst into a different kind of laughter—one of revelation. The audience had had its mind changed. It doesn't happen that often. And it usually isn't the work of a college dropout who tosses off his new ideas as just "sort of obvious when you think about it." Horner has made numerous great discoveries precisely because he happily questioned the oldest views about dinosaurs. He looked at the most notorious predator of all time and thought—wait, how *precisely* did he kill?—a question that unraveled generations of macho assumptions about what is now seen as a very large proto-bird.

III. Serious Comedians

When Ben Franklin began thinking about breaking with his apprenticeship in Boston and striking out for a personal (and, ultimately, revolutionary) freedom, he pretended to be a woman. It was a pose that he'd continue off and on for a lifetime. His earliest writings—posing as the querulous forty-year-old "Silence Dogood" (or, later as Martha Careful or Celia Shortface and Alice Addertongue)—involved women observing the inanities of the authoritative men around them. Franklin's characters brought humor to the tedious journalism of his day. Then, the early colonial media were infected with a tiresome pomposity. The papers were filled with earnest declarations, often little more than reprints of the previous Sunday's sermons. At that time, women were widely seen as grown-up children, silly versions of adult men who might say anything! So, Franklin's female voices granted him a freedom to make sharp observations (many would now be considered radically feminist). This was a new voice on the American literary scene—colloquial, profane, funny, casual, and alluring. It was a tone that no one would have heard if Franklin had tried to create it in his actual voice—a sixteen-year-old boy apprentice working for his solemn older brother.

When Stephen Colbert and Jon Stewart—both of whom pose as "serious newsmen"—first appeared on cable news, it was widely understood by the traditional media to be mere comedy. But fairly soon there appeared articles worried that these "fake anchors" were more than phony blowhards. People were actually *getting* their news from them. The comedy was working on several levels. The real anchors on television fretted about what this all "meant," and the actual blowhards on cable, like Bill O'Reilly, got angry and called them all stoners and subversives. The line from the improvisations of Ben Franklin to the comedy of Stephen Colbert is as American as pie.

Colbert and Stewart happened at around the same time that the blogosphere rose up and challenged, mostly, calcified newspapers and magazines. But TV media had long before degraded into something worse. Prime-time news had become a haven for stiff "presenters" (even their hair) who recited little more than what the professional press spokesmen for powerful players in Washington *said* was the truth. If comedy typically emerges out of the space between what we say and what we suspect is actually true, then Colbert and Stewart had wandered into a gold mine. Terrified of being labeled either liberal or conservative, mainstream television anchors long ago retreated behind words like "balanced" and, as a result, had abandoned analysis or even truth-telling for the ratings sanctuary of simply repeating what the establishment had instructed them to say.

In a sense, the regular TV anchor and the "action reporter" had already become parodies of serious newsmen. It's just that the wooden professionals didn't get the joke until Stewart and Colbert showed up.

There is a certain playfulness that comes with pretending, and that, too, is the animating spirit of amateur pursuits. Every study confirms that getting a person into a spirit of play not only puts them in their most creative posture but also, they will say later, made them happier than they had ever been. When a book came out about summer camp a few years ago, I remember being struck by how many adults were quick to confess that summer camp was *the* happiest memory of their lives. They had moved on to professional pursuits, but their fondest memory was this halcyon time of pretend, of being in the woods with bows and arrows, of encountering strangers in the guise of a wholly invented persona, of wearing ridiculous costumes.

The lightness of being that comes with pretend, of being unmoored from everything you think you know and skimming effortlessly across the surface of something profound and deep—that sense, too, pervades this fundamental idea of the American character. We are the people who literally created playtime for adults. It's not a coincidence that as America's industrial might began to emerge in the early twentieth century and the world came to see us as the embodiment of the Protestant work ethic that we simultaneously created a new space for playfulness. America invented the "weekend" and all that flows from that word—leisure, vacation, time off, mental-health days, etc. In other words, playtime.

This concept was so radical at the time—and still is in many cultures where work is constant and uninterrupted—that they had no word for it. The French word for "weekend" is *le weekend*. In Europe, the educational system that developed long ago pegged your lifetime pursuit early on. Claude-Anne Lopez had been scheduled at age seventeen to become a schoolteacher. Europeans still take the "test" that determines their future. Meanwhile, the traditionalists there love to honk in editorials about America's "extended adolescence" and how our immaturity and general ignorance and refusal to play by the rules are all signs that we are a nation of Peter Pans, an entire people who refuse to grow up.

Europe has always judged America's intellectual and artistic productions as childish versions of much finer things. We invented the musical, a banal corruption of opera. We invented the op-ed piece, a secular withering of the noble sermon. We invented the short story, a novel for a nation afflicted with ADD.

But the improvisation that comes with that playfulness yields all kinds of new things. Sure, that superficial lightness of being means we are the nation of unending Top-40 hits, a place where novelty trumps gravitas-burdened tradition every time. The architectural essayist J. B. Jackson liked to praise the temporary buildings and structures of our culture—the malls, the suburban creations, the strips on the edge of town—as the true American architecture in part because it so lacked any sense of tradition and permanence. American architecture was transitory, improvisational, and amateurish precisely because we were always tearing it down and building it up all over again, our permanent frontier.

Despite whatever America is going through now, this American idea still remains, for many people, the lure—this sense that here one can escape a past and create something new. A 2011 poll, in the midst of global terrorism and worldwide financial cataclysm, found that people still think that America is "the coolest nation" on earth. That may change, and perhaps this spirit of the amateur pursuit will flee elsewhere as America assumes the dreadful role of "empire." But probably not.

The essential contradiction of the American ideal survives here—the nation of dedicated hard workers who've never grown up. We are all Californians—babes in bathing suits and hunky boys in convertible jeeps who somehow managed to create the seventh most productive economy on the planet. The rest of the world is still enchanted with a country whose most authoritative and credible newsmen are comedians faking it.

The kind of creativity one finds here can drive outside observers insane. Consider religion. Abroad, religion is the ultimate repository of tradition. The Vatican is arguably the oldest continuous bureaucracy in the world. In America, religion is largely improvisational and inventive. We are not a Catholic nation or even a Christian nation. We are inventing religions almost as fast as hits on iTunes. America is the land of Mormons and Scientologists, storefront Pentecostal shacks and weird rural cults. The Church of England stands as a mighty bulwark of tradition in a country that grows increasingly bored by religion. Here, religion is its own cycle, with Great Awakenings pulsing throughout the nation as rhythmically as amateurism.

So, we reinvent God every generation or so. No biggie. There really is nothing that can't be reinvented here. Wine-tasting? Who could compete with the erudite palates of Europe? Wine-tasting was once the province of certain old-school, largely French, experts who could boast a lifetime of sipping Burgundies. Then along came this alleged "million-dollar nose," Robert Parker, who created a cockamamie scoring system that awarded "Parker Points." There's something very American about creating a pseudoscience out of something almost by definition unquantifiable. But quantify we shall.

What is the actual difference between Robert Parker scoring a new Bordeaux as a 97 versus a 98? Who knows? The infuriated French vintners do: millions in sales.

Almost no realm of human pursuit, no matter how abstract, is immune from some improvisational entrepreneur coming up with a scorecard and, of course, a company that charges for the result. Love has been Robert Parkerized at eHarmony.com, which boasts 29 "compatibility" measures to ensure "accuracy." Emotional intelligence can be scored. Even the oldest of these measurements—the IQ test—is privately regarded as bunk (like the bogus Nielsen ratings), but as with wine, hell, it's helpful to have a number. In fact, *any* number. Just as long as we all agree to it.

Happiness is another one. We are currently living through a renaissance of happiness studies and metrics. You can choose among dozens of tests to find out how happy you are. The most popular course at Harvard University these days is Psychology 1504, also known as "How to Get Happy."

The word "happiness" has a strong pull in America. Amateurs lay claim to it—it's another word for Csíkszentmihályi's flow or Meredith Patterson's codespace. But it's also the one odd word that stands out in our Declaration of Independence. The pursuit of happiness. This is supposed to be our national mission, the American Dream, yet we've always been a little uncertain of what it meant.

IV. Flying a Kite

In the early 1950s, President Truman proposed that the papers of the Founding Fathers be collated by scholars and made available to the public. Thus began a series of seemingly endless efforts to annotate all the papers of the heroes of the American Revolution. Princeton University was assigned Thomas Jefferson's papers. UVA got Madison's and Washington's papers. Yale would work with Ben Franklin's papers. Money was appropriated and the process began.

The original editor of this effort in New Haven was a solemn and stately historian named Leonard Larabee. In 1954, he assembled a half-dozen workers and took over Room 220 in the august edifice at Yale known as Sterling Library. Like medieval monks, the small crew of historians pored over the documents under Larabee's watch, eyeing the papers as though with a jeweler's loupe, providing notes of explanation and clarification, putting these thousands of pages in order and creating a lifetime narrative of the written record of Ben Franklin. As he looked at the decades of work ahead, Larabee realized that some of Franklin's later papers were in French and he remembered hearing some faculty wife had "a funny accent and that it was probably French."

So he hired this young housewife, Claude-Anne Lopez, to perform the grunt work of typing some of these later papers so that the real historians could, one day, get to them.

"I was hired as a transcriber," Lopez told me. "It could not have been lowlier." And the atmosphere in that Sterling sanctuary could not have been more solemn. The work was done in near silence and moved at a glacial pace. The Franklin Papers opened for business in 1954 and produced "Volume 1" in 1959. The effort continues to this very day. They are on Volume 40 and intend to finish the entire project sometime in the next fifteen years. The work began with the beginning of Franklin's life and moved slowly forward—almost in real time. When I visited the project, I once asked one of the scholars when she was hired. "Oh," she said in a soft voice, "it was around the time Franklin left for Paris." The chronology of Franklin's life so structured the place, it had become a kind of calendar.

"I was paid sixty-five cents an hour and in order to get a pension you had to work nineteen hours, and Larabee had me working eighteen hours a week," Lopez said. "They had weekly meetings and I was never invited because my work was completely separate. There were three men and three women. Larabee was the head and Whitfield Bell was number two, and he was my friend."

The other reason Lopez had no one to talk to was "because the French letters came later in Franklin's life, and others were doing Boston"—in other words, Franklin's earliest years. So she worked alone, apart from the scholars.

Being European, Lopez confessed, "I knew nothing about American history; all I knew was what I had read in *Gone With the Wind*." One day, when she encountered an unfamiliar name, "I raised my voice and said, 'Was there somebody named John Jay?' And who came tiptoeing to my booth but Whitfield Bell, and he whispered to me, 'I must show you the American Dictionary of Famous People. I will bring that to you!'"

Larabee was very restrictive when it came to Lopez's work. She was not encouraged to think or have an opinion, simply to transcribe and be done with it. She told me that she just couldn't help taking notice of little details that she knew something about. So, after a while, she would simply insert a little note in a document's file folder for a future reader. Historians who have worked there over the years still delight in coming upon a Lopez note from three or four decades ago.

"In my own way, I was trying to edit, but Larabee wouldn't hear of it," Lopez said. One day, when she realized that an "unidentified" letter of Franklin's was, due to a misspelling, actually a letter from the famous French chemist Antoine Lavoisier—the man who discovered oxygen and hydrogen, co-invented the metric system, and helped standardize much of modern chemistry (and was also, incidentally, guillotined during the French Revolution for selling inferior tobacco)—she wondered what she was to do with this discovery.

Her husband's reply was what he knew: "Publish or perish."

So, she wrote a little article, and it was accepted for publication by a German magazine. And later, people talked about the article (although not Len Larabee, who never mentioned it to Lopez). She was asked to give a talk at Smith College about her paper. In the cozy outpost of Ben Franklin scholarship, there was a tiny bit of news. A new voice was in town. Claude-Anne Lopez.

As years passed, Lopez spent a lot of time with Franklin in that era when he was notoriously bedding all those women—a simple fact of history that was presumably indisputable. Lopez wrote a book called *Mon Cher Papa: Franklin and the Ladies of Paris.* The book was widely reviewed and well received. "Larabee was still running the papers and he never said a word about it." Lopez actually went on to write three notable books about Franklin and is now regarded as one of the great Franklin scholars of our time.

When a new editor, William Willcox, arrived to take over from Larabee in the 1970s, he was stunned to learn that Lopez was still considered a "transcriber" and was not even listed as a staff member of the Franklin Papers.

"What?" Willcox said incredulously to Lopez. "You are the only person here I've heard of." And so Claude-Anne Lopez, the amateur academic, was officially recognized to exist eighteen years after she was hired. Her name appears for the first time in 1972 with the publication of *The Papers of Benjamin Franklin, Volume 15.* Or, to put it in Papers' time—just before Franklin printed his maps charting the Gulf Stream and the birth of his grandson, Benny.

Coming to Franklin as a self-made scholar, Lopez brought the kind of eye that a Leonard Larabee would never appreciate. She saw a completely different man from the one seen repeatedly by the professionals who had pored over his words. Probably the most controversial and unacceptable discovery Lopez made was realizing that Franklin was not really some colonial lothario. It took a complete newcomer to his letters to see what's actually right there.

"I paid a lot of attention to his letters to women—to Catherine Ray and the other girls," she told me over a glass of wine, "and these letters are so delicate and so grandfatherly." There are three great letter exchanges with three women in Franklin's oeuvre, and Lopez believes they are widely and commonly misunderstood.

"I was always particularly interested in the wooing side of Franklin. It doesn't necessarily mean sex. Americans are so peculiar about sex. When I arrived here, people still wrote 's-x.' Many American men are virgins when they marry. It's astonishing." The question remained: was Ben Franklin our founding Casanova?

"I am sure he tried; he was a man after all," Lopez said with a laugh. "With Polly [Stevenson, his London landlady's daughter], he never tried. He thought of her as his daughter and he encouraged her to marry."

Lopez acknowledges what is indisputable: Franklin had a wild time as a young single man. He wrote, almost humiliatingly, about it. "After his youth, he settled down," Lopez told me. "People say it was a terrible marriage with Deborah, but it wasn't a terrible marriage. They had fantastic cooperation. It was her doing. Deborah ran the shop and kept the accounts. When he was away, she was the postmistress."

And it's true that Deborah Franklin wasn't as social as Ben and feared crossing the Atlantic. So he traveled alone and she became his trusted surrogate in Philadelphia for the rest of their lives. Ben loved the society of women, but Lopez observed a far less dashing reality.

"As soon as I read Catherine Ray," Lopez said, "I realized that *she* was the one going overboard and he was the one calming her down." Lopez referred to an incident often cited about Ray, when Franklin watched her sail off for a long, long time. This anecdote is always presented as being evidence of him as a smitten man.

"He was visiting his brother in Boston at Christmas," Lopez said. "She was going back to Block Island and then he wrote he stood on the shore and watched her disappear through his glass. The French talk about *amité amour*, a loving friendship. It's platonic, and for a woman it can be quite nice." She looked away for a moment. "You don't get pregnant."

As to the years in Paris and the famous story of Franklin playing chess with Madame Brillon in the tub, Lopez reminded me that women bathed beneath a board that covered everything except their heads. Socializing with a bathing person wasn't so unusual then. And there was one other thing, Lopez said. "Franklin had gout. He had kidney problems. He had stones. Marie Antoinette loaned him her litter. He was in real pain! Adams wrote that Franklin lost his head with the women of the court." But the truth is that "he didn't frequent the court much; he wasn't invited that often, only special occasions. It's a completely false idea that Adams had." She paused and looked at me as if we were gossiping about somebody we both knew personally. "John Adams—I hate his self-satisfaction, his arrogance—so many alcoholics in that family."

So, the reality of Ben Franklin in all probability is that he was not a sex maniac but a busy man with a functional marriage who flirted with younger women in a grandfatherly way. It's a truth as difficult to hear as the claim that T. rex was a giant buzzard.

"Anytime I take a cab in Philadelphia," Lopez added, "that comes up—'Oh, yes, Franklin was quite a woman chaser, wasn't he?'—I don't even try to dissuade them anymore."

Looking back on her career, Lopez's only regret is that she wishes she had marketed her books better. Still: She spent her later career awash in academic approval, giving prominent lectures, publishing all over, and being regularly honored as the great Franklin expert—all achieved by a series of self-motivated actions that Franklin would have recognized as arguably his greatest invention—the pursuit of happiness.

That troublesome phrase appears in Thomas Jefferson's final draft of the Declaration of Independence, a document edited by two men—John Adams and Ben Franklin. Surely Adams had vetted it for the constitutional and legal arguments that were his expertise. He was the Harvard-trained lawyer after all. But it was probably Ben who brought his own lightness of style to the sentences.

The main idea of personal happiness at that time was not some hedonistic notion of pleasure but the other, more philosophical, kind.

The Greek philosophers believed that discovering one's own talents and then taking the pleasure of exploiting them (finding out that you had a singing voice, could write well, start a company, or invent new things), *that* was the deeper pleasure the founders had in mind and the freedom they sought.

We don't know for certain who put that phrase in the Declaration, but it was probably Ben. He wrote a good deal about happiness. The common phrase that would have rung familiar two hundred years ago, particularly as it pertained to government, came from John Locke—that governments were instituted to protect "life, liberty, and property." Locke's term ends with such a solid and limiting *kerthunk*. It's hard not to suspect that the rascally Franklin, who broke with tradition himself, envisioned the future of American citizens as something far more open-ended than the mere accumulation of property and careted in that phrase. *The pursuit of happiness.* Even in the founding document, the sense of playfulness is there.

The other image that Franklin loved to invoke in this vein was the kite. He wrote about how, as a child in Boston, he would lie on his back on the surface of the harbor and get pulled along by his kite. It's almost certainly a fiction. But that image is so compelling, such a wonderful sense of a child at play, drifting about, pulled here and there by a kite. His other usage of that image is a good bit more famous, the most famous image from the founding era: Ben flying his kite to prove that electricity existed in clouds and was the source of lightning.

Several Franklin mavens believe that that story—the kite and key on a string—is *also* a probable fabrication. (I am one.) The fact is that Franklin had given away his theory of electricity by publishing his ideas and letting others—Europeans!—prove his theory by setting up electrical rods. The experiment was to put one's knuckle near the rod during an overcast, pre-thunderstorm afternoon, and if the clouds were as charged with electrical "plasma," as Franklin believed, then you would feel a nice kick of intense static electricity. And that *was* proven in Europe. (Proven too well in St. Petersburg, where a Swedish scientist named Georg Wilhelm Richmann put his knuckle near the rod when a bolt of lightning struck and he was killed.)

The famous kite story was one Franklin told *many* years later—not at the time he allegedly performed it. His only witness was his son William. Franklin's account is unusually vague. My own suspicion is that Franklin feared that the discovery of electricity was his greatest achievement. So he tried to retrofit the story of his experiment so that the history books would give him proper credit. He laid claim to the achievement not by setting out the details of his experiment—like I said, the account is vague—no, rather he put in the minds of all of us an image more indelible than the scribblings of a thousand historians. He improvised his own rewriting of history, in other words, by conjuring the world's first beta-test version of what we might now call a photo-op.

He did it by invoking an image that is at once playful and profound, practically the logo of the amateur's childish spirit, of liberty, of leisure—the emblem of the lightness of being, where creativity thrives. It can be American, not out of nationalist pride, but because this sense emerged at our founding and is the inheritance of anyone born or driven to come here. While we might list the great liberties—speech, assembly, due process, trial by jury—the one that goes unstated, almost presumed, is the revolutionary decision to abandon one's past and one's self, as well as one's culture, tradition, and history. To walk away from everything that one is—whether it's fleeing a repressive nation for this new place or simply out the back door for the garage—*that* is real freedom. It's a story that everyone who lives here or comes here recognizes in their gut is true, that the amateur's dream is the American Dream.

Acknowledgments

Every idea starts somewhere, and this one began over lunch with Eric Nelson, a book editor who first asked me if I had ever noticed how many of my stories seemed to involve some self-invented crank wandering off to the outskirts of an obsession. The way he spoke made it sound like he was talking about me, but soon enough the idea was getting kicked around to collect a number of pieces from magazines and radio and shape them into an anthology. But that didn't happen in part because, at the time, I was beginning the research for an article for my editors at the *New York Times Magazine,* Paul Tough and Gerry Marzorati. The original draft was about NASA's awards program—a half dozen or so massive monetary prizes dangled in front of America's backyard tinkerers to seduce them into inventing a new generation of cheaper and better space gear. They pushed me to do more reporting and expand the focus (maybe this is how one can tell a magazine idea is a possible book: the rare phenom of an editor telling you: write *more*). I wound up with a reported story called "The Amateur Future of Space Travel." And that reporting, which didn't make it into this book, managed to get me poking around the edges of this idea as something larger and more fundamental to what often goes on in our nation's metaphorical garages. By this time, I found myself eating several lunches with David McCormick, who's a good bit more than a literary agent when he gets around half an idea and some ragged paragraphs on paper. A few hundred e-mail exchanges later and I had a book proposal in my hand. So I want to thank them all for getting me started.

Once committed to a book, though, there's a long period of wondering just what it was that you said in that proposal, which all of a sudden reads as vaguely as a found spiral notebook filled with notes from a long lost high school English class. This inspires frantic reactions that typically involve hiring research assistants and giving them half-cocked requests to find out everything about, say, self-taught dinosaur experts, homemade gasoline distillers, open-source anything, local "historians," the newest religions, DIY submariners, amateur chefs, and the latest version of creation science. But then you realize what you really need is information on, say, self-taught dark-matter theorists, ethnic innovators coining new races, the ongoing jet-pack dream, the last 500 patent applications, high school kids building nuclear reactors in the suburbs, the latest Howard Finster, the latest Steve Jobs, the latest Lana Del Rey, anything to which the prefix wiki- has been added, and space elevator designers. But, wait, that's nowhere near enough, so you tell them you also need a research file on, say, this year's MacArthur Genius Grant winners, amateur porn pioneers, pranksters, weekend warriors curdling into militias, storm chasers, uncredentialed archaeologists, the collected triumphalist blog posts of Jeff Jarvis (a lot of heavy lifting, that one), cutting-edge agronomists in the medical marijuana field, self-appointed terrorist hunters, that whole smart mob business, competitive eaters, amateur rocketeers, microbrewing dudes, top fan-fiction writers, horticultural pioneers, latter-day radio pirates, and the surprisingly hefty crowd of people describing themselves as time travelers, some of whom, curiously, have recently disappeared.

The first person who got sent off on these quixotic missions was the indispensable and brilliant Kirsten Weld. And when she fled to South America for a real research job, I handed the reins to Will Sedlack, Aliza Shvarts, and David Huyssen, who rode off on many a quest and in at least one case—and I totally understand—never found the way back.

After the writing starts, there is a whole set of people who might read something or just listen to you talk through some vague notion until it begins to sound like a newish idea. First and foremost is Lisa Sanders, who sits in the other chair in our living room, and who has figured out the sweetest ways to say things like, "I don't understand this whole chapter, really" and "signposts, Jack, signposts" and "Is this chunk in English, or did you accidentally set the font to dingbats?" When the writing's all over, there's this moment when you really need a single reader who can sit down with the manuscript and tell you in fresh terms exactly what it was that you actually said. Thank you, Michael Pollan. Throughout all this, there were those who did their share of listening and I am told this can be a fun but at times trying experience: Ian Ayres, Jessica Bauman, Jennifer Brown, Kevin Baker, Kaveh Khoshnood, Sarah Koenig, David Mikell, Jon Mooallem, Stephen Sherrill, Vera Titunik, and the itinerant scholars at Lulu's.

Then there are the other ears I have counted on all my life: Joan Algar, Dianne Moore, Nancy Miller, and Bobby Hitt. Thanks for everything that happened at 38 Gibbes Street—somehow connected here, I think.

Toward the end of any book, there is the guy who was there every step of the way. Sean Desmond, my editor, is someone who managed a Jobian patience when he should have lost it and a no-drama steadiness not seen outside of the White House. For letting me supply the counterpoint, Sean, I am grateful. And all those at Crown—Sarah Breivogel, Julie Cepler, Annie Chagnot, and Courtney Snyder—and that riot of fun e-mails and ideas, thank you.

Finally, to Tarpley and Yancey, who in the course of all this somehow managed to follow the plot, going from scuffed-up little girls to brilliant young women. You're why this book and I are here.

Index